I0540776

João Paulo Guimarães (ed.)
Aging Experiments

João Paulo Guimarães holds a PhD in English from SUNY Buffalo, was an Irish Research Council postdoctoral fellow at University College Dublin and is currently a junior researcher at the Universidade do Porto. His research concentrates on experimental poetry and science studies.

João Paulo Guimarães (ed.)

Aging Experiments

Futures and Fantasies of Old Age

[transcript]

Bibliographic information published by the Deutsche Nationalbibliothek

The Deutsche Nationalbibliothek lists this publication in the Deutsche Nationalbibliografie; detailed bibliographic data are available in the Internet at http://dnb.d-nb.de

First published in 2023 by transcript Verlag, Bielefeld
© João Paulo Guimarães (ed.)

Cover layout: Maria Arndt, Bielefeld
Cover illustration: WWeiser / photocase.de

https://doi.org/10.14361/9783839462836
Print-ISBN: 978-3-8376-6283-2
PDF-ISBN: 978-3-8394-6283-6
ISSN of series: 2702-8968
eISSN of series: 2702-8976

Contents

Acknowledgements 7

Introduction: Unnatural Aging
João Paulo Guimarães 9

Fantasies of Agelessness and Age Hierarchies in *Mary Poppins Returns*
Mariana Castelli-Rosa 17

Doris Lessing's Eccentric Old Women
Carmen Concilio 33

The Old Child in Susan Cooper's *The Dark Is Rising* Series
João Paulo Guimarães 47

Life after Youth
Elves and Elders in Medievalist Fantasy Literature
Jiwon Ohm 53

"how to dance / sitting down"
Aging, Innovation and the Graying of Disability"
Michael Davidson 73

Dancing Relational Bodyhood
Older Disabled Artist-Activist Tuuli Helkky Helle (1933–2018)
Heunjung Lee 97

A Recognition of Certain Realities
Keith Rowe's *Absence*
Ryan Bell... 125

A Measure of Dignity?
Age & the Abject Body in Clarice Lispector's Short Fiction
Patrícia Silva.. 141

Crones, Care Homes, and Crises
'the material culture of growing older' in Leonora Carrington's
The Hearing Trumpet (1977)
Jade Elizabeth French.. 155

Eternity is Nothing but a Second
A Reflection
Sofia Matos Silva 175

Queering Time, Questioning Ageism Through Speculative Siction
Maricel Oró-Piqueras and Sarah Falcus 199

Authors 219

Acknowledgements

The idea for this book sprung from a symposium with the same title that I organized at the Humanities Institute of University College Dublin in 2020 (via Zoom) as an Irish Research Council Postdoctoral Fellow. Many of the papers included in this volume were first presented at that event. I then continued to work on this volume as an Portuguese Foundation for Science and Technology CEEC Junior Researcher at the Comparative Literature Institute (ILCML) of the University of Porto.

I would like to thank all of scholars that participated in the 2020 event and in particular those that decided to continue working with me on this book for the two years that it took me to put everything together. I am especially grateful to Professor Michael Davidson, the keynote of the *Aging Experiments* symposium, for accepting my initial invitation and letting me reprint here the essay he went on to publish in the *Journal of Modern Literature*. I am also very happy that I got to work with my colleagues from SUNY Buffalo, Jiwon and Ryan, who immediately accepted my challenge, despite having a dissertation to write and not having done work in Aging Studies before (they had to step outside of their comfort zones and I think it paid off beautifully). My friend Mariana must also be mentioned not only because she helped me pick the cover for the book (her choice, really), but also because she maintained her motivation and kept working very hard through a period during which she was extremely ill. Finally, a note of appreciation to my student and current MA advisee, Sofia, for her courage and the enthusiasm with which she embarked on this project despite having a million other things to do.

Introduction: Unnatural Aging

João Paulo Guimarães[1]

In "Cheating Death", an article about the medical advances that promise to expand average longevity during the next couple of decades, The Economist tells us that as life expectancy increases, it is conceivable that the elderly will feel emboldened to make nonstandard late life decisions like finding a new partner or taking up a new profession. In the future, the newspaper suggests, life might thus become "more a series of new beginnings than one single story". Summed up, someone's life would look somewhat like a collection of correlated but not organically integrated fragments.

Although similarly sceptical of so-called "decline narratives" which naturalize the idea that old age inevitably denotes physical and/or mental deterioration, Aging Studies (henceforth AS) scholars nonetheless believe that alternative discourses about aging have useful cultural work to do in the present and that discussions of this nature need not be subordinated to the progress of science and medicine. In the view of these scholars, the well-being and social lives of elderly people might be improved if we attend to and tackle certain stereotypes and assumptions about old age. American literary critic Kathleen Woodward, for example, claims that pervasive "gerontophobia" has led to a "relative lack of ambiguity in our representation of aging" (1999: 284), the paucity of research done on late life creativity being particularly notorious. Responsible for this, according to behavioural scientist Martin Lindauer, is the widespread belief that "nothing really new happens in the later decades

---

1   University of Porto (ILCML).

when there are no fundamental changes comparable to youth" (2012: 5). In reality, says Lindauer, "creativity diminishes with age for some, is left unaffected for others and for a few emerges for the first time in late life" (2012: 21), the cognitive loss normally associated with old age being often related to manageable lifestyle habits and psychosocial forces. On a different note, literary critic Heike Hartung explains that accounts of old age generally follow a tragic formula that disregards how certain late life events, even painful ones, can transform someone's life trajectory in ways that are not always strictly negative. Taking a cue from Mary Russo, who advocates for the "inclusion of risk and randomness" in scholarly studies of old age, Hartung observes that a "focus on contingency makes it possible to incorporate illness, mourning and death, as well as [...] acting against one's age and other departures from normative ideas of aging into narratives of life" (2015: 15). Rather than see life in terms of progress and decline, notions rooted in a rigid understanding of ability and strength, one might, Hartung notes, attend to its unpredictability as a series of potential turning points.

AS has focused predominantly on realist, confessional and (auto) biographical fiction, so much work remains to be done about genres that seek to challenge our views of reality, rather than mirroring or describing it. The central claim of this book is that experimental writing, science-fiction and fantasy (henceforth SFF) "denature" aging, proposing strange images of the body, the self and the lifespan that configure nonstandard, but nonetheless normal, modes of embodiment. They complicate so-called "decline narratives" in various and oftentimes contradictory ways, critiquing naive fantasies of immortality and adaptability without lapsing into technophobia or a refusal to think beyond the boundaries of "the natural", too often conceived, in aging studies, as an immutable category used to describe the limits of (mortal) humans, who must inevitably age and die.

For their part, experimental works that dwell on the topic of aging often challenge the idea that old age is a time of recapitulation, reconciliation and resignation. Experimentalism excavates and shakes up the symbolic and ideological foundations upon which mainstream conceptions of the "normal" are based. Avant-gardists like those whose work we discuss here position themselves against a poetics of summation, sobriety and depth, highlighting instead the importance of immaturity, incompleteness, skepticism, error, forgetfulness, plasticity, playfulness and everydayness for literary prospection and late life wellbeing. Their work is, most importantly, fully rooted in the present and retains the prospective and future-oriented tendencies that characterize experimental projects.

SFF and experimental art offer us perspectives on aging that are strange, speculative and sometimes downright unrealistic, which might make it seem like they have little to contribute to the discussion about a sensitive topic like that of old age. The latter is, nevertheless, often treated with exaggerated caution and seriousness, reinforcing stereotypes and limiting the array of social roles available to older people. Some research has been done on how aging is represented in experimental writing: for example, Kathleen Woodward's study of how Eliot, Pound, Stevens and Williams reached a more detached style in old age, Scott Herring's defense of Djuna Barnes's poetics of endless revision in her late phase or Elizabeth Barry's work on Beckett and his idea that loss of memory and concentration in old age actually made his writing more true-to-life in its vagueness and fragmentariness. Aging in SFF is also not a new area of study: we have, for example, Amelia DeFalco's article about how caregiving robots can become intimate companions or Ulla Kriebernegg's analysis of Margaret Atwood's apocalyptic "Torching the Dusties", a "burden story" about the segregation of the old), our aim is to take this research further, as well as to compile and synthesize, in a single volume, perspectives from multiple genres which are often seen as unrelated but nevertheless equally offer us perspectives on aging that undermine expectations of credibility and seek to expand the horizon of possibility. Rather than focus on the everyday challenges of the elderly, the works we explore here intentionally concentrate on seemingly otherworldly issues like immortality and monstrosity (for example, Ohm's chapter on Tolkien and Silva's chapter on Lispector and the abject), or they force us to reimagine what it means to be normal, healthy and creative (for example, Davidson's chapter on the life-affirming aesthetic/formal innovations William James, William Carlos

Williams and Merce Cunningham derive from their disabilities – or alternative abilities, if one sees them, as Davidson suggests we do, as other-abled rather than deficient vis-à-vis a standard model of bodily and cognitive competence).

By focusing on aging in SFF, this project also answers the call of aging studies veteran Kathleen Woodward for scholars in the field to turn to other aesthetic traditions and genres, highlighting "speculative and posthuman fiction" as modes of writing that allow us to inhabit other worlds with different youth-age value systems. Our aim will thus be to assess how the representations of aging we find in SFF differ from those provided by mainstream fiction and other marginal forms, like avant-garde literature. In spite (or precisely because) of their strangeness and irreverence, SFF provide us, we will argue, with important perspectives about aging that have thus far received little academic scrutiny.

There is a clear connection between Queer Studies' alternative views on time and the literary genres we propose to explore. Scholars like Cynthia Port and Linda Hess have done important work on the way queer theory can productively be used to make sense of the contradictions of old age, a time that is normally seen as unproductive and past-oriented (whereas heteronormativity is, according to Lee Edelman, for example, mandatorily future-oriented). In her essay on Benjamin Button, Port draws upon Edelman's critique of modernity's fascination with the redeeming features of youth and futurity to point out that "older adults whose economic, physical and/or cognitive resources are compromised may well find themselves outside mainstream temporal structures" (2012: 3). Like queer subjects, older people often put conventional ideas of progress to the test, either because they require vital but unproductive forms of care or are "preternaturally" active and creative. Queer Theory might also allow us to harness the creativity of SFF for the purposes of Aging Studies. In Queer Universes, Pearson et al. argue that, at its most progressive, science fiction is a genre that is particularly effective at conjuring up vistas of "a future that opens out, rather than forecloses, possibilities for becoming real, for mattering in the world." They point out that, for science fiction writers, "life does not remain static; what we know today may be entirely different tomorrow." In other words, the pleasure we derive from science fiction partly stems from the way it "denatures" the world we know, challenging inevitabilities and probing the kinds of futures that are possible and desirable. Taking a cue from Tzvetan Todorov, Eugene Thacker notes that fantasy too is a genre that invites us to rethink the categories of the possible and the natural. "Aging Experiments" carries out an unprecedented survey of these two genres, our aim being to find and scrutinize SFF (science fiction and fantasy) texts that focus on aging and old age, as well as, whenever pertinent, the adjacent topics of life-extension, rejuvenation, immortality, body enhancement and time travel. SFF texts pose difficult questions about the inevitability of death, the desirability of immortality (or a very long life), the digitization of the self, the plasticity of one's lifelong talents, or the idea that one must try to lead a (long) healthy life. Our key assumption, based on a cursory overview of these genres, is that there is a vast array of relevant texts that have received little attention from the AS community.

It should be noted that, because some of the books in question engage with technoscientific fantasies about life-extension, this does not mean that they do so uncritically. They would otherwise not merit the close analysis that we here propose to undertake. Our goal is not, after all, to reinforce the prevailing culture of "juvenescence" nor to promote unrealistic and unjust ideas about how one can "age successfully", an endeavor that is always already constrained by race, class and sex inequalities that are often not taken into account. Like Pearson et al. point out about queer science-fiction, the texts of that genre we wish to examine here "are narratives that extend . . . cognitive estrangement precisely to those areas which a focus on the science of science-fiction tends to elide: the very world in which science takes place, the world of bodies and social systems" (2008: 3). The novels in question do not, that is, take the merits of science for granted. Crucially, however, they also do not reject science (or magic, in the case of fantasy) wholesale, choosing rather to pose provocative questions about the nature of necessity, progress and the good life.

As Michael Drout points out in his lecture series about these genres, SFF are immensely popular genres, topping sales charts not only in literature but also in other media like film and videogames. This not only means that these genres have a significant impact on mainstream discourse but also that they take up problems that speak to a vast array of people, much as the epic literature of the remote past used to do. One of these fundamental problems is that of death and immortality, which has fascinated the popular mind at least since the epic of Gilgamesh. Both genres create speculative worlds in which abstract concepts can be externalized (as fantasy does with its immortal elves, for example) or possible future scenarios be tested. Although informed by scientific debates, science-fiction, for one, does not merely follow the lead of science. Rather, it drives discovery and frames how we talk about the future, posing questions about the many paths human culture can take. Fantasy, for another, is not merely about romanticizing and escaping to some sort of ideal past. Rather, it gives us a glimpse of worlds that are oftentimes better than our own and empowers us to think and act in the here and now with a renewed perspective. In short, SFF offers us what realism can't: imaginary worlds and alternative social systems that allow us to put our mundane reality in perspective.

Such perspectives are readily available to us in such critically acclaimed novels as Larry Niven's Ringworld (1970), which sees his 200-year old protagonist, physically healthy but bored with ordinary earthly affairs, embark on a recon mission to the eponymous planet, home of an ancient civilization; Robert Heinlein's Time Enough for Love (1973), about the 2000-year old Lazarus Long, object of a life-extension experiment who, putting a spin on the Arabian Nights' premise, agrees to not commit suicide for as long as a relative keeps listening to his stories; Dan Simmons's Hyperion (1989), structured, like The Canterbury Tales, as a series of stories told by fellow pilgrims, in this case on their way to a planet in which time flows backwards, a phenomenon that makes one of the characters, who had already been to the planet on a research mission, to become progressively younger and gradually lose her memories; Tim Powers's Expiration Date (1996), which pits a young boy and a middle-aged man against a pair of elderly antagonists who seek to attain immortality by ingesting ghosts; John Scalzi's Old Man's War series (2005 – present), which centers on a vast array of old characters that enroll in a mass recruitment program set up by the US government to fight aliens and colonize other planets, giving old people their youth back in exchange for a life-long commitment to the war; Robert J. Sawyer's Rollback (2007), which narrates the drama of a husband and wife who both undergo a rejuvenation treatment but end up following different temporal trajectories, the first regaining his youth but the second (due to the therapy's ineffectiveness) staying on course towards a progressively older age.

Throughout this collection we explore works that interrogate the concepts of flexibility, longevity and immortality, but we also wish to discuss how the genres in question foreground risk, vulnerability, disability and nonstandard forms of embodiment. Taking a cue from Stephen Katz, we acknowledge that the notions of flexibility and risk, undoubtedly valuable for the experimental approaches to aging we wish to explore, need to be clarified with due caution and responsibility in an age of increasing fragmentation and precarity. Above all we are interested in perspectives on aging that challenge the predominant narratives of decline as well as the equally prevalent fantasies of invulnerability and eternal youth. Our goal is ultimately to plumb and promote alternative conceptions to the good life as defined by neoliberal notions of health, able-bodiedness, agency, self-improvement, progress, plasticity and productivity.

Works Cited

Barry, Elizabeth (2016): "Samuel Beckett and the Contigency of Old Age." In: *Samuel Beckett Today/Aujourd'hui* 28.2, pp. 205–217.

Calasanti, Toni and Stephen Katz (2015): "Critical Perspectives on Successful Aging: Does it 'Appeal More than It Illuminates'?" In: *The Gerontologist* 55.1, pp. 26–33.

DeFalco, Amelia (2010): *Uncanny Subjects: Aging in Contemporary Narrative.* Columbus: Ohio State University Press.

Drout, Michael (2006): *Rings, Swords and Monsters: Exploring Fantasy Literature.* Prince Frederick: Recorded Books.

Hartung, Heike (2015): *Ageing, Gender and Illness in Anglophone Literature*, London: Routledge.

Herring, Scott (2015): "Djuna Barnes and the Geriatric Avant-Garde." In: *PMLA* 130.1, pp. 69–91.

Hess, Linda (2019): *Queer Aging in North American Fiction*. London: Palgrave.

Kriebernegg, Ulla (2018): "Time to Go. Fast Not Slow: Geronticide and the Burden Narrative of Old Age in Margaret Atwood's 'Torching the Dusties'." In: *European Journal of English Studies* 22:1, pp. 46–58.

Lindauer, Martin (2012): *Aging, Creativity and Art*, New York: Springer.

Mangum, Teresa. (2002): "Longing for Life Extension: Science Fiction and Late Life." In: *Journal of Aging and Identity* 7.2, pp. 70–81.

Pearson, Wendy Gay, Veronica Hollinger and Joan Gordon, Eds. (2008): *Queer Universes: Sexualities in Science Fiction*. Liverpool: Liverpool University Press.

Port, Cynthia (2012): "No Future? Aging, Temporality, History, and Reverse Chronologies." In: *Occasion: Interdisciplinary Studies in the Humanities*. https://arcade.stanford.edu/occasion/no-future-aging-temporality-history-and-reverse-chronologies.

Thacker, Eugene (2016): *Tentacles Longer than Night*. London: Zero Books.

The Economist (2016): "Cheating Death" (Aug. 16), https://www.economist.com/news/leaders/21704791-science-getting-grips-ways-slow-aging-rejoice-long-side-effects-can-be.

Woodward, Kathlyn (1980): *At Last, the Real Distinguished Thing*, Columbus: Ohio State University Press.

Woodward, Kathlyn (1991): *Ageing and its Discontents*, Bloomington: Indiana University Press.

Woodward, Kathlyn (2019): "Afterword: Literary Antidotes to the Toxin That Is Ageism." In: *Studies in American Fiction* 46.2, pp. 373–381.

Fantasies of Agelessness and Age Hierarchies in *Mary Poppins Returns*

Mariana Castelli-Rosa[1]

Abstract: *In my paper, I investigate how aging and the passing of time are depicted in the film* Mary Poppins Returns *(2018) and how they shape the narrative and give it ageist undertones. As a sequence to the 1964* Mary Poppins *original film, the 2018 film hints at the passing of time which is evident in the age of the Banks children who have grown up. However, time has not passed for Mary Poppins as she is portrayed by a young actor (Emily Blunt). I explore how this casting choice affects the film and which ideas it reveals about aging, and especially, women aging in Hollywood. I also focus on Mary Poppins' role in the domestic realm organizing intergenerational relations and its effect on the film plot. Lastly, I connect the casting of Mary Poppins as a young woman to the erasure of older people in film and the childhood nostalgia promoted by Disney, the producer of the film.*

Keywords: *Agelessness; intergenerational relations; older women; Mary Poppins; age socialization*

In 2018, Disney released *Mary Poppins Returns*, a sequel to the 1964 *Mary Poppins* classic. In this return to the Mary Poppins universe, the titular nanny gains ageist implications. This is obvious considering that in the 1964 film, when Mary Poppins produces a measuring tape that provides

---

1   Trent University.

insight into the characters' personalities, the tape reads "practically perfect in every way" when the nanny measures herself. This scene functions as both Mary Poppins's introduction to the Banks' home and the children she will look after, and her introduction to the film-going audience. Soon, because of her magic powers and her ability to almost effortlessly take care of the children in a fun manner, both the Banks children and film viewers are convinced that Mary Poppins is indeed nearly perfect.

The narrative of *Mary Poppins Returns* takes place during the Great Depression, about twenty years after the narrative of the original film, which was set in 1910 as George Banks emphasizes in the song "The Life I Lead." In this film, she reappears to help Michael and Jane Banks, who are in their late 20s, save their childhood home from being repossessed by the bank where Michael, a depressed, widowed, aspiring artist with three children, works part-time. To prove that Michael and Jane have enough money to pay the loan and keep their house, they need to find a certificate of shares left by their father and present it to the bank on Friday by the last stroke of midnight. Unsurprisingly, in *Mary Poppins Returns*, many, if not most, of the characters have aged accordingly. The notable exception is Mary Poppins herself who similarly to the first movie still continues to be in her mid-thirties. In the beginning of the 2018 film, Michael Banks recognizes his former nanny and says: "Good heavens, it really is you. You seem hardly to have aged at all." Mary Poppins dismisses the comment as sheer rudeness, but astute viewers should not be so quick to dismiss this fact.

Michael's comment draws attention to how out of place an unaged Mary Poppins is, especially since the narrative of *Mary Poppins Returns* heavily relies on the passing of time and the importance of adhering to age hierarchies and culturally assigned intergenerational relationships. The compulsory lack of aging ascribed to Mary Poppins points to the ageism of the film industry, a realm that often excludes older women. Moreover, as both films frame Mary Poppins as "perfect," the refusal to let her age alongside the other characters feeds into this ageism, suggesting that perfection and old age are mutually exclusive. In this chapter, I argue that *Mary Poppins Returns*, through Mary Poppins's lack of aging, coupled with the plot's focus on organizing intergenerational relationships and framing aging as a decline, reflects the ageism of the entertainment industry. The combination of ageism within the industry and the ageism present in the plot and appearance of Mary Poppins reinforces ideas of childhood idealization and nostalgia that Disney deploys to sell films, products, and experiences. Even though my analysis is directed at 2018 film, because the Mary Poppins universe is made of self-referential parallels, I will also analyse some key scenes of the 1964 film.

An important theme of the Mary Poppins films that is often overlooked is time and its passing. There are countless examples. The film's audience and some of the characters know, for instance, that Mary Poppins's sudden departure is just a matter of time. Admiral Boom, a retired member of England's navy and a neighbor, fires a cannon twice a day from the rooftop of his house to mark the time, even if he is nearly always some minutes behind in *Mary Poppins Returns*. In this film, the plot is driven by Michael's deadline of Friday by the last stroke of midnight to produce the shares that can save his home. Time works both for and against the protagonists: Michael has not paid his loan for three months, resulting in the bank's impending repossession of his house, but in the end it is time in the form of the hidden shares that helps the Banks family save their home. These shares are, in fact, the result of a tuppence investment that was made for Michael Banks in the 1964 film. The resolution of the 2018 film is only possible as a result of the passing of time and the consequent accumulation of interest of these shares. It is only the natural progression of time that allows the Banks to save their home and guarantees a typical Disney happy ending. Finally, to ensure that the Banks will be able to meet their deadline, Mary Poppins actually turns back time as seen in the Big Ben scene.

As a sequel, *Mary Poppins Returns* also underscores that time that has passed by aging the characters the audience is familiar with, as evident in the age of the adult Banks children and the visible aging of their housekeeper and neighbors, as well as introducing new characters such as Jack, the lamplighter, and Mary Poppins's cousin Topsy Turvy that, respectively, are substitutes for two characters (Bert and Uncle Albert) from the original movie. Jack tells Mary Poppins that Bert is travelling the world, but the disappearance of Uncle Albert from the plot is left unexplained thus also hinting at the passing at time, i.e., his possible death. And yet, while time has a crucial role in the film, in the twenty years that separate the plot of original movie from its sequel, it is only Mary Poppins who does not show any signs that time has passed: it is only she who has not aged.

Perhaps it is a bit hasty to say that Mary Poppins has not aged *at all*. Michael Bank's comment is more on point: she has *barely* aged. It is difficult to write about movies not acknowledging that casting decisions affect the film as a final product, especially when a character has the quality of perfection attached to it. *Mary Poppins Returns* was released in 2018 and Emily Blunt, the actor playing the part of Mary Poppins, would have been around 35 years old at the time. When the 1964 *Mary Poppins* was released, Julie Andrews, who played Mary Poppins in the original film, was around 29 years old. If casting decisions are observed, there was a slight increase in the actors' ages while ensuring that both remain below the forty-year-old threshold that separates women into the categories of old and young in Hollywood (Dolan 2017: 17). Yet, this small increase does not correspond to the time that has passed from the narrative of the original narrative to the sequel, and is relatively unnoticeable, especially in comparison to the aging of the other characters as outlined above.

An argument might be made that Mary Poppins's lack of aging is a result of her powers and position as the "practically perfect" equivalent of a superhero. According to Wilson Koh, the "superheroic body must remain healthy and vital. It must not be seen to age" (2014: 492). This happens because superheroes are usually caught up in what Umberto Eco calls "the illusion of a continuous present" (1979: 116) or an "oneiric climate [...] where what has happened before and what has happened after appear extremely hazy" (ibid: 114). This is the device that allows for the circulation of multiple Superman stories, some of them portraying him as a boy, others as an adult. However, this argument falls apart in the face of the importance of time and aging to the film's narrative. The universe of Mary Poppins, and especially the diegetic part of this universe, is relatively small compared to Superman. Moreover, there is a noticeable continuity from one film to the next which eliminates the possibility of being trapped in a continuous present, even if in the end of the film, in a superhero fashion, Mary Poppins literally turns back time by moving Big Ben's hands counter-clockwise to ensure that the Banks can save their house. Eco's ideas about a continuous present cannot completely explain why Mary Poppins is the *only* character that barely ages. Additionally, the framing of Mary Poppins in the films refuses her the status of superhero by relegating her to the domestic sphere through her position as a nanny, an occupation that is often devalued and underpaid. Since her position in the domestic sphere, which is usually associated with and prescribed to women, rather than the public sphere of superheroes, usually prescribed to men, is a fundamental part of her role in the film, Mary Poppins's youthful appearance seems to point at bigger issues in the entertainment industry and the ageist exclusion of older women in lead roles.

Due to the success of the original movie and of its soundtrack, fans and producers had high expectations for the new Mary Poppins. Andrews, who played Mary Poppins in the 1964 film, was unable to reprise her role because her voice was damaged in an operation to remove a polyp from her vocal cords ("How Julie Andrews's Voice Was Stolen by a Medical Disaster"). As a result, she no longer fulfilled the musical's basic requirement as she could not sing. The decision to cast Blunt in the role indicates a very deliberate choice on the part of the film's casting directors to refuse to allow Mary Poppins to age. While Blunt does a very good job, her casting purposefully juxtaposes Mary Poppins's lack of aging with the aging experienced by all the other characters common between the two films. In essence, those in charge of the 2018 film deliberately chose an actress in a manner that excluded the representation of an older woman in the lead role.

The erasure of older women from the entertainment and film industries is notorious. In the introduction to *Women, Celebrities and Cultures of Ageing: Freeze Frame*, Deborah Jermyn and Su Holmes note that, in 2013, German supermodel Heidi Klum surprised party-goers and fans alike by attending her own, extravagant Halloween party in New York dressed up as an old woman (2017: 1). According to the authors, her "costume" is a confirmation that older people are seen as the "Other" (Jermyn and Su 2017: 2), that is, as those that do not belong in a culture so obsessed with youth. Additionally, by choosing to dress as an old woman in a Halloween party, where costumes are supposed to be scary, Klum's choice implies that being old is frightening and not glamorous (ibid: 2). More importantly, in their analysis of Klum's "costume" choice, Jermyn and Holmes point to the perceived impossibility of conciliating being old with being a celebrity at the same time, something that Klum's choice reflects.

Through her "costume" choice, it is also likely that Klum was both being ironic and self-deprecating, thus making a statement about how women over forty, the age she had reached a few months before her Halloween party, are often excluded from celebrity culture and the entertainment industry. If this was her intention, Klum had a point: old women celebrities and women over forty in the entertainment industry are much rarer than men (Dolan 2017: 17). This rarity suggests that these industries give preference to women who display youthful and so-called perfect bodies, and the combination of gender and age-less expectations for female celebrities creates a double standard, as male actors are more likely to continue to get lead roles at older ages. In *The Double Standard of Aging*, after observing that in the cultural imagination growing old is "a moral disease, a social pathology" (2013: 746), Susan Sontag recognizes that being youthful is often equated with happiness and, in the case of women, to beauty (ibid: 747). Sontag's awareness that ageism affects women and men, even though it is much harsher to women, and her insight that beauty is equated with youth and perfection further explains the choice of casting a young actor about the same age as Mary Poppins in the first movie. But there is more to it.

While Andrews' absence from the 2018 production can be explained by her medical condition and her refusal of a cameo in order to not detract from Blunt's performance ("'Mary Poppins Returns': Why Julie Andrews Turned down a Cameo"), the decision to cast a young Mary Poppins and refuse to give visibility to an older woman is conspicuous in the face of Dick van Dyke's cameo appearance in the 2018 film and the portrayal of older men in both films. In the 1964 movie, van Dyke plays two roles: he is Bert, Mary Poppins's sidekick, a chimney sweeper and artist, and he also plays Mr. Dawes Sr., the chairman of the bank where George Banks, Jane and Michael's father, works. Van Dyke portrays Mr.

Dawes Sr. in the 1964 film as a typical "grumpy old man" in a very decrepit and declining image of old age, especially as he is hardly able to get his message across to Michael Banks because fits of coughing continually interrupt him. Suffice to say that the use of "gray face" in the portrayal of Mr. Dawes Sr. along with a characterization that is not very flattering emphasizes the undesirability of aging and old age. Likewise, in *Mary Poppins Returns*, van Dyke plays the role of Mr. Dawes Jr., the retired chairman of the bank. In his scene towards the end of the movie, van Dyke is exaggeratedly dressed as an old man with white hair and a long white beard, and he performs a musical number with movements and characterization that exaggerate his age and that imply that old age equals decline. Moreover, in his scene, before he starts to sing, he says: "I may be circling the drain, but I got a few steps left in me," which is then followed by the lyrics: "So when they tell you that you're finished/ And your chance to dance is done/ That's the time to stand/ To strike up the band/ And tell 'em that you just begun." While van Dyke's characterization and number echo the caricature of male old age in the 1964 film, the mere presence of his characters in the 2018 film shows a willingness to allow men to age in public and on screen; but only if they engage in what Shary and McVittie (2016) call "elder kitsch."

In *Fade to Gray: Ageing in American Cinema*, Shary and McVittie explain that starting in the 1960s, initially, older male actors and then older female actors, began to appear in films commercialized to a teenage audience (2016: 88). In these films, they often played stereotypical older characters whose purpose was to emphasize their own characters' anachronism (ibid: 89) in relation to the younger characters who were often more central to the plot. The inclusion of older characters in these movies was both to repurpose older stars and to capitalize on their previous public personae (ibid: 98). To do so, actors were supposed to play the roles of people looking old while, at the same time, performing so-called "youthful activities" (ibid: 97), which, in turn, contributed to an exacerbated representation of old age and the anachronism that their characters entail. Shary and McVittie call this type of performance "elder kitsch." In *Mary Poppins Returns*, van Dyke's character appears older than the actor actually is, but he can only do so in the guise of elder kitsch, as his costume and song suggest. Van Dyke's performance stands in sharp contrast to Meryl Streep's portrayal of Topsy Turvy, Mary Poppins' cousin. Unlike van Dyke, Streep's character barely has any physical signifiers of age, even though the actress was nearly seventy at the time of the filming. Of particular note is the use of cosmetics to remove the most obvious signifier of age: wrinkles. The difference in depiction of both characters reflects Sontag's double standard of aging. Additionally, while Topsy Turvy does activities that parallel van Dyke in terms of elder kitsch, i.e., so-called youthful activities such as dancing on top of a table or doing a handstand, Streep's number doesn't touch on the subject of aging at all. By diminishing Topsy Turvy's physical signifiers of age and emphasizing those signifiers on Dawes Jr., the film shows different standards of aging for men and women, coupling age diminishment and elder kitsch in van Dyke's performance to suggests that old age is an undesirable end, even if one is alive, and, as such, should be avoided at all costs.

This view of age as a decline has a particular effect on how the 2018 film represents the passage of time when it is viewed in conjunction with the 1964 film. *Mary Poppins Returns* repurposes characters and dialogue to create self-referential parallels within the Mary Poppins universe. These parallels are characteristic of the franchise. Georgia Grilli (2007), focusing on the Mary Poppins books by P.L. Travers, analyzes different themes in the Mary Poppins universe. One theme Grilli identifies is the constant repetition that structures these books (2007: 10), and which creates parallels especially in relation to the plot and characters. Even though Grilli (2007) highlights that the Mary Poppins 1964 movie is different from the books, when the 1964 and the 2018 films are compared, several parallels that buttress the filmic Mary Poppins universe surface. In addition to the reappearance of certain characters (the Banks family, Admiral Boom, etc.) and themes (political activism now in the figure of Jane Banks instead of her mother; the importance of order, and the fundamental role of fun in establishing it), new characters are included to substitute those that have disappeared from the plot (Topsy Turvy replaces Uncle Albert, Mary Poppins gains a new sidekick, who is about the same age as her previous one, in Jack). Lines from the 1964 film are also referenced ("Michael, close your mouth. We're still not a codfish" and "Practically perfect in every way") and certain objects from the original film are shown again (the kite, the carpet bag, etc.). The genealogy connecting the two older van Dyke's characters, both of them chairmen of the bank, is also an important parallel. However, a crucial parallel that is of special interest to an Age(ing) Studies analysis of the film, is the reprisal of Mary Poppins's role in reorganizing intergenerational, familial relationships.

Before Mary Poppins's arrival in *Mary Poppins Returns*, the Banks' life is upside down. Losing their childhood home is just the biggest symptom of the chaos that has ensued. The economy is bad, and Michael Banks is depressed after the death of his wife, which prompts his two older children, John and Annabel Banks, to act as grown-ups by running errands for the family while taking care of Georgie Banks, their wild, youngest little brother. For this reason, when Mary Poppins arrives, there is not only a financial crisis in progress, but a domestic one that affects intergenerational relationships. This is a crisis that also bears relation to time, a key theme of the film, as children and adults have unknowingly reversed age roles and the responsibilities attached to them, which is dangerous as it keeps them from finding the certificate of shares.

In *Declining to Decline: Cultural Combat and the Politics of Midlife*, Margaret Morganroth Gullette argues that Age Studies should not be conflated with gerontology and proposes that all ages be included in age theory (Gullette 1997: 207). She highlights that the full extension of the life course should be studied and emphasizes that there still are many gaps in this area (ibid: 201). Gullette is interested in how bodies are first and foremost aged by culture and believes that if scholars focus on how we learn and internalize the master narrative that aging equals decline, and how we begin to associate certain age cohorts to certain characteristics in age socialization (1998: 9), we will begin to fill in research gaps and produce meaningful research.

Mary Poppins Returns offers a good opportunity to look into age socialization and the master narrative of decline. Not only is the 2018 film a means through which viewers learn what aging can or should look like as seen in the example of a Mary Poppins, whose aging is barely noticeable, or of Mr. Dawes Jr., who looks exaggeratedly old and frail but engages in "youthful" activities, the audience also learns that different age cohorts should behave in certain ways as represented by the construction of social relationships. As mentioned above, when Mary Poppins arrives, John and Annabel have taken on many of the household responsibilities: they take care of Georgie, go to the supermarket, and tell Ellen, the housekeeper, that they will make lunch when they get back. The film, through Mary Poppins, makes it clear that John and Annabel have taken on tasks not appropriate for their age. Instead, they are fulfilling the responsibilities of their father who, because of his depression, is unable to perform his role in the age hierarchy. This inversion is presented negatively. In fact, upon Mary Poppins's arrival, Jane asks her what brings her back, and the nanny ambiguously replies: "Same thing that brought me back the first time. I've come to look after the Banks children," while not specifying *which* Banks children she means. Mary Poppins and film viewers are aware that what can save the Banks family is not only finding the certificate of shares: there must also be a reorganization of the family according to age hierarchy and the roles associated with these ages.

The idea of chronological age and of identity connected to age is not as natural as it may seem. Quoting Bill Bytheway, Pamela Gravagne explains that "chronological age itself is a social construct, instituted in the eighteenth and nineteenth century by lawyers, bureaucrats, [...] who, in the interest of quantification, required specific numerical ages for the assignation of certain duties and rights" (2013: 27). As a result, this quantification resulted in the creation of socially and culturally reinforced age categories and identities. In *Mary Poppins Returns*, the audience is presented with a world in which these age categories have been overthrown and must be returned to expected norms. These norms include a gendered aspect. According to Cristina Pérez Valverde, it is not uncommon in children's literature to have a female character with magical powers (2009: 264). These characters, as seen in the example of Mary Poppins, are usually single women with a maternal role who "question family relationships, disclosing the gaps in the established social order inasmuch as they, as outsiders, are required to sustain that order, on the verge of collapse" (ibid: 264). In both Mary Poppins films, the nanny takes on a maternal role that rearranges familial relationships by calling into question the misaligned nature of these relationships. In the 1964 movie, Mr. and

Mrs. Banks are so busy with their own lives that they have lost touch with the children's needs. In the 2018 sequel, the death of Michael Bank's wife has affected his mental health and his ability to look after his children. In both films, Mary Poppins's maternal role is fulfilled as she reorganizes familial relations, situating the parents back into their parental roles and the children back into their, well-mannered, child roles. Although there is a temporality to Mary Poppins's role, the effects of her actions are expected to remain past her departure.

In both films, Mary Poppins effects change by reminding the family that that children are supposed to act as children and not have the responsibilities that Annabel and John Banks were burdened with in the beginning of the film. Similarly, adults finally learn to take the lead even though they are occasionally allowed to act as children, especially if it is for the sake of keeping the family together and creating stronger familial bonds. This is evident in the final scene of the movie, when the Banks family goes to a Spring Fair where they all buy balloons that take them up in the air while the cast sings "Nowhere to go but up." The person who sells them the balloons is an old woman who reminds Michael of the importance of remembering what being young feels like. In their conversation she tells him that he should be the first to pick a balloon.

> MICHAEL BANKS. Those days are long behind me. I don't think I've held a balloon since I was a child.
> BALLOON LADY. Then you've forgotten what it's like!
> MICHAEL BANKS. To hold a balloon?
> BALLOON LADY. To be a child!

As previously stated, there are not many older people in the 2018 film that *look* their age. In fact, old age is equated with decline, as seen with Admiral Boom's decreased punctuality coupled with his use of a wheelchair, and Mr. Dawes Jr.'s display of elder kitsch. The balloon lady, portrayed by Dame Angela Lansbury, also reinforces the idea that aging is a decline through the above lines that emphasize that feeling like a child, embracing youth, is important and preferred to old age. In fact, her exchange with Michael Banks and some of the lyrics of her song ("Life's a balloon/ That tumbles or rises/ Depending on what is inside/

Fill it with hope/ And playful surprises/ And oh, deary ducks/ Then you're in for a ride") echo ideas about "aging graciously" present in van Dyke's song mentioned above.

The film's choices to cast a young Mary Poppins, employ elder kitsch and anachronism through van Dyke's and Streep's performance, and centre the secondary plot around realigning intergenerational relationships in accordance with culturally reinforced norms, all point to a prizing of youth over age and suggests that age decline can be staved off by continuing to be young at heart. This messaging reflects the inherent ageism of the entertainment industry by marginalizing the true experience of age from its plots and casting. It implies that youth and youthfulness will guarantee a more pleasant experience to characters and film viewers alike. In addition, as this film is a Disney production, it is impossible to overlook that many Disney productions have a similar kind of message, either by not having many older characters[2] or by profiting on products that promote childhood idealization and nostalgia. For instance, Disney amusement parks are often advertised as a sort of fountain of youth that grownups can visit and feel young again, even if it is just for one day. In *Mary Poppins Returns*, the narrative and the titular character's mandatory youthfulness, coupled with the idealization of childhood reinforces societal and cultural age expectations that in turn fuel the Disney marketing machine, reminding viewers that childhood is the age that is desirable and even adults can experience it if they continue to consume Disney products and watch Disney productions. Finally, by casting a young actress as Mary Poppins in the 2018 film, the directors and producers not only establish and reinforce the idea that

---

2   According to a study conducted by Zurcher and Robinson, Disney animated films tend to lack representations of old age. Moreover, when there is an older character in an animated film, it is more likely that it will be male (2017: 9). In comparison to a previous study, Zurcher and Robinson have noticed an overall decrease in the number of older characters with a primary role in the plot, while older characters with secondary, or smaller, roles have increased (ibid: 10). Another important finding from Zurcher and Robinson that resonates with my analysis of *Mary Poppins Returns* is that the number of older characters with physical signifiers of age (wrinkles, grey hair, etc.) has decreased (ibid: 10–11).

perfection is embodied in youthfulness, but also ensure that the Disney universe will continue to provide experiences where ordinary people can have the feeling time, and the undesirable decline of age, may be stopped by consuming Disney services and products.

Age(ing) Studies is not only concerned with representations of older people, but the way constructions of age shape and inform culture and healthcare. As a whole, *Mary Poppins Returns* engages with age and time in a way that reveals an ageist construction idealizing childhood that is inherent in the entertainment industry and fuels the marketing efforts of its main players, such as Disney. By linking Mary Poppins's mandatory youthfulness to her identity as someone "practically perfect in every way," the film demonstrates the ageism of the cultural industry that Jermyn and Holmes discuss in their book. Moreover, by complying to Sontag's double standard of aging as shown in van Dyke's and Streep's cameo, the 2018 film makes us questions why Mary Poppins is not allowed to age on screen. The absence of an older Mary Poppins and the reinforcement of socially constructed age identities demonstrate how the entertainment industry can reproduce and perpetuate ageism. As the aging population in most countries continues to grow substantially and as film sequels become a safe bet for big studios wanting to make profit, it begs the questions: Will Mary Poppins continue to be youthful in possible upcoming sequels, or will the (aging) public want to see more representations that mirror themselves and contain natural signifiers of old age?

Acknowledgments

I am in great debt to Jessica Anne Carter for her help editing and proofreading this chapter. text was originally written for a course taught by Prof. Emeritus Stephen Katz and I would also like to acknowledge his instructive feedback. Last but not least, thank you to the editor, João Guimarães.

Works Cited

"'Mary Poppins Returns': Why Julie Andrews Turned down a Cameo," Nov 30, 2018 (https://variety.com/2018/film/awards/mary-poppins-retu rns-julie-andrews-1203065856/).

"How Julie Andrews's Voice Was Stolen by a Medical Disaster," March 19, 2015 (https://www.washingtonpost.com/news/morning-mix/wp/2 015/03/19/how-julie-andrewss-voice-was-stolen-by-a-medical-disa ster/).

Dolan, Josephine (2017): Contemporary Cinema and 'Old Age': Gender and the Silvering of Stardom, London: Palgrave Macmillan.

Eco, Umberto (1979): The Role of the Reader: Explorations in the Semiotics of Texts, Bloomington: Indiana University Press.

Gravagne, Pamela H (2013): The Becoming of Age: Cinematic Visions of Mind, Body and Identity in Later Life, Jefferson, North Carolina and London: McFarland & Company, Inc., Publishers.

Grilli, Giorgia (2007): Myth, Symbol and Meaning in Mary Poppins: The Governess as Provocateur, New York and Milton Park: Taylor & Francis Group.

Gullette, Margaret Morganroth (1997): Declining to Decline: Cultural Combat and The Politics of The Midlife, Charlottesville and London: University Press of Virginia.

Gullette, Margaret Morganroth (1998): "Midlife Discourses in the Twentieth-Century United States: An Essay on the Sexuality, Ideology and Politics of 'Middle-Ageism.'" In: Richard A. Shweder (eds.), Welcome to Middle Age!: (And Other Cultural Fictions), Chicago and London: Univ. of Chicago Press, pp. 3–44.

Jermyn, Deborah/Holmes, Su (2017): "Introduction: A Timely Intervention – Unravelling the Gender/Age/Celebrity Mix." In: Deborah Jermyn/Su Holmes (eds.), Women, Celebrity and Cultures of Ageing: Freeze Frame, London: Palgrave Macmillan, pp. 1–10.

Koh, Wilson (2014): 'I Am Iron Man': The Marvel Cinematic Universe and Celeactor Labour. In: Celebrity Studies 5/4, pp. 484–500.

Marshall, Rob, director. *Mary Poppins Returns*. 2018.

Pérez Valverde, Cristina (2009): "Magic Women on the Margins: Ec-Centric Models in Mary Poppins and Ms Wiz." In: Children's Literature in Education 40/4, pp. 263–274.

Shary, Timothy/McVittie, Nancy (2016): Fade to Gray: Aging in American Cinema, Austin: University of Texas Press.

Sontag, Susan (2013): "The Double Standard of Aging." In: David Rieff (eds.), Essays of the 1960s & 70s: Against Interpretation, Styles of Radical Will, on Photography, Illness as a Metaphor, Uncollected Essays, New York: Library of America.

Stevenson, Robert, director. *Mary Poppins*. Walt Disney Productions, 1964.

Zurcher, Jessica D./Robinson, Tom (2017): "From 'Bibbid-Bobbidi-Boo' to Scrooge: An Update and Comparative Analysis of the Portrayal of Older Characters in Recent Disney Animated Films." In: Journal of Children and Media 12/1, pp. 1–15.

Doris Lessing's Eccentric Old Women

Carmen Concilio[1]

Abstract: *The aim of the present contribution is to introduce, analyze and discuss a short story by Doris Lessing (1919–2013), which is capable of surprising the reader with its unconventionality. The short story title is "The Grandmothers" (2003), but the two women protagonists are nothing but a pale portrait of stereotypical elderly women. Ageing, gender and sex create such an eccentric discourse, in this piece of prose, which is able to subvert any predictable thematization of the story. The framework of ageing studies is not necessarily enough to explain the text, it is rather more appropriate to discuss the concept of "juvenescence", as elaborated by American scholar Robert Pogue Harrison (2014), in order to critically frame the short story.*

Keywords: *Doris Lessing; grandmothers; juvenescence; ageing; eternal youth*

The aim of the present contribution is to introduce, analyze and discuss a short story by Doris Lessing (1919–2013), which is capable of surprising the reader with its unconventionality. The short story title is *The Grandmothers* (2003), but the two women protagonists are nothing but a pale portrait of stereotypical elderly women. Ageing, gender and sex create such an eccentric discourse, here, which is able to subvert any predictable thematization of the story. The framework of ageing studies is not necessarily enough to explain the text, it is rather more appropriate to discuss

---

1   University of Turin.

the concept of "juvenescence", as elaborated by American scholar Robert Pogue Harrison, in order to critically frame the short story.

The protagonists of the novella are two women, who do not allow any stereotype to touch them, particularly "stereotypical beliefs which make old age, sexual attractiveness and, thus, interest in sex, utterly incompatible" (Oró Piqueras 2019: 85). In a nutshell, the two women reciprocally "fall in love" with the other's young son. Their eccentric life experiment, or life experience, shakes and undermines normative meanings of home and family quite seriously (Watkins 2007), while strongly questioning aging, per sé. In relation with the two women protagonists, rather than age, ageing or ageism, it is rather more appropriate to resort to the category of "sexy oldie" (Gott 2005: 23).

The novella later became a drama Film, entitled *Adoration*, popularly known as *Adore*, directed by Anne Fontaine in 2013, which was presented both at Sundance Film Festival and at the 57th BFI London Film Festival. Although discussing the film and the adaptation is out of the scope of this contribution, only one annotation might suffice here: The two (grand)mothers look much younger in the film, whereas in the short story they already have grandchildren and are in their sixties.

* * *

Doris Lessing, Nobel Prize winner for Literature, in 2007, is well-known for her long-lasting career as activist, as a member of the Communist party, as a voice in the anti-nuclear campaign, but above all, as anti-apartheid and feminist writer. Not by chance, the motivation for the Nobel Prize reads: "that epicist of the female experience, who with skepticism, fire and visionary power has subjected a divided civilization to scrutiny."[2] Last but not least, besides being among the first sci-fi women-writers with her five volumes of space fictions, *Canopus in Argos: Archives* (1979–1983), she was a pioneer writing about old age, when it was not jet a fashionable topic. In *Diary of a Good Neighbour* (1983), she created the character of an old and decrepit woman, Maudie Fowler,

---

2   Cf. https://www.nobelprize.org/prizes/literature/2007/lessing/facts/.

with touches of gothic (Goldman 2017: 216–237), describing her almost as a witch in a fairy tale, living in a dark cave of a London basement, with neither proper electricity nor heating, yet capable of enchanting a career woman in her fifties thanks to her storytelling. This well-known novel can be considered a classic in coming of age literature; an emblematic novel about ageing in the twentieth century; more precisely, of women ageing, and, above all, voicing the invisibility of elderly people in our modern city life and city scape.

Thus, Maudie Fowler is the embodiment of the mythical and iconographic "crone" described by Barbara Walker in her homonymous essay (1985; Concilio 2001: 128). When Jane Somers spots her in a London Chemistry, she believes she sees "an old witch. I was staring at this old creature and thought, a witch. [...] A tiny bent-over woman, with a nose nearly meeting her chin, in black heavy dusty clothes" (Lessing 1983: 20). Maudie has got fierce blue eyes and characteristically always says "NO" to anyone and to any imposed rule, including medicaments. Moreover, also characteristically, she is extremely slow. Thus, when Jane has to slow down her pace and her life's rhythm, she is suddenly conscious of what she has expunged from her sight:

> I thought how I rushed along the pavements every day and had never seen Mrs Fowler, but she lived near me, and suddenly I looked up and down the streets and saw – old women. Old men too, but mostly old women. They walked slowly along. They stood in pairs or groups, talking. Or sat on the bench at the corner under the plane tree. I had not seen them. That was because I was afraid of being like them. (Lessing 1983: 21)

In this passage Doris Lessing voices "ageism" in its form of social indifference, to the point that elderly people are actually invisible to the gaze of the passers-by. Lessing's feminist engagement is here evident, for she is indirectly quoting Simone de Beauvoir, who, in her essay *The Coming of Age* (1996 [1970]), denounced our modern "conspiracy of silence", erasure and concealment (De Beauvoir 1996: 2). Thus, one way to recover the elderly from marginality is to portray the old woman as a transfigured modern Mother Goddess, or Great Mother of ancient times, particularly for feminist writers and thinkers. The "crone" according to Barbara Walker gives back empowerment to old women, otherwise neglected. What is the power of old age, then? Simone de Beauvoir (1996) claims it is lived experience, whereas to the eyes and the gaze of onlookers, old age is only a perception, a cognition.

A similar conclusion is reached by Robert Pogue Harrison, who claims that "modern Western societies, especially in the United States, have institutionalized age segregation by confining the young to educational institutions, adults to the workplace, and the elderly to retirement homes. Consequently the generations spend most of their time alongside rather than with one another" (Harrison 2014: 63). We might parenthetically add that Covid-19 has exasperated this aspect of "living along" rather than "with" the elderly. This "apartheid", Harrison goes on saying, "deprives elderly of their mentorship roles, deprives the young of a sense of larger kinship, and deprives families of 'generativity,' which in more traditional societies fosters dialogue and interaction between the various age groups" (Harrison 2014: 63).

In this context, I would like to focus on this concept of "generativity", for it is precisely pivotal in Lessing's novel. Generativity is defined as "transmission of legacies from one generation to another within the domestic sphere, leading to the mutual 'embeddedness' of those who inhabit it" (Harrison 2014: 63). The reason why the protagonist of Lessing's novel, Jane Somers, is so fascinated and mesmerized by Maudie Fowler is Maudie's storytelling. This is the gift she receives from the old woman: that is to say, a bunch of stories about life in London in the 1940s and 1950s, that Jane cannot avoid listening to and craving for. This cements the strange friendship between a 50 years-old journalist and a woman on the verge of death, whose only testament and legacy is an unavoidable and inexhaustible narrative flow. Perhaps, just another version of the ancient Mother Goddess's "generativity".

* * *

Doris Lessing, however, also wrote a very original type of story in *The Grandmothers* (2003). As already hinted at, never title could be more misleading. We expect – perhaps stereotypically enough – grandmothers to be women in their seventies, with a halo of whitish hair, and a strong sense of responsibility, particularly in relation to their grandchildren. On the contrary, here very atypical grandmothers are presented, for the two women protagonists and their sons are entangled in quasi-incestuous relations. If title and thematic content converge in creating an experimental piece of writing, the genre of this novella also introduces a novelty. Side by side with *Buildungsroman*, by which it is possible to describe the two young men's evolution from children to married husbands and fathers, Lessing introduced the genre of *Reifungsroman* (or, novel of ripening), mentioned in Oro Piqueras' study (2019: 89), which describes the two women's progress towards old age. This seems to confirm what critic Susan Watkins wrote about the fact that "Lessing's interest in formal experimentation tends to operate at the level of genre and narrative perspective" (2007: 247). Picking up from this consideration, Watkins also notices how innovation and experimentation in Lessing does not involve so much syntax, but rather "manipulation of free-indirect discourse and performative play with the idea of 'omniscence'" (2007: 247). In particular, she claims that in the short story the main difficulty is finding the appropriate vocabulary to define the two women's sexual and emotional life, as in the following example, where they "need to be told", rather than being able to tell for themselves:

> "Roz, did Harold say that we are lezzies?"
> "Well, we aren't, are we?" enquired Lil, apparently needing to be told.
> "Well, I don't think we are," said Roz. (Lessing 2003: 17–18)

The setting of the story is a protected bay in Australia, named after a legendary, lonesome seaman, Baxter, whose boat crashed against the seven black rocks that prevent the open ocean to enter the idyllic gulf. This is a colonial exotic paradise, of sun, sea and summer – under a sky that was so different from the British sky – only vaguely reminiscent of ancient, hospitable and peaceful Aborigines, now peopled by blond-haired and blue-eyed, healthy, tanned and sporty people, who look like happy tourists all their life.

In particular this is the portrait of the family of the protagonists. A happy, shining and beautiful family, when looked at, with envy, by the waitress who serves them a healthy breakfast of fresh fruit juice and wholebread sandwiches. She was enchanted in looking at *the family*. *That family* was her passion. But, as Susan Watkins notices:

In this story, the family seems to be a rigid structure which is in no way flexible enough to incorporate the idea of middle-aged women's sexual and emotional intimacy with younger men, much less the suggestion that this intimacy is connected in some way to their intimacy with each other. Whether or not the family should be capable of containing mother son incest is a question that also exists as an uncomfortable resonance. (2007: 250)

Like the institution of the family, also home is a problematic category, for it might become synonym with violence and unspoken secrets, inclusion and exclusion, where "Membership is maintained by bonds of love, fear, power, desire and control [...] They are places of violence and nurturing" (Watkins 2007: 250; George 1996: 9).

First the husbands, later the daughters-in-law feel excluded from the quartet of mothers and sons, who create a sort of enclosed family. Even Tom, one of the boys, while visiting his by now divorced father, claims to feel free "up here", while feeling entrapped and imprisoned "down there" (Lessing 2003: 37), meaning his mother's and his friends' home. Therefore, also the concept of motherhood and ageing undergo a twisting and bending which is quite unusual. The age of the two women protagonists is about sixty, but the story develops retrospectively and is narrated by an omniscient narrator.

Yet, what is age exactly? How can it define a person's identity?

My body is at once sixty years old and several billion years old, since all of its atoms originated a few seconds after the Big Bang, hence are as old as the universe itself. Moreover, a body does not age uniformly in all its parts. The age of a weak heart is not that of a sound kidney. One may turn old in one part of the body and not in another over the course of years. As John Banville's protagonist remarks about his Italian neighbors in the novel *Shroud*: "They age from the top down, for these are still the legs... they must have had in their twenties or even earlier" (2014: 3–4). In sum, the body too is heterochronic. (Harrison 2014: 8)

Each individual is representative of this heterochronicity, of multiple times, condensed, some more visible or prominent than others, as Banville underlines, by noticing "youthful legs" in Italian elderly people.

The story's title, *The Grandmothers*, creates a short circuit in the identification of the two protagonists. If both fictional and scientific literature seem to generally agree with those who "recognize the 'grandmother' as one of the very few accepted female literary images in old age" (Oró Piqueras 2019: 88), here the grandmothers shatter this reassuring portrait. Lessing's story is one which includes heterochronicity, at least in the relationship between the social and familiar role of the grandmothers and their biological age. The novella's genesis is a story that an old man once told the writer as worth narrating, as Doris Lessing claims in an interview:

The Grandmothers was told to me some years ago by a man who has been a friend of the two boys, and who envied them and wished he was in their place. But when he approached older women the response was usually on the lines of "Run along, sonny." The convention is that boys are the prey of lustful older women, but usually it is the youngsters who approach the older women. And it is nearly always the older women who end it. But conventional morality has to have its say. I was struck by how the man telling me this tale repeated, again and again, that the women had been cruel to the end of the affairs. I kept asking him, "But what did you think could happen?" They were in their early fifties by then, and they were right to end it before they got too old. But he couldn't see it. "They were all so happy," he kept saying. His view of the thing as ten years of unmitigated bliss did rather influence the writing. Though my view of the story was darker than his. Life seldom comes up with ten years of perfect bliss. This man, my informant, was very funny: he was much older, and was putting past heartaches into perspective.[3]

This is a good piece of narrative, but why? Susan Watkins provides a suggestion, perhaps it is because this short story presents "women's sexuality and reproduction", and more in general "relationships outside the sanction of the patriarchal family" (2007: 249). Moreover, it is a story about how not to accept ageing passively and inertly, on the part of women. It is the story of two female's whimsical, eccentric, and brazen refusal of coming of age. Thus, when "Brennan and Hepworth argue that the main reasons why the figure of the grandmother remains an accepted image of female ageing is the fact that she is devoid of sexual implications; her role being mainly that of carer and emotional support when needed in the family" (Oró Piqueras 2019: 88–89), they might not be farther away from Lessing's daring imagination.

In the short story, the two boys in their twenties embody Apollonian beauty, while the two mothers incarnate Juno-like, mature beauty. Roz has divorced from her husband, right because her relationship with her best friend, Lil, is so pervasive and invasive, that they hint at being lesbians. Lil is a widow. Both their young boys suffer in different ways for the loss of their fathers. They end up in bed with their mother's best friend, partly to find consolation and maternal cocooning, partly as a safe initiation rite to sexual life with an intimate person, and partly as a vacation from life's responsibility, in a mockery of ancient Greek myths, where Gods and Goddesses descended on Earth to seduce mortals for their own leisure and recreation.

The resort, where they live, seems characterized by an a-temporal summertime: the time of eternal youth, at least according to the tradition in Shakespeare, who identified the summer with youth and the winter with old age.

In Sonnet n. 2 winter is a metaphor for old age, it is seen as an enemy besieging beauty, and the wrinkles in old age are seen as trenches in a battlefield:

---

3   Cf. https://b0f646cfbd7462424f7a-f9758a43fb7c33cc8adda0fd36101899.ssl.cf2. rackcdn.com/book-interviews/BI-9780060530112.pdf.

When forty winters shall besiege thy brow
And dig deep trenches in thy beauty's field,
Thy youth's proud livery, so gazed on now,
Will be a tattered weed, of small worth held.
(Shakespeare 1966: 3; n.2, ll. 1–4)

In Sonnet n. 18, famously Shakespeare mentions summer. In its opening line, "Shall I compare thee to a summer's day?" (Shakespeare 1966: 11;
n.18, l. 1), the mysterious Fair Youth is compared to the summer season
for his ripen beauty. More relevantly, perhaps, Sonnet n. 5 does neither
mention the Fair Youth, nor the marriage that might preserve his beauty
in his children, but speaks rather of a beauty that transcends time and
decadence, and is preserved almost forever. Thus, the last lines declare:

Then were not summer's distillation left,
A liquid prisoner pent in walls of glass,
Beauty's effect with beauty were bereft,
Nor it, nor no remembrance what it was:
But flowers distilled, though they with winter meet,
Leese but their show; their substance still lives sweet.
(Shakespeare 1966: n.5, ll. 9–14)

This idea, of a beauty that transcends the effects of time, is the status, the
suspended atmosphere in which the quartet of Lessing's protagonists
live. Their happiness has not so much to do with physical countenance
but with the bliss of the prolonged moment. The two mothers' beauty is
extra-temporal. The two couples do not live immorally, but a-morally in
a hedonistic reality, where beauty is intrinsic in the situation of shared
bliss of juvenescence and not so much in the carnal incident per sé, immersed as they all are in summer time, swimming and sun-bathing, always laying on the sea-shore like mermaids, as if in a never-ending holiday from life and responsibility.

Socially, the two women's way to procrastinate winter and old age
strongly questions morality, social norms and common sense. Their
love challenges "normative understanding" of love, gender and sexuality
(Oró Piqueras 2019: 90) it is almost incestuous and endogamous, for

it pertains to the domestic sphere; the friend's son is a substitute for the missing husband and at the same time mirrors, as in a twinship, their own child. Besides being ever present, consoling, and sheltering neighbors, both women have always been like second mothers to the boys. Their love is scandalous not only because they are mature women having sex with much younger men, but also because they keep the boys in their houses, thus preventing them from exogamous relationships. An aggravating element in this dangerous relationship is that they favor neoteny. In a sense the two mothers pursue rejuvenation, while the two boys are not allowed to abandon childhood entirely, and persist in protracted youth and dependence, as in:

> "Fetalization theory": humans are basically juvenile apes whose natural development (into adult apes) has been indefinitely retarded. Thanks to this retardation, humans remain "paedomorphic," or child-like in form, throughout their entire lives. (Harrison 1983: 17)

The two boys in the story are like child-apes. Although here Oedipus's myth is evoked, or better Lessing seems to produce an anti-Oedipus, for the boys have to symbolically kill the father, that is to say, acknowledge and come to terms with his absence, then they sleep with their substitute mothers not to kill them as in the classical myth, but right on the contrary to remain in that oedipal, child-like, or ape-like idyll for as long as possible. Literally they embody "Man, in his bodily development, a primate fetus that has become sexually mature" (Harrison 1983: 17).

Eventually, they get married and have their own children, two girls, loved by their grandmothers. Yet, the mother-son bond persists in the love letters that one of the boys has been writing, although not always sending, till then, to one of the women, thus creating an unacceptable scandal to the eyes of his young wife.

Here, the grandmothers preserve their juvenescence rather than accepting their ageing, proclaiming sexual rights also for ageing women. In this story, Lessing touches on another social taboo, that is having a young lover for a mature woman. This is something that is socially stigmatized, much more than a mature man having a younger female partner.

This prejudice is another case of ageism, a discrimination against older women who gain power over younger males, whereas older men are admired for patronizing over younger partners. If, on the one hand, "With this highly suggestive short story Lessing blurs the boundaries of time between the older women and the younger men, and, thus, ageing and the Western limitations attached to the ageing body" (Oró Piqueras 2019: 94), on the other hand, the story ends when the two women put an end to it. Suddenly, they seem to recover their wisdom, almost becoming old and wise. Yet, Doris Lessing admits that "they were right ending it before they got too old". She, too, seems unable to believe fully in her invention. She retreats from the very eccentricity she produced, in the end withdrawing her pawns from the game. This might be an autobiographical trait, for Doris Lessing herself, in spite of being a clever woman, an intellectual and an activist, admired by peer artists, refused to engage in a late love-affair, for she believed she was just too old.

Anyway, the writer did not dare to stretch the consequences of her own plot to the extreme. Elderly women in the end retreat in their right place within the family and within society. And only at the very end of the short story, the two women become real Grandmothers, although by now the two daughters-in-law threaten to prevent them from seeing their grandchildren ever again, as a form of extreme revenge. In this case, the generation gap seems inevitably to widen, and the family idyll is shattered.

After all, Doris Lessing's would-be adoptive daughter, Genny Diski provides a portrait of the artist as a withdrawing woman:

> She had had two serious affairs, with Clancy Sigal, an American writer ... The other affair was with a psychiatrist from the Maudsley who, she said, had been the love of her life, but who was married and not prepared to leave his wife. When I arrived there, there were a few one-night stands and weekends away with new men she met, [...] she seemed rather to have withdrawn or to be withdrawing from the idea of a settled relationship with a lover. [...] She explained that a son should not be a witness to his mother's sex life. Six years later, at her fiftieth birthday party, she told me that she was not going to have sex

any more. At her age it was demeaning to trail a younger man around, and there didn't seem to be any available and interesting old men. In any case, her interest in that sort of things was over. (Diski 2016: 85)

We might say that Doris Lessing did experiment in writing what she would not dare to put to the test in real life. After all, she surrendered to social conventions and standardized behavior, which define the role of women, particularly of elderly women, socially and culturally. She died at ninety-four, in 2013, having written remarkable works on old age and grandmothers, but still bringing with her the secret formula of happy ageing, unless we consider her storytelling as her gift to humanity, her contribution to "generativity", a legacy that comes from the past but looks straight into our future.

Works Cited

Concilio, Carmen (2001), "'Old Woman' e l'incontro con la morte in *The Diary of a Good Neighbour* di Doris Lessing e in *Fire on the Mountain* di Anita Desai." In Elsa Linguanti (ed.), *Personaggio – Donna. Lo sguardo dalla fine*, Urbino: QuattroVenti, pp. 127–152.

De Beauvoir, Simone (1996 [1970]): *The Coming of Age*, New York: Norton.

Diksi, Jenni (2016): *In Gratitude*, London: Bloomsbury.

George, Rosemary Marangoly (1996): *The Politics of Home: Postcolonial Relations and Twentieth-Century Fiction*, Cambridge: Cambridge UP.

Goldman, Marlene (2017): *Forgotten. Narratives of Age-Related Dementia and Alzheimer's Disease in Canada*, Montreal: McGill-Queen's University Press.

Gott, Merryn (2005): *Sexuality, Sexual Health and Ageing*, Oxford: Oxford University Press.

Harrison, Robert Pogue (2014): *Juvenescence. A Cultural History of Our Age*, Chicago: The University of Chicago Press.

Lessing, Doris (1983): *The Diary of a Good Neighbour*, London: Michael Joseph.

Lessing, Doris (2003): *The Grandmothers*, London: Harper Collins.

Oró Piqueras, Maricel (2019): "Representations of Female Ageing and Sexuality in Penelope Lively's *Moon Tiger*, Angela Carter's *Wise Children*, and Doris Lessing's *The Grandmothers*." In: Andrew King, Kathryn Almack and Rebecca L. Jones (eds), *Intersections of Ageing, Gender and Sexualities. Multidisciplinary International Perspectives*, Croydon: Policy Press, pp. 83–96.

Shakespeare, William, *The Sonnets*, Cambridge: Cambridge University Press, 1966.

Walker, Barbara G (1985): *The Crone, Woman of Age, Wisdom and Power*, San Francisco: Harperson.

Watkin, Susan (2007): "'Grande Dame' or 'New Woman': Doris Lessing and the Palimpsest." In: *Literature Interpretation Theory*, 17:3–4, 243–262, https://www.doi.org/10.1080/10436920600998829.

The Old Child in Susan Cooper's
The Dark Is Rising Series

João Paulo Guimarães[1]

When I started organizing this collection, some scholars to whom I showed the outline of the project voiced some concerns about the idea of putting together essays about experimental writing, science fiction and fantasy (SFF) side by side. These are, those people claimed, genres that simply do not belong together, with very different goals, audiences and traditions. To be sure, in *Re-Enchanted: The Rise of Children's Fantasy Literature in the Twentieth Century*, Maria Sachiko Cecire suggests that this might indeed be the case, when in the first few pages of her book she contends, apropos of J. R. R. Tolkien and C. S. Lewis, who were responsible for propelling the genre of fantasy to new heights of popularity in the postwar era: "[F]ar from wanting to 'make it new,' to quote the catchphrase of Modernism, they sought to step outside of relentless linear narratives of progress and instead spark a return to the medieval past that they loved" (2019: Kindle 3). Fantasy's fascination with the past does not, however, make it necessarily any less thought-provoking and epistemologically challenging, as I have argued in the introduction and as other chapters in this book try to show. In this essay I will pursue a similar line of thinking: fantasy can indeed be as de-familiarizing and de-naturalize reality just as much as an experimental text, even if the events it depects are not real (or even plausible) and its style is not realistic.

---

1   University of Porto (ILCML).

My piece focuses on Susan Cooper's "The Dark Is Rising" saga, which began in 1965, with *Over Sea, Under Stone*, and was concluced in 1977, with *Silver on the Tree*. The series is especially interesting when read from an Aging Studies perspective because its protagonist is, paradoxically, a child (born to a moder-day British family) who finds out he is the encarnation of an ancient undying spirit. Will Stanton is one of the so-called "Old Ones", tasked with defending humanity from the rise of the forces of the Dark. Alongside him are other allies of the Light, like Merriman Lyon (according to medievalist Jennifer Bryan, he is a Merlin figure with the trappings of our time: a professor with magical abilities) and Bran, a Welsh descendent of King Arthur. Throughout the series, Will learns how to control his power as an Old One, he collects (with the help of his companions) a set of magical signs and uses them in combination with a crystal sword to defeat his foes.

One could certainly argue that the overarching plot of the series is simplistic and its conceptions of good and evil rather naive. As Cecire points out, however, Cooper was responding to the straightforward moral reality of nazism and WW2 which she experienced first-hand (in particular the bombing of London). As Bryan observes, Cooper was "also indebted to T. S. Eliot and his quest for mythic origins in the midst of social and personal breakdown" (2017: 29). Moreover, the scholar reminds us that "according to models developed in the nineteenth century, Arthurian stories [provide] children with ethical role models to guide them in the acquisition of values and character." (2017: 29). The quasi-medieval framekwork of good vs. evil that we find in the series no doubt provides us with the comforts of a world in which characters can act with purpose and conviction, a valuable and edifying milieu especially in a time like ours, increasingly fragmented, murky and lacking clear asnwers as to what a truly progressive future would look like.

Most relevant for our purposes, "The Dark Is Rising" books take two different groups of people that we normally see as disenfranchised – children and old people – and mashes them together in the character of their protagonist. According to fantasy scholar Maria Nokolajeva, the figure of the child in children's literature is usually mobilized to probe the terrain of innocence and potentiality that one leaves behind when one climbs to the plateau of adulthood. Childhood, from the vantagepoint provided by stories like that of Peter Pan, is a phase one ultimately must grow out of. Nevertheless, children's literature grant children abilities that (temporarily, at least) make them more powerful than adults. Such is the case in "The Dark Is Rising", in which Will, an otherwise unremarkable boy, is given special status as a major player in the struggle for the fate of humanity, a role that many a child surely wishes she one day could play, especially given how children are normally excluded from the "serious" affairs of adults.

Will is treated as a child by his parents and sublings and many times acts like one, displaying as much puzzlement and uncertainty as a normal kid would. Although he is still getting used to it, we know that he is special, the last of the Old Ones. This "time-shift" mechanism gives him access to a timeless form of knowledge and wisdom. As Nikolajeva points out, "time-shift fantasy seems a more prominent genre in children's literature than in mainstream fiction . . . not least, time displacement focuses on change, growth, ageing and death, major issues in serious children's literature" (2012: 153). Will is granted immortality (and thus complete mastery over death) and acquires the wisdom of old age, of someone who has been alive since the beginning of human history.

As an admiror of T. S. Eliot's work, Cooper knows how valuable knowledge of the past can be for a grounded uderstanding of the present. In her essay about "The Dark Is Rising", Bryan links Merriman's statement that all times co-exist to Eliot's assertion that "a poet is not likely to know what is to be done unless he lives in the present moment of the past" (qtd. in Bryan 2017: 35). Knowledge of the past is not something that one acquires passively or automatically (i.e. it does not come naturally with old age), as Robert Pogue Harrison points out in his about about aging, titled *Juvenescence*. Harrison notes that "wisdom does not depend on age" and that "a man of a hundred may be full of empty talk" (2014: 44). In fact, he goes on to say that the acquisition of wisdom should begin at an early age (with an journey into the past, like Will's, who actively goes out in pursuit of the symbolic "signs of power") and that wisdom is something that needs to keep being renewed and reinvented with a childlike creative spirit. In order to be fully experienced, the past needs the present as much as the present needs the past. Moreover, one should add that it is a mistake to presuppose that old age necessarily leads to wisdom, and this is something that does a disservice to the unique histories and experiences of particular old people. At best, an older person will have a greater empirical understanding of the specific historical time she lived through, she may have amassed a unique set of memories and, as Harrison points out, she may have may have indeed worked to acquire greater learning or self-knowledge.

Another interesting way "The Dark Is Rising" can be put in conversation with Aging Studies requires us to attend to the way Cooper puts a spin on the figure of the child, which in this series does not fuction as a mere symbol of the future, unmoored from the past. Taking a cue from Cynthia Port's work on queer aging (she builds upon Lee Edelman's insights, in *No Future*, about how mainstream culture glamorizes children), Aging Studies scholars have been paying significant attention to how our age's obsession with the child as a quasi-messianic figure of redemption in effect leads to a further disenfranchisement and dismissal of older people, who ought to be treated as fully part of the present and as important as everyone else for ongoing discussions about the future.

Cooper is not, however, interested in presenting the child as a symbol of the future. Progress for progress's sake is rather the enemy of fantasy writers that follow in the footsteps of Tolkien and Lewis, as I have noted above. Instead, Cooper's "old child", Will, is bound to the past and he represents the hope in a future that draws its creative energies from an older, more cohesive and simple, time. Immortality as infinite longevity has no interest for Cooper. The author simply needs her main characters to be immortal so that they can tap into their culture's ancient traditions and use this knowledge to defeat evil. For Cooper, the noble values of Arthurian legend do not represent merely an interesting curiosity from the remote past. The middle ages do not simply conjure up a world we can escape to in order to avoid the complex challenges of the present. More than anything, the Arthurian mindset is useful. In a world in which one feels ever more impotent to change the course of things, a character like Will Stanton gives us hope and motivation. Cooper makes us believe that age-old values do matter, after all, and that, sticking to them (even if in a somewhat quixotic manner) renders one less vulnerable to the stagnating cynicism that defines the age that we live in.

Works Cited

Bryan, Jennifer (2017): "Memories, Dreams, Shadows: Fantasy and the Reader in Susan Cooper's *The Grey King*." In: *Arthuriana* 27.2, pp. 29–54.

Cecire, Maria Sachiko (2019): *Re-Enchantment: The Rise of Children's Fantasy Literature in the Twentieth Century*. Minneapolis: University of Minnesota Press.

Harrison, Robert Pogue (2014): *Juvenescence. A Cultural History of Our Age*, Chicago: The University of Chicago Press.

Nikolajeva, Maria (2012): "The Development of Children's Fantasy." In: Edward James and Farah Mendlesohn (eds.), *The Cambridge Companion to Fantasy Literature*. Cambridge: Cambridge University Press, pp. 50–61.

Port, Cynthia (2012): "No Future? Aging, Temporality, History, and Reverse Chronologies." In *Occasion: Interdisciplinary Studies in the Humanities*. https://arcade.stanford.edu/occasion/no-future-aging-temporality-history-and-reverse-chronologies.

Life after Youth
Elves and Elders in Medievalist Fantasy Literature

Jiwon Ohm[1]

Abstract: *The Middle Ages, despite its real existence, is often seen and used by fantasy writers as a tabula rasa to engrave their imagined stories. Its seeming state of blankness due to its distant time and lack of recorded histories allows the period to be used as a background for imaginative creations of creatures, peoples, and stories to engage with social issues pertaining to specific periods and places as well as the same issues that arise in different forms depending on the period and location. This article explores J.R.R. Tolkien's works on Middle-earth and Kazuo Ishiguro's The Buried Giant to illustrate how fantasy literature engages with the concept of (eternal-) youth and ageing. While Tolkien disrupts the idealization of (eternal-) youth through the fates of humans and imaginative races, Kazuo Ishiguro presents the value, growth and meaningfulness of life up until its very end by having readers follow the quest of an elderly couple. Both Tolkien and Ishiguro illuminate the meaningfulness and value of the lives of the aged up until the brink of death.*

Keywords: *Ageing; Tolkien; Ishiguro; Neo-medieval; Fantasy*

---

1   University at Buffalo.

Fantasy of Youth

Romanticization of (eternal-)youth has often been discussed, questioned, and challenged in many literatures, such as in the genre of
fantasy literature; this article will look specifically into how the topics
of youth and ageing have been contemplated in specifically *medievalist*
fantasy literature. Umberto Eco points out in *Travels in Hyperreality:
Essays* that a longing for the medieval period began soon after the period
ended, which caused it to "always [be] messed up in order to meet the
vital requirements of different periods, [so] it was impossible for [the
period] to be always messed about in the same way" (1973–1983: 65–68).
In the same vein as Eco, Geraldine Heng argues that, "The fantasy of
the medieval past itself, constructed and reinforced by postmedieval
periods, delivers material effects: The fantasy of a pre-political, pre-
racial, pre-nationalist, and pre-imperial time that is the Middle Ages—a
zone of freedom [...]" (2003: 15)[2]. Thus, the Middle Ages—"a zone of
freedom"—has been reimagined and reproduced at different times in
history to be used in ways its appropriators needed or wished to. Indeed,
the use of the medieval period has many strengths, such as in invoking
nostalgic feelings or nationalist sentiments, and for its seeming state of
blankness or malleability; a period of time so distant and with too few

---

2   This "zone of freedom," I believe, is the reason that fantasy literature has often been associated with escapism and therefore ostracized from the academic realm. Tolkien's works have only started to be taken seriously in the
past decade due to its continuing popularity. At the turn of the new century,
when the work was chosen as "the greatest book of the twentieth century" in
a survey conducted by a major bookstore in England and "the greatest book
of the millennium" in Amazon.com, numerous literary scholars "retched and
kvetched, wailed and flailed, gasped and grasped for explanations. One said
that they had failed and wasted their work of 'ed-u-ca-tion'" (Kreeft 2005:13).
Many Tolkien scholars, such as Tom Shippey, Joseph Pearce, Peter Kreeft, Brian
Rosebury, Bradley J. Birzer, Stuart D. Lee, Elizabeth Solopova, David Day, Ver-
lyn Flieger and Douglas A. Anderson have resisted the academic contention
against the fantasy genre, and examined Tolkien's works through the lenses of
medievalism, linguistics, Catholicism, mythology and fairy tales.

recorded histories that it could be used as a background for imaginative creations of creatures, peoples, and stories to engage with social issues pertaining to specific periods and places as well as the same issues that arise in different forms depending on the period and location, with an example being, one which J.R.R. Tolkien deemed significant, "Death and Immortality" (2000: 246).

Using medievalist fantasy literature, specifically J.R.R. Tolkien's works on Middle-earth and Kazuo Ishiguro's *The Buried Giant* as examples, this article will illustrate how medievalist fantasy engages with the concept of (eternal-)youth and ageing. In his works, Tolkien disrupts the idealization of (eternal-)youth through the fates of humans and the imaginative races of Hobbits and elves, as well as by writing older protagonists as great heroes who go on grand quests that change their lives. Kazuo Ishiguro presents the value, growth and meaningfulness of life up until its very end by having readers follow the final journey—or quest—of an elderly couple, Axl and Beatrice, and the elderly Sir Gawain, who joins them to fulfill his final duty. Both Tolkien and Ishiguro illustrate the potential of the aged for fruitful life and growth until the brink of their death as well as the value of such growth despite the elders' proximity to death.

Mortality as a Gift in Tolkien's Middle-Earth

J.R.R. Tolkien's *The Lord of the Rings: The Fellowship of the Ring*, begins with the announcement of the celebration of Bilbo Baggins's a hundred and eleventh birthday. Bilbo, who is the hero of the book's prequel, *The Hobbit* is described to be famous not only for his sudden disappearance and reappearance with riches, but also for "his prolonged vigour" (1954a: 21):

> Time wore on, but it seemed to have little effect on Mr. Baggins. At ninety he was much the same as at fifty. At ninety-nine they began to call him well-preserved; but unchanged would have been nearer the mark. There were some that shook their heads and thought this was too much of a good thing; it seemed unfair that anyone should

possess (apparently) perpetual youth as well as (reputedly) inexhaustible wealth. 'It will have to be paid for,' they said. 'It isn't natural
[...]!' (ibid: 21)

Describing Bilbo's "perpetual youth" on top of his wealth as being "unfair," Bilbo is the envied subject in the Shire just as he would be in our
societies. However, the envying Hobbits are not only right to say that
"It isn't natural," as Bilbo's youth comes from the power of an evil magic
Ring. Bilbo does indeed pay for it, as he is not happy with the eternal
look of youth that the Ring has given him. In fact, when Bilbo describes
how he feels to Gandalf before he departs the Shire, home of Hobbits,
for good, he says: "'I am old, Gandalf. I don't look it, but I am beginning
to feel it in my heart of hearts. *Well-preserved* indeed!' he snorted. 'Why, I
feel all thin, sort of *stretched*, if you know what I mean: like butter that has
been scraped over too much bread. That can't be right. I need a change,
or something'" (original emphasis ibid: 34). Contrary to everyone's belief,
Bilbo feels bitterness towards his "Well-preserved" body as it is not how
he feels mentally. He does not simply wish to find a place where he would
be able to "*rest*" away from bothersome relatives and other Hobbits, but
where he would like to finish his book with the ending lines, "*and he lived
happily ever after to the end of his days*" (original emphasis ibid: 34), insinu-
ating his expectation that he will, one day, hopefully, pass. Bilbo's journey, however, does not end even at the end of *The Lord of the Rings* when
he is a hundred and thirty-one years old. In fact, the last of Bilbo we see
is his travel to Valinor, home of the gods. Though he is barely able to stay
awake due to his old age, he joyfully says, "I think I am quite ready to go
on another journey" (1955: 337), exemplifying that one's life continues as
long as they continue to live it. Bilbo's life and his attitude towards extra
longevity and youth is connected to a prevalent and important theme in
Tolkien's works on Middle-earth, such as in *The Silmarillion*[3].

---

3   Amazon has recently adapted the appendices of *The Lord of the Rings* into a show
     titled, *The Lord of the Rings: The Rings of Power* (2022-), although much of its sto-
     ries seem to be inspired rather than adapted. The show does depict the corrup-
     tion of many Númenóreans who hate the elves and wish to enslave the elves,
     though the reasons are not elaborated on. Some scenes do engage with the

The Silmarillion is a collection of mythologies of Middle-earth, which includes the creation of Middle-earth and of its peoples such as the elves, dwarves and humans. It is in the third part of this book that what Tolkien called "the real theme" of his works— "Death and Immortality" (2000: 246)—are explicitly presented. The third part of this book, titled "Akallabêth," or "The Downfall of Númenor," narrates the downfall of the most noble and blessed humans, who are called "Númenóreans." Númenóreans, who were created after the elves. Númenóreans were not given the immortality that the elves had, but nonetheless were given long life spans of hundreds of years as well as stronger bodies that are immune to diseases. Although the Númenóreans were happy and satis-fied with their lives for many centuries, they began to envy the elves for their immortality. In our ageist perspective, such sentiment may seem natural. However, as shown by the title of this section, "The Downfall of Númenor," Tolkien believed that envying the elves' immortality was the downfall of these humans, as he writes that mortality, not immortality, was the "gift" bestowed to men. Moreover, he claims that many including the elves will come to, in reverse, "envy" the mortality of men: "Death is their fate, the gift of Illúvatar [the One God], which as Time wears even the Powers shall envy" (1977: 36). Contradicting the romanticization of eternal youth and immortality, Tolkien describes immortality as though it is a curse:

> [...] the children of Men dwell only a short space in the world alive, and are not bound to it, and depart soon whither the elves know not. Whereas the Elves remain until the end of days, and their love of the Earth and all the world is more single and more poignant therefore,

---

topic of elven time in relation to mortals' time. In one particular scene between Elrond, an elf, and Durin IV, a dwarf, who are friends, Durin is upset that El-rond had been absent from his life for twenty years, and his negative feeling exacerbates when Elrond asks, "Has it been only twenty [years]?" Durin angrily responds, "Twenty years may be the blink of an eye to an elf! But I've lived an entire life in that time!" (Hutchison 2022). However, the theme of ageing and time is not a striking theme that the show engages with, at least in the first season.

and as the years lengthen ever more sorrowful. For the Elves die not till the world dies, unless they are slain or waste in grief (and to both these seeming deaths they are subject); neither does age subdue their strength, unless one grow weary of ten thousand centuries; and dying they are gathered to the halls of Mandos in Valinor, whence they may in time return. But the sons of Men die indeed, and leave the world [...]. (ibid: 36)

More than anything, immortality results in sorrow or weariness for the elves; such as that of seeing the world itself pass before them, and that which is so intense it could result in their deaths, although even after death they do not truly die like humans do. This fate does not bring joy to the Elves, as exemplified through the elf Míriel, who, after giving birth, no longer wished to live, but could not truly die because her soul would live even after leaving her body (ibid: 63–65). Thus, for Tolkien and his elves, preserved youth and immortality do not necessarily bring joy.

Ungrateful for the gift of mortality bestowed upon them, envy overpowers the Númenóreans's minds, and they confront the gods and elves, and express their desire for immortality. However, the only response they receive is that they should accept their fate and gift of mortality just as the elves accept their fate and the consequences of immortality, which is "neither reward nor punishment, but the fulfilment of their being" (ibid: 315–7). Dissatisfaction towards the answer grows overtime, and as a result, so does "madness and sickness" which did not affect them before (ibid: 328). Such result insinuates that the real madness and sickness is the unyielding desire for immortality which caused the Númeóreans "to seek wealth rather than bliss" (2000: 155)[4] and lead to their complete downfall of rebelling against their creators and being forever exiled away from the blessed land of Númenór to the continent

---

4   Tolkien has used the word "sickness" to describe greed in *The Hobbit* while narrating the fate of the Master of Lake-town: "Bard had given him much gold for the help of the Lake-people, but being of the kind that easily catches such disease he fell under the dragon-sickness, and took most of the gold and fled with it, and died of starvation in the Waste, deserted by his companions" (1937: 305).

of Middle-earth. Mortals in Middle-earth who find a way for immortality are only able to achieve a "counterfeit" one, "lead[ing] the small to Gollum, and the great to a Ringwraith" (ibid: 286), neither who eternally exists as fully Hobbit nor human but as a ghoul or a wraith. Thus, although Tolkien sympathizes with the human desire for immortality, he warns against the reality of such fantasy.

Life After Youth

Stories dealing with a hero's journey usually have young protagonists who, like in a bildungsroman, grow physically and in mind through the experiences they have gained and relationships they have built in their journey. These stories end with the hero(es)'s coming-of-age and maturity into adulthood, in its own vague "and she lived happily ever after," as life is assumed to be stagnant once old. Such trope in literature has created a stereotype that life ends after one reaches adulthood. However, Tolkien's works do not follow this trope; most of the heroes in Tolkien's works are not children and are, at the least, middle-aged. In other words, for Tolkien, life *can* and in some cases *will* begin at a later age or continue despite old age.

In *The Hobbit*, Bilbo is fifty years old when Gandalf—an elderly wizard—appears with a group of mostly elderly dwarves to take him to a quest to find the dwarves' long-lost treasure as well as territory by defeating the great dragon, Smaug. Before Gandalf appeared, Bilbo was "considered very respectable" by other Hobbits because he was a Baggins, and "they never had any adventures or did anything unexpected" (1937: 2). Just like his father, a stereotypical middle-aged person, Bilbo, in his comfortable hobbit-hole, "had in fact apparently settled down immovably" (ibid: 3). When asked—or demanded—to go on the adventure with the dwarves, Bilbo declines and feels a pinch of regret having done so, but convinces himself that he has made the right decision saying to himself, "Don't be a fool, Bilbo Baggins! [...] thinking of dragons and all that outlandish nonsense at your *age!*" (ibid: 28) Though there is no doubt that Bilbo refused to go on the adventure because he felt settled in his life, this thought reveals that Bilbo refuses mostly because of his age. Eventually, Bilbo does go on the journey to become a hero of the quest, and despite his older age, returns to his home a changed Hobbit who has a wider perspective on the world, later visiting elves, spending time with dwarves and writing poems. Gandalf notices such change and exclaims, "My dear Bilbo! [...] Something is the matter with you! You are not the hobbit that you were" (ibid: 302). The only way that the Hobbits can accept Bilbo's change after his return is to consider he had perhaps lost his mind, as "few believed any of his tales" and would call him "queer" and "Poor old Baggins" (ibid: 304). The Hobbits' discomfort of Bilbo is not unlike the perspective people may have of old people who do not abide to societal rules of what ageing and the aged should look like, but as the narrator—or Tolkien—writes, "I am sorry to say [Bilbo] did not mind" (ibid: 304). Indeed, Bilbo departs on his final adventure when turns a hundred and thirty-one when he sets sail to Valinor.

Bilbo is not the only middle-aged protagonist who goes on an adventure and returns changed and emotionally matured. As aforementioned, aged and older characters such as Gandalf, most of the dwarves, and Bard who slayed the dragon Smaug, have all played major roles in *The Hobbit*. In *The Lord of the Rings*, Frodo Baggins sets out from the Shire to destroy the Ring at the age of fifty just like his uncle Bilbo. Other characters like Aragorn, the King of Gondor, is eighty-seven[5], Boromir, the first-born of the Steward of Gondor, is forty-one. Another noticeable character is Théoden, the King of Rohan, who is seventy-one years old.

Théoden had been ill-advised by a servant of the corrupted wizard, Saruman, for a long period of time which causes his mind and body to stiffen, and becomes witless and weak as elderly men are deemed to be. However, once the veil of ill-advice lifts, he swiftly regains his sanity and strength as he was under a spell. As his conscious returns, and Théoden notices that "It is not so dark," Gandalf answers, "No [...] Nor does age lie heavily on your shoulders as some have you think"

---

5   Hobbits are considered to come-of-age at the age of thirty-three and Aragorn
     is a descendant of the Númenórean line, so that even as a human he lives to be
     two-hundred and ten.

(1954b: 127), urging Théoden to not let age trick him into undermining his strength. Still, Théoden laments his survival as he hears the news of many deaths including the death of Boromir, exclaiming, "Alas for Boromir the brave! The young perish and the old linger, withering" as "He clutche[s] his knees with his *wrinkled* hands." Immediately after the description of Théoden's hands, Gandalf responds, "Your fingers would remember their old strength better, if they grasped a sword-hilt" (ibid: 129), again emphasizing that Théoden's age should not deter him from his potentials. Soon after, Théoden proves Gandalf right, "As his fingers took the hilt, it seemed to the watchers than firmness and strength returned to his thin arm" and "they looked at their lord in amazement" (ibid: 130). Théoden dies fighting in a great battle, after he plays multiple great roles in saving his people.

This is not to say that Tolkien writes that only the old can play significant roles, as that itself would be stereotyping the aged into the wise and know-it-all. Furthermore, there are younger characters who play big roles, such as Éowyn, who is twenty-four. For Tolkien, age should not be a determining factor in an individual's value, and both the old and young are neither perfect and equally prone to human mistakes and faults. Ageing does not necessarily mean growth for the young, as the young can be stagnant and unchanging as Bilbo was until he turned fifty. Likewise, the old will be witless and weak if they decide to remain so like Théoden did until Gandalf reminded Théoden's strength. Simultaneously, Tolkien does not romanticize eternal youth as he writes of the elves' envying of human mortality and through Bilbo's fatigue of life not only despite, but also because of the deceitful youthful appearance.

Kazuo Ishiguro's *The Buried Giant* as Fantasy

Set in a post-Arthurian England, Kazuo Ishiguro's *The Buried Giant* mainly follows the story of two Britons, Axl and Beatrice, who are an elderly couple. With their memories clouded by a mist, the couple sets out on a journey to find not only their son, but also the memories they have lost. While on this journey, the couple gets roped into a larger quest to defeat the dragon, Querig. When this work was published, Ishiguro was not sure how his work would be received, and wondered whether people would consider it a work of fantasy (Alter 2015). Many fantasy writers such Ursula K. Le Guin, Lev Grossman and David Mitchell responded by confirming that *The Buried Giant* is, indeed, fantasy (ibid; Cain 2015) despite Ishiguro's lack of intentionality[6].

Notwithstanding his unintentional entrance to the fantasy realm, the reason Ishiguro chose to set *The Buried Giant* in a medieval past is the same as those writers' who cho(o)se to use medievalist fantasy for its "zone of freedom." Richard Rankin Russell agrees, though not specifically regarding *medievalist* fantasy, in Ishiguro's choosing of fantasy which "enables [Ishiguro] to explore the territory of 'universal human experiences'" (2021: 305). Explaining his choice of his book's setting, Ishiguro stated that "The Buried Giant's fantasy setting served as a neutral environment [...]" (Cain 2015) and that the setting is a "historical never-never land, so that it could be applied to all kinds of settings" (Russell 2021: 305). Similar to Tolkien, the medieval setting offered Ishiguro the space to write about what he believes to be universal themes.

The Elders in Kazuo Ishiguro's *The Buried Giant*

One of the most striking themes in Ishiguro's *The Buried Giant* is the loss and (re-)gaining of memory; not only on a national level, but also on an individual level with the focus on elderly characters. More specifically, the memories of these individual are tied to the memories of the nation and vice versa. Ishiguro claims, "I wasn't just interested in nations [...] and that question about when do we need to remember, when do we need to forget things. I was also interested in that same question applied to a marriage" (2015b). The main protagonists of *The Buried Giant* are an elderly married couple, Axl and Beatrice, seeking for answers about their past which they have forgotten much of, but as readers are to quickly find

---

6   "And by and large I've rather enjoyed my inadvertent trespassing into the fantasy genre, too, although I wasn't even thinking about *The Buried Giant* as a fantasy – I just wanted to have ogres in there!" (Gaiman 2015)

out, *not due to ageing*. Like Bilbo, Frodo, and many other characters from Tolkien's works, the story revolves around old characters' journey and quest, rather than that of the young. Axl and Beatrice's goal is to reunite with their son, which turns into a quest in which they encounter knights, an ogre, and eventually Querig, the dragon they must slay to recover their lost memories. Thus, at the forefront of the story is the journey of a couple whose lives and memories are entangled with other individuals and communities whom, together, form a nation; most importantly, the elderly couple goes on a quest in which their relationship grows instead of wither, and in which they gain memory instead of losing it[7].

At the beginning of the story, it is easy to fall into the trap of believing that Axl and Beatrice are suffering from memory loss due to their age. After all, readers are first introduced to the elderly Axl questioning himself and the community he lives in, and his inability to answer any of these questions, as he suffers from memory loss. When Axl remembers something while others do not, he is "almost ready to admit he had been mistaken [...]. He was after all an ageing man and prone to occasional confusion" (2015a: 9) and doubts his own memories because he believes it is a result of his ageing. With the ageist bias and with Axl's amnesia, it is easy to presume that Axl may be suffering from dementia or Alzheimer's. However, as though foreseeing and challenging the bias

---

7   An important article written in regards to in Kazuo Ishiguro's *The Buried Giant* and ageing is Sarah Falcusa and Maricel Oró-Piquerasb's "Ageing without Remembering: Neomedieval Fantasy, Memory and Loss in Kazuo Ishiguro's *The Buried Giant*." This article argues that "What is significant about this novel's exploration of memory, trauma and history, however, is the way it links cultural and national memory to individual experience, the life course and generational identity, making ageing itself central to the exploration of time and history in the novel" (2020: 5). Naturally, the article elaborates on the generational relationships in connection to memory, trauma and history, the empowerment of the aged and the questioning of the youths' futurity. Meanwhile, I will focus specifically on how Ishiguro uses three elderly characters in order to subvert the trope of quests-for-youths in literature, how he reflects ageism in societies, uses readers' ageist biases to challenge ageist notions of mental and physical frailty in *The Buried Giant*.

judgment, the narrator asks, "You may wonder why Axl did not turn to his fellow villagers for assistance in recalling the past," and proceeds to explain that the memory loss is caused by a mist which everyone suffers from collectively: "[...] in this community the past was rarely discussed [...] it had somehow faded into a mist [...]. It simply did not occur to these villagers to think about the past—even the recent one" (ibid: 7). Ishiguro also clarified in an interview that in this imagined medieval Britain, there is "some sort of memory loss nothing to do with ageing or you know, dementia" (2015b). Rather, Axl is the one who has the most memories. For example, he remembers a red-haired woman who used to heal people in the village, and Marta, a child who went missing, both of whom nobody else seems to recall. He also experiences other "steady run of such puzzling episodes" (2015a: 7–12) in which only he remembers someone or something. Thus, contrary to ageist biases, Axl is the one who has the strongest memory.

The attitude of villagers towards Axl and Beatrice as elderlies is also disparaging. The narrator strongly insinuates that Axl and Beatrice have been pushed to live at the outer border of the village, "where their shelter was less protected from the elements and hardly benefitted from the fire in the Great Chamber where everyone congregated at night" because of their old age. Axl suspects that he and his wife may have lived closer to the Great Chamber when they were younger (ibid: 5). Additionally, candles, which are distributed to younger villagers, are not given to the old couple. Depriving them of candles angers Beatrice, who generally has a sweet temperament. She complains to Axl:

> "It's an insult, forbidding us a candle through nights like these and our hands as steady as any of them. While there's others with candles in their chamber, senseless each night from cider, or else with children running wild. Yet it's our candle they've taken, and now I can hardly see your outline, Axl, though you're right beside me" (ibid: 9) [8]

---

8   It is possible that candles could have been taken from them for specific reasons. For example, though not fully elaborated, there is an incident when Beatrice almost lost one of her nice cloaks in a fire which might have caused villagers to believe that she was not to be trusted with a candle. Nonetheless, from the

Although Beatrice notes that she and Axl are as productive and healthy as anyone else, they are still deemed less worthy of the warmth and light from both the Great Chamber due to their age.

The couple's anxiety about being perceived as useless is demonstrated when Beatrice rushes her husband back to work as he is already considered "slow": "Then go on with your business, husband, for I'm sure they'll be complaining again how slow you are at your work, and before you know they'll have the children chanting at us again." Although Axl rebukes, "I've never heard a word of such complaint and I'm able to take the same burden as any man twenty years younger," and Beatrice responds that she was just "teasing" (ibid: 15–16), that the couple have been pushed to the edge of the village and are revoked of having candles insinuate that Beatrice may be right, and that the couple is not a valued part of the community even despite the fact that "advanced though they were in years, [they] had their burden of daily duties" in the village (ibid: 27).

The villagers' maltreatment of the elderly couple reaches a climax when a child gives Beatrice a candle and the villagers try to take it from Beatrice by force, while others in the crowd watch with "amusement," "shouting" and "laughter" as the old woman wrestles with all her power to protect "a squat, somewhat misshapen candle" (ibid: 20–21). When the pastor of the village arrives to the scene, instead of showing empathy, he orders people to take the candle from Beatrice and feigns kindness once the candle is taken from her using her old age as an excuse for her behavior: "Leave Mistress Beatrice in peace and none of you speak unkindly to her. *She's an old woman who doesn't understand all she does*" (ibid: 22). After the debacle, once the crowd disperses and the old couple are left alone, Axl asks Beatrice why she is so fixated on the candle when they had lived without one for so long, Beatrice simply responds, "They think us a foolish pair, Axl," indicating that it is not the candle itself that Beatrice truly wants, but basic human respect and rights. Beatrice claims that

---

villager's short-term memory of not even remembering the lost child, Marta, it is difficult to say that they would remember such small incident to the point in which they would ban an elderly couple from having candles.

if they had their son with them—someone younger—he would be able to protect them (ibid: 23). This event becomes the final catalyst which triggers Axl and Beatrice to set out on the journey to a neighboring village to reunite with their son, which they kept forgetting or pushing off, as they believe that people would treat them more respectfully if they had someone *younger*, their son, to protect them. In short, the couple departs the village because, although they have the most comprehension and memory regarding the village and its inhabitants, they are neither treated with respect nor dignity due to their age which is a reflection of ageism prevalent in societies.

Quests of the Elders: The Axl, Beatrice, and Sir Gawain

The Buried Giant challenges most mainstream literature where the protagonists are children or young adults and in which their lives, stories and growths seem to end once they become adults. Similar to Bilbo and Frodo in *The Hobbit* and *The Lord of the Rings*, Axl and Beatrice initially set out of their village to find their son and *unexpectedly* end up becoming part of an important quest which is to determine not only their own fate, but also the fate of their nation and peoples. Although the old couple's original goal was to reunite with their son, their desire to remember their shared memories becomes more important for them which results in their joining the quest to kill Querig once they find out that the dragon's breath is the cause of the mist.

Axl and Beatrice's determination to aid in the quest to kill the dragon was provoked by their desire to regain their memory. The old couple resists against the natural urge to blame their loss of memory on ageing. Although the couple is eager to regain their memories, they do sometimes wonder if their love is stronger due to the fact that there are events which they do not remember. Nevertheless, trusting in the strength of their love, the old couple keeps pushing forward. This decision causes the old couple to experience adventures from fairy tales such as, out of many things, smuggling a young knight, Wistan, and a boy, Edwin, past Briton's soldiers who wish to capture or kill them, meet with the legendary Sir Gawain, escape a monastery of corrupted people through an underground tunnel, combat a monstrous hound and fight pixies.

After the many adventures, stereotypically unsuitable for an old couple, Axl and Beatrice finally reach the dragon with Sir Gawain and Wistan. After witnessing Wistan slay Querig, the old couple remembers what were forgotten as the mist which had caused people's mysterious loss of memories dissipate. Once their memories fully return, the old couple remembers the event which caused the breach in their relationship: Beatrice's infidelity which led their son to leave and eventually die from a plague. This remembrance, however, does not end the couple's relationship, but instead makes it stronger as they are able to accept the past events and understand that they have grown out of the spite they had for each other, as their love also grew. Such possibility of growth until death is portrayed with the couple's final conversation with each other and their respective private conversations with the boatman as they must part due to Beatrice's final journey with the boatman to the island where their son awaits[9].

Of course, their journey is not glamorized in any way as the couple experiences many drawbacks due to their aged bodies. For example, the old couple takes up the difficult detour up a mountain in order to visit Father Jonus, who is known for his medicine, in a monastery due to a physical illness Beatrice suffers. They also take longer to reach places due to their aged bodies which becomes more explicit once the young boy, Edwin, joins their journey and often becomes frustrated by the couple's sluggishness. At the beginning of their journey together, Edwin asks himself, "[...] why travel with these two elderly Britons who required rest at each turn of the road?" and thinks, "they had so far been kind [...], but they were frustrating companions all the same" (2015a: 92–93). Nevertheless, as Edwin and the couple experience tribulations together, the boy grows to, if not love the couple, respect them and accept them as people who are more than just a burden. Even Wistan who is vengeful towards all

---

9   The boatman in *The Buried Giant* resembles Charon. In Greek mythology, Charon
     is the ferryman who carries the dead souls across the river Acheron or Styx to
     the afterworld. The island therefore symbolizes the afterworld.

Britons grows to respect the old couple's kindness and tenacity, as does the legendary Sir Gawain. Thus, although the story is of an elderly couple's final journey together, it is not of deterioration, but of living, growing, venturing and being affected by and affecting others until the brink of death.

Another notable elderly character in *The Buried Giant* is Sir Gawain. Ishiguro's Sir Gawain is the same legendary knight who is the nephew of King Arthur. Axl and Beatrice run into him soon after they depart the second village with Edwin and Wistan. The moment Sir Gawain enters the narrative, the couple becomes part of a bigger legend—the remnant of the Arthurian legend. Sir Gawain in *The Buried Giant*, however, is not the young and mighty Sir Gawain as popularly known from the Arthurian legend, but an elderly—though not frail— knight, who remains to fulfill his uncle's final order to defend the dragon until his death. Ishiguro dedicates two chapters of Part III of the book with Sir Gawain's internal thoughts, titled, "Gawain's First Reverie" and "Gawain's Second Reverie" giving weight to the significance of the character.

Despite the fact that Sir Gawain is a legendary knight, he is depicted as a normal elderly person, with his body having been also susceptible to ageing. The first impression of Sir Gawain is through Axl's perspective, in which his outer appearance presents a frail old man:

> Axl saw that the knight was no threatening figure. He appeared to be very tall, but beneath his armour Axl supposed him thin, if wiry [...]. The face protruding from the armour was kindly and creased; above it, several long strands of snowy hair fluttered from an otherwise bald head. He might have been a sorry sight, fixed to the ground, legs splayed before him [...]. (ibid: 104–105)

Axl's view of Sir Gawain is almost as though of an old man who is decaying, with the realistic depiction of the legendary knight's ageing becoming almost a rude awakening to the readers that the legendary Sir Gawain is, after all, just an old man.

However, although Sir Gawain's aged body even requires Axl and Beatrice's help "to bring the old knight [himself] to his feet" (ibid: 114), readers—alongside Axl—must reassess the rash judgment as we are soon to discover that Sir Gawain is no weak man: "when finally he straightened to his full height in his armour and pulled back his shoulders, he was an impressive sight" (ibid: 114). Sir Gawain often proves his vigor and skills in moments such as when he sees the monstrous hound and laughs at it (ibid: 175). Regardless of what Sir Gawain says, the characters draw a hasty conclusion that the old knight has failed to kill the monster when they see monster's body running even after Sir Gawain swung his sword. However, they soon find out that Sir Gawain had actually successfully cut off the monster's head and it was only its body running, once again dispelling the belief that the old knight is weak.

In the same vein, ageism in *The Buried Giant* deceived its people into assuming that Sir Gawain's weakness is what kept Querig alive, as the belief is that Sir Gawain was the one entrusted to slay the dragon. However, it is later revealed that Sir Gawain used the ageist bias against others and feigned this weakness, as his actual role is to defend the dragon. Sir Gawain's reveries expose that both age and the weight of his guilt—having been the cause of so many deaths—has worn the old knight down to the point that he is almost looking forward to his death. Nevertheless, as Axl and Beatrice are determined to see the dragon killed, Sir Gawain is determined to defend the dragon (ibid: 214). Sir Gawain perseveres even knowing that he must fight the powerful and younger knight, Wistan.

Despite his awareness of his physical disadvantage due to his aged body, Sir Gawain is still able to analyze Wistan's combat movements to find a "small weakness" he believes might give him a chance for victory (ibid: 205). Wistan understands the advantage of his youthful physique and accepts Sir Gawain's request to let them begin the combat with their weapons unsheathed, as Sir Gawain's slower body would ensure his loss otherwise. Although Sir Gawain eventually loses, he was given the chance to die with dignity and Wistan acknowledges that it was the most difficult combat he had fought (ibid: 292). Thus, although Sir Gawain is a knight from the legends, his ageing was not glamorized as the consequences of ageing was not undermined. Simultaneously, rather than depicting a helpless old knight, *The Buried Giant* depicts a knight who set out on a quest in his youth, and whose quest continues even after ageing. Similar to Axl and Beatrice, Sir Gawain is but an old man still living and going through life-changing journeys while in the midst of an extraordinary quest. In short, Axl, Beatrice and Sir Gawain's lives continue as aged people's and are not less valuable, significant, impactful or uneventful than those of younger; even the final word, experience, and change of mind at the brink of death are invaluable.

Fantasy of Ageing in Fantasy

With the colossal success of *The Lord of the Rings*, the eternally young, beautiful and healthy Tolkienesque elves have become prevalent in popular culture. However, the popularized version of elves is stripped of the complexity of eternal youth and life which Tolkien explicitly highlights in *The Silmarillion*. Such simplification is ironically a result of our likemindedness as the Númenóreans of Middle-earth, who romanticized and envied the elves' eternal life and youth without considering its implications and consequences. As Tolkien wrote succinctly in a letter answering a question about elves, "they were not unageing or unwearying [...] a burden may become heavier the longer it is borne" (2000: 325) which is also echoed in Ishiguro's *The Buried Giant* when Sir Gawain reflects on the fatigue he feels ageing due to the weight of his guilt. Indeed, ageing does not simply mean a deterioration of the physical, but also eternally bearing the accumulation of burdens such as regret and loss.

One notable medievalist fantasy writer who has taken a step farther than Tolkien in deromanticizing the longevity of elves is Andrzej Sapkowski—"the Polish Tolkien" (Purchese 2019)—in his *The Witcher* series. Also set in an imaginary medievalist fantasy world, unlike in Tolkien's Middle-earth from which the elves sailed away to a haven, the elves in Sapkowski's world stayed in the same world as humans, dwarves and halflings who are equivalent to Tolkien's Hobbits. Although the initial instinct may be to believe that the elves are respected as the wise, in Sapkowski's world, they are overpowered by humans who kill the elves, take their lands and enslave them. The elves who survived must suffer the longevity of their lives hiding from and fighting humans who have also affected nature itself: "The sun shines differently, the air is different, water is not as it used to be. The things we used to eat, made use of, are dying, diminishing, deteriorating" (1993). Sapkowski's elves must suffer either their slaughter or must die with the world.

Rather than placing the elves who are physically youthful and wise in mind at the center, Tolkien instead chooses older and commonplace characters who are past their middle-age, such as Bilbo and Frodo as the main protagonists of his works. Furthermore, for Tolkien, although older in age, these characters are not the wiser: realistically depicting old people who lived insular lives in naïveté or ignorance, Bilbo and Frodo are rather like children despite their older ages. Unlike little children or young adults going on adventures and returning home wiser after experiencing trials and tribulations and accomplishing goals and quests, it is the aged characters who go on such journey and return home wiser.

Similarly, Ishiguro's main characters are elders who go on a great journey which change their lives, albeit right before their deaths. Impending death is not reason for individuals to sit at wait for it to arrive. The lives of the aged continue, be it amongst themselves or younger people, and their lives continue to have an effect, just as they continue to be affected by life. Death is not something that the aged passively to resign to, but an occurrence which must be accepted; until death arrives, the aged too, will and should live. Thus, exemplified by Tolkien's and Ishiguro's medievalist fantasy works, the concept of ageing has been a prevalent conversation in the genre and will continue to remain so as the genre itself opens boundless spaces for such timeless topic.

Works Cited

Alter, Alexandra (2015): "For Kazuo Ishiguro, 'The Buried Giant' is a Departure." In: The New York Times February 19.

Cain, Sian (2015). "Writer's indignation: Kazuo Ishiguro rejects claims of genre snobbery." In: The Guardian March 8.

Eco, Umberto (1986 [1973–1983]): Travels in Hyperreality: Essays, Translated by William Weaver, New York: Harcourt.

Faculsa, Sarah/Oró-Piquerasb, Maricel (2020): "Ageing without Remembering: Neomedieval Fantasy, Memory and Loss in Kazuo Ishiguro's *The Buried Giant*." In: Journal of Aging Studies vol 55.

Gaiman, Neil (2015): "'Let's talk about genre': Neil Gaiman and Kazuo Ishiguro in Conversation." In: The New Statesman June 4.

Heng, Geraldine (2003): Empire of Magic: Medieval Romance and the Politics of Cultural Fantasy, New York: Columbia UP.

Hutchison, Gennifer (2022): "Adrift." In: The Lord of the Rings: The Rings of Power September 1, Amazon.

Ishiguro, Kazuo (2015a): The Buried Giant, New York: Alfred A. Knopf.

Ishiguro, Kazuo (2015b): "Kazuo Ishiguro: The Buried Giant." In: The Agenda with Steve Paikin July 22, Youtube.

Kreeft, Peter (2005): The Philosophy of Tolkien: The Worldview behind The Lord of the Rings, San Francisco: Ignatius Press.

Purchese, Robert (2019): "Seeing Red: The Story of CD Projekt." In: Eurogamer May 15.

Russell, Richard Rankin (2021): "Ishiguro's *The Buried Giant*: The (Re)turn to Fantasy from *the Remains of the Day*." In: The Comparatist vol. 45, pp. 300–323.

Sapkowski, Andrej (2008 [1993]): The Witcher: The Last Wish, trans., Danusia Stok, London: Orbit Books, Kindle.

Tolkien, J.R.R (1937): The Hobbit, New York: Del Rey.

Tolkien, J.R.R (1999 [1977]): The Silmarillion, Glasgow: Harper Collins.

Tolkien, J.R.R (2000): The Letters of J.R.R. Tolkien: A Selection, ed., Humphrey Carpenter, London: Houghton Mifflin.

Tolkien, J.R.R (2012 [1954a]): The Lord of the Rings: The Fellowship of the Ring, New York: Del Rey.

Tolkien, J.R.R (2012 [1954b]): The Lord of the Rings: The Two Towers, New York: Del Rey.

Tolkien, J.R.R (2012 [1955]): The Lord of the Rings: The Return of the King, New York: Del Rey.

"how to dance / sitting down"
Aging, Innovation and the Graying of Disability"

Michael Davidson[1]

"What is age anyway? Something
you don't understand."
– Leonora Carrington, *The Hearing
Trumpet*

Abstract: *The topic of aging has been somewhat overlooked in disability studies,
perhaps owing to the adage that "everyone is disabled if they live long enough." If
the life course is simply a state of debility, why create a distinct category for bodily
and sensory impairment? Disability in old age, I argue, is not a mark of precarity but of capability. The work of writers and artists who continue to experiment
formally while becoming increasingly disabled in later years (Beethoven, Henry
James, Merce Cunningham) offers an opportunity to complicate "late style" as developed by Theodor Adorno and Edward Said and account for the role of complex
embodiment in the production of new work. Finally, I consider Samuel Beckett,
whose characters are often aging and disabled and for whom bodily and sensory
decline are central to their ability to "go on."*

Keywords: *disability; debility; aging; Samuel Beckett; "late style"*

---

1   University of California, San Diego.

Precarious New World

In the spring of 2020, many of us became old. I don't mean that we became aged by exposure to COVID-19 but that we emerged as a distinct epidemiological category. Where elderly persons in a market-driven society are often invisible or else channeled into the ideology of "successful aging," we are now a statistical category, a vulnerable demographic that must be protected.[2] Our new visibility was registered in special elder hours at markets, meal delivery services, expanded on-line shopping, conversations with grandchildren through nursing home windows, and headlines like those in a *New York Times* article early in the pandemic advising "How to Protect the Elderly. "And an emphasis on the age and health of older political figures increased in light of their vulnerability to the virus. A 2020 cartoon featured the image of the then-living Chief Justice Ruth Bader Ginsberg floating in a bottle of hand sanitizer expressing, perhaps, the fervent hope that she could be protected through the duration and fight on through the next election.[3]

There is a more insidious undercurrent to the outing of aging persons during the pandemic concerning the bioethics of national identity. The paucity of testing equipment, masks, medical supplies, and hospital beds revived eugenics era concerns about who should live or die, who is "at risk" and who is "safe." Correspondingly, the Trump Administration was far more concerned about the economic bottom line than a vulnerable population. At a rally in Ohio Trump offered the comforting opinion that the coronavirus only "affects elderly people, elderly people with heart problems and other problems... But it affects virtually nobody. It's an amazing thing" (Bella: 2020). Notice the quick segue between "elderly

---

2   On "successful aging" discourses, see Hailee M. Gibbons, "Compulsory Youthfulness."

3   The hope this cartoon expressed could not stave off the inevitable. Ruth Bader Ginsberg died on September 18, 2020. Trump invoked vulnerable elderly persons in a campaign ad that depicted an older woman living at home alone when an attacker breaks in: "She's unable to reach anyone at 911 in Joe Biden's America," the ad read.

people" and "virtually nobody." His cancellation of nursing home oversight and infection-control regulations early in the pandemic, his refusal to receive counsel from epidemiologists and scientists, resulted in the illness and deaths of countless patients and helped to normalize an attitude that the disabled and the elderly were dispensable. Getting old in this climate can also mean getting dead. But there's a silver lining. The Lieutenant Governor of Texas suggested that older people should return to work and risk infection—as their "patriotic duty"—to save the economy for the younger generation (Rodriguez: 2020).

I introduce the contemporary pandemic here to suture the relationship between aging and aesthetic experiment, since those two terms resonate differently when the life course becomes, for good or ill, a site for social innovation and bioethical revision. In the name of progress, we have all become members of what Viet Thanh Nguyen calls "the precariat" (2020: 10). But I want to approach risk as an aesthetic imperative that is not a liability but rather a value, a state of being in "uncertainties, mysteries, doubts without any irritable reaching after facts and reason" as Keats famously said. Taking risks in art is the very requirement for change, even if—perhaps because—it is dangerous. Unlike the brave new world of Huxley's titular novel in which aged persons are sent to "dying hospitals" at age sixty, the precarious new world is one that embraces both the challenges and the capabilities produced by being at risk.[4]

The True Gerontology

Among the many depictions of aging humans in Samuel Beckett's *oeuvre*, perhaps the most moving is that of Nagg and Nell in *Endgame*. Forced by their son, Hamm, to live in trashcans and survive on Spratt's Biscuits, they emerge from time to time to reminisce about lost love and grumble about their lot. "Me pap," shouts Nagg, to which Hamm responds, "Accursed progenitor!…the old folks at home! No decency left! Guzzle, guzzle, that's all they think of" (9). Nagg and Nell in their ash bins reflect a

---

4   On Huxley's novel and aging, see Maren Linett, *Literary Bioethics* (2020: 61–88).

common belief, implicit in Trump's remarks that persons once past their prime have ceased to be productive. Theodor Adorno calls Hamm's treatment of his parents, the "true gerontology" (1998: 32). We could understand this as a statement about disability in Beckett's oeuvre in general in which aging, disabled, and dependent individuals are faced with the prospect of "going on" despite society's indifference. The "endgame" of *Endgame* is not the end of the game but the evidence of the game's potential repetitions—the life course reduced to an endless cycle of interdependent relationships.

Beckett's work in its entirety is a brief on the ideology of decline, often depicted as a comic attempt to confront what society regards as a tragic loss of power. Vladimir and Estragon in *Waiting for Godot*, Krapp listening to tapes of his past life, Winnie in *Happy Days* laying out her possessions as she is swallowed up by the earth. It is less often said of this narrative that it grows out of disability. In *Endgame* Hamm is blind and lacks the use of his legs; Clov has a stiff leg and is losing his sight; Nagg and Nell have lost their limbs in a bicycling accident. The ideology of decline is countered, in Beckett's work, by forms of abject dependency as characters create uncomfortable alliances with each other while waiting for Godot. "Uncomfortable" because dependency is often regarded as weakness or hated subservience in a society that values independence and autonomy. If we bracket such relations from the social contract, we fatally ignore, as Alasdair Macintyre says, the "virtues that we need, if we are to confront and respond to vulnerability and disability both in ourselves and in others" (1999: 5).[5]

Adorno's remark about "true gerontology" recognizes aging not as a biological but a cultural fact—a set of social meanings imposed on the aging body. When the body is no longer useful in a productivist society, it becomes a problem that needs to be diagnosed, medicalized, or institutionalized. In this respect Adorno anticipates more recent theorists who are challenging the binary of ability/disability by introducing

---

5   I have discussed Beckett's thematics of dependency in *Invalid Modernism* (2019: 83–101).

the term "debility" as a pervasive human condition of neoliberal society.[6] When personhood is defined by progress, privatization, and profit, the body, as Jasbir Puar says, "is always debilitated in relation to its ever-expanding potentiality" (2017: 13). In the US where universal healthcare is a distant dream, where medical costs are prohibitive, and where "compulsory youthfulness" dominates the media, debility is the unintended consequence of privatization and biopolitics.[7] We live, as Sarah Locklain Jain says, in "prognosis time" that defines life lived in a biomedical future: not quite cured while awaiting the next test, scan, or biopsy. Although Jain is using "prognosis time" to describe the uncertainties of persons living with cancer, the phrase has special relevance for older persons. When I retired from teaching, one of my doctors joked, "aren't you glad that you've retired? Now you'll have more time to spend with us." True enough!

While I welcome the challenge that debility theory offers by specifying the economic implications for and on disability, I worry that it will become a substitute for that term, effacing the long history of activism for disability rights and re-framing disability around frailty and vulnerability. Disability as a rights-bearing category has been a target of debility theory, since a key goal of achieving equal rights imagines an embodied norm to which all aspire. As David Mitchell and Sharon Snyder suggest, "neoliberal inclusionism tends to reify the value of normative modes of being developed with respect to ablebodiedness, rationality, and heteronormativity" (2015: 2). As a general theory of how neoliberalism interpellates bodies around a model of ability, debility generalizes a population on a wide spectrum of capabilities—from the prelingually deaf person whose first language is sign-language and who lives in a vibrant community of culturally Deaf persons to the late-deafened indi-

---

6   Although he is not associated with debility theory, Tobin Siebers in *Disability Theory* provides an early and important summary of the relationship between the two terms: "For better or worse, disability often comes to stand for the precariousness of the human condition, for the fact that individual human begins are susceptible to change, decline over time, and die" (2008: 5).

7   The phrase "compulsory youthfulness" was coined by Hailee M. Gibbons, "Compulsory Youthfulness: Intersections of Ableism and Ageism in 'Successful Aging' Discourses" (2020).

vidual who lives within hearing culture; from the person born with cerebral palsy to the person who develops a spinal cord injury later in life; from a person who lives with chronic pain to the person who lives with occasional migraines. And where do persons with intellectual or cognitive disabilities fit into the debility paradigm? Those of us who conduct our daily lives with a disability may find "frailty" or "debility" inadequate descriptors for our condition. We are not all living in a diagnostic present, nor are we passive before the neoliberal state of exception. This future targeted temporality, grounded (implicitly) in a medical model, may apply to able-bodied persons who fear the diagnosis of cancer or Alzheimer's disease, but it seems reductive to assume that we all are, to paraphrase Lauren Berlant, "haunted by the disability to come [while] disavowing the debility that is already here" (qtd in Puar 2017: 12).

Given the limitations of a debility-based theory of embodiment, I want to interject the word "disability" between two seemingly opposed terms—aging and aesthetic experiment—to emphasize that the relationship between them is always a matter of being at risk, of making one's bodily vulnerability a site for change and innovation. And this is important in relation to the debate over debility since the term stresses a socio-political rather than a bodily condition, a condition of "living toward" some kind of endlessly thwarted fulfillment rather than living with a form of "complex embodiment."[8] Artists who become disabled later in life not only live with various bodily and psychological impediments but also create new work out of impediments that defy traditional aesthetic standards for a given medium or genre.[9]

Disability studies has not always dealt with the aging body or the specific impairments and social barriers that attend later life, perhaps due to limits in the mantra that "we'll all be disabled if we live long enough."

---

8   On the debate between disability and debility, see Margaret Shildrick, "living on; not getting better" (2015). On "complex embodiment." see Tobin Siebers, *Disability Theory* (2008: 22–33).

9   On aging and innovation among older writers, see Herring (2015). See also the following: Gallop (2019); Hamraie (2015); Woodward, "Feeling Frail (2015); Gilleard (2016); Straus (2008).

This formulation, however therapeutic, tends to neutralize the differences of embodiment and the meanings that attach to them as we grow older. A broken arm from a skiing accident at age 25 is different than the same impairment due to as fall at age 75. To adapt Simone de Beauvoir, one is not born disabled; one becomes disabled culturally in a society that venerates youth, independence, health, and agility.[10] In the graying of disability studies we first need to interrogate the term "aging," which to most people implies the biological and physical process of getting older. But when does this begin? There's a birthday card that some of us have received whose cover reads, "Happy Birthday. You'll be hearing a lot of comments and wisecracks about the end of your youth, the waning of your powers, the unmistakable signs of advancing age and so on." And the inside of the card reads, "Don't pay any attention. 30 is a Great Age!" (Gullette 1997: 4). And as I can testify, the joke gets funnier with each decade.

What follows are attempts to look at "aging experiments" through the "late style" of older artists and writers and the representation of older figures in Beckett's plays. Both examples treat aging as a matter of recognition, where Subjects are formed through representation and are likewise constituted by those representations. We may all become disabled if we live long enough, but some may embody that recognition differently through an "unaltering wrongness that has style" (Duncan 2014: 57).

---

10   The cultural construction of aging parallels the "social model" of disability in which the non-traditional bodymind is defined not by medical diagnoses but by social barriers to access and accommodation. For those whose bodies and minds are in pain, whose medical insurance is in peril, whose access to medicines, clean water, and care are vulnerable, there is little comfort and knowing that our disabilities are merely a function of social opprobrium or architectural barriers.

Unaltering Wrongness

> It is toward the old poets
>   we go, to their faltering,
>   their unaltering wrongness that has style (57)

In his "Poem Beginning with a Line by Pindar," Robert Duncan's celebration of the "old poets" is specifically addressed to Walt Whitman,
William Carlos Williams, and H.D., all of whom had strokes in later
life that impacted their physical and verbal abilities. Duncan imitates
Williams's post-stroke vocal slur by remembering,

> A stroke. These little strokes. A chill.
>   The old man, feeble, does not recoil.
> Recall. A phase so minute,
>   only a part of the word in-jerrd.
>   *The Thundermakers descend,*
> demerging a nuv. A nerb.
>   The present dented of the U
> nighted stayd. States. The heavy clod?
>   Cloud. Invades the brain. What
> if lilacs last in *this* dooryard bloomd? (57)

Duncan continues with a litany of presidents ("Hoover, Roosevelt, Truman, Eisenhower") whose limited poetic potential contrasts vividly
with Whitman's love for Lincoln in his elegy, "When Lilacs Last in the
Dooryard Bloom'd." But in imitating the aphasic difficulty of speaking,
the errors in pronunciation that lead from "nerve" to "nuv" to "nerb,"
Duncan hears linguistic residues that reveal "recoil" in "recall." The
"heavy clod" becomes the mushroom "cloud" that hangs over Cold War
America in William's late poem, "Asphodel that Greeny Flower." The
word "aphasia" is itself revealed in the phrase "a phase so minute," yet in
such substitutions can be heard echolalic resonances of words hidden
at the boundaries of sense. The American potential and inclusiveness,
memorialized in Whitman's Lincoln elegy, give way to misspellings and
misspeakings that embody the inadequacies of subsequent presidents

("Hoover, Coolidge, Harding, Wilson / hear the factories of human misery turning out commodities" [58]) at the same time that they enact possibilities of a new poetics by the then young poet (Duncan was 36 when he wrote these lines).

Reference to poets' strokes generates the patterned rhythmic structure of the poem, stroke upon stroke, a variable meter that occupied Williams's later musings on free verse rhythm. Critics have argued that Williams's speech impediment coincided with his typographical move to the stepped, triadic line in his late work. There is no direct evidence that impairment produces a new line, but it is important to recognize, as Charles Olson says in "Projective Verse," the limits that the body and breath impose on the poem. Poets of Olson and Duncan's generation seized upon precisely such limits as guides to new measures, lineations, and uses of the page. Or as Olson said, "Limits / are what any of us / are inside of" (1983: 21).

Duncan's poem reminds us that in speaking of an artist's late style, we forget that their innovations were often the result of a disability: cancer (Henri Matisse, Audre Lorde) deafness (Ludwig Beethoven, Francisco Goya, Gabriel Fauré) chronic pain (Frida Kahlo), diminished sight (J.M.W. Turner, Claude Monet, Jorge Luis Borges, John Milton), dementia (Willem deKooning, Aaron Copeland, George Oppen) severe arthritis (Merce Cunningham, Pierre-August Renoir, Henry James). It is tempting to place a triumphalist narrative on the late work of such artists and describe how they "overcame" challenges, but this denies the aesthetic gains produced *through* disability. Two examples come to mind.

Beethoven's *Grosse Fuge*, op 133 (1825–6) might be a prime instance of a work whose radical structure almost certainly was influenced by the composer's deafness. Edward Said has written movingly about many artists whose late style was their crowning achievement, but he notes that "artistic lateness" may also be revealed "as intransigence, difficulty, and unresolved contradiction" (2008: 7).[11] Beethoven epitomizes these

---

11   Said notes that for Adorno, "lateness" is the idea of surviving beyond what is acceptable and normal [and] includes the idea that one cannot really go beyond

features of late style, but Said omits almost entirely the role of deafness in producing that "intransigence." And it is clear, thanks to a recent book by Robin Wallace, that as early as 1801, Beethoven was composing music *not despite* of but *through* hearing loss. The distinction is important. Originally intended as the finale to the String Quartet in B-flat Major, op. 130, *The Grosse Fuge* was written when the composer was almost totally deaf. Its dissonances, sudden shifts of tempo, leaping thematic figure, sudden silences and sheer difficulty are radical, even by today's standards. The work occasioned consternation in the Viennese Press, causing one journalist to remark that "it was incomprehensible, like Chinese" (qtd. in Wallace 2018: 182). But the reviewer understood its potential by acknowledging that "perhaps the time is yet to come when that which at first glance appeared to us dismal and confused will be recognized as clear and pleasing in form" (Wallace: 183). To describe the opus 133 fugue as a triumph over adversity ignores its evolution through hearing loss and equally through the anger and depression Beethoven experienced along the way.

Another case of late style as "disability gain" may be seen in the later work of Henry James, who, in 1897, at the age of 53, developed rheumatism that became so painful that he hired a typist to take dictation.[12] James grew to appreciate a technology that curiously allowed him to "speak" his novels, and since his various amanuenses became a kind of audience, to "perform" them. He continued to write letters in longhand, but with *What Maisie Knew* (1897) and *In the Cage* (1898) began to dictate most of his subsequent fiction. What Leon Edel calls the style of "The Master"—convoluted, long—often very long—sentences, filled with subordinate elements, indirections, pronominal confusions and parentheses—was enhanced by a technological prosthesis. James apparently became reliant on the rhythmic "click" of the keys on his favorite

---

lateness at all…"(2008: 13). But this could as easily lead to a disability analysis of late style as a critique of normalcy.

12   The phrase "disability gain" is a modification of "deaf gain" as formulated by Dirksen Bauman and Joseph Murray. It refers to the advantages and diversity offered by deafness rather than its limitations in a hearing world.

Remington typewriter—so reliant that once when it broke down and he was forced to use a substitute machine, he was unable to dictate.[13] Apparently, the rhythm of the machine contributed to the rhythm of his speech, as he paced the floor of his office at DeVere Gardens. He was aware that his ability to extemporize verbally had its limits. In a remark to his last typist Theodora Bosanquet, he said "I'm too diffuse when I'm dictating…. It all seems to be so much more effectively and unceasingly *pulled* out of me in speech than in writing." (qtd. in Campbell 2008: 209).[14]

That "diffuse" speech, as we now know, was that of a person with a stutter. Reports of James's speech concur on the fact that his sentences were often drawn out by "hems" and "mmmmm's" and "ah's" and other space-filling sounds characteristic of someone attempting to control a stammer. Although he never stammered in French, when speaking English he tended to elongate his words and sentences, with much repetition and deferral. Edith Wharton commented that,

> His slow way of speech, sometimes mistaken for affectation—or, more quaintly, for an artless form of Anglomania!—was really the partial victory over a stammer which in his boyhood had been thought incurable. The elaborate politeness and the involved phraseology that made off-hand intercourse with him so difficult to casual acquaintances probably sprang from the same defect. (Qtd. in Campbell 2008: 168)

The only record we have of James's speech is provided by his friend Elizabeth Jordan, who asked him whether he thought Savage Landor's *In the Forbidden Land* was a "true account." She transcribed his response:

> "[…] eliminating, ah-h—eliminating nine-tenths—nine-tenths—nine-*tenths* (slowly)—of—of—of (very fast)—of what he claims—what he claims (slowly)—what he claims (very slow)—there is still

---

13   On James' use of the typewriter see Edel (1969: 168).

14   Apparently, he thought of Bosanquet as more than a typist, inscribing a copy of one of his novels "from my collaborator."

(fast)—there—is still—there is still (faster)—enough left (pause)
enough left (pause) to make—to make—to make (very fast) a remarkable record (slow)—a remarkable record—ah—ah—(slower)—a
re-markable re-cord." (Qtd. in Shell 2005: 45)

It is interesting to consider how a lifelong stammer might have contributed to the delays and deferrals in his last novel, *The Golden Bowl*
(1904). In the opening pages, Prince Amerigo contemplates the romantic
element that his American fiancé, Maggie Verver, brings to his European
background. "Oh I'm not afraid of history!" she says; "Call it the bad part,
if you like—yours certainly sticks out of you" (31). Against the phallic history that "sticks out" of him, the Prince is submerged, according to
Maggie, in a salubrious, if figurative, bubble bath that "sweetened the
waters in which he now floated" (32):

Maggie scattered, on occasion, her exquisite colouring drops. They
were the colour—of what on earth of what but the extraordinary
American good faith? They were the colour of her innocence, and yet
at the same time of her imagination, with which their relation, his
and these people's was all suffused. What he had further said on the
occasion of which we thus represent him as catching the echoes from
his own thought while he loitered—what he had further said came
back to him, for it had been the voice itself of his luck, the soothing
sound that was always with him. 'You Americans are almost incredibly
romantic.' (34)

The elliptical movement of the free indirect style captures the efferves-
cent quality of the trope but knowing that this passage was dictated by a
person with a stammer, its repetitions and delays reinforced by the typewriter's sonic properties, makes James's late style as much an elocution-
ary and technological phenomenon as a purely aesthetic one.

Krapp Sits

I want now to return to Beckett, whose representations of aging occupied him in all of his work, from the blind Mr. Rooney in his early radio play *All that Fall* (1957) and the nonstop "voice" in *Not I* (973) through the octogenarian mother in *Footfalls* (1976) and the aging unnamed woman in her rocking chair in *Rockaby* (1981). Given the attention that Beckett paid to disabled and aged figures, it might seem that they embody the condition of debility described earlier, a socio-economically imposed existential condition of being-toward-death. I see these figures not as signs of failure or frailty, but of capability: how individuals constantly revise the trajectories of "normal" human life to suit the lived condition of bodily and mental change. Winnie in *Happy Days* (1961) provides a tonic riposte to her own limited mobility, buried up to her waist in a mound of dirt, as she addresses her husband Willie's difficulty in returning to his den: "What a curse, mobility!" (1989: 46) The comic routines of Vladimir and Estragon, the formulaic dialogues between Hamm and Clov, Winnie's attempts to engage her husband Willie in conversation all reflect the human condition as an exasperated recognition of interdependent relationships. Beckett never offers a paean to solidarity or mutuality but strips humanist narratives down to their basic components: how to "go on" and by what means? What early critics of Beckett called his "absurdism" we might now call his realism. The palette from which he draws his monochromatic mise en scène is often that of disabled, older persons compensating not for a loss of power but for society's unremitting will to improvement.

It is worth remembering that in many of these works, Beckett experimented with new technologies in rendering voices that struggle to respond to the passage of time. In his radio plays, the idea of creating works for disembodied voices extended an interest already explored in his earlier prose fiction. In his 1957 radio play, *All that Fall*, Beckett uses the radio medium to create an acoustic environment of rural life—farm animals, creaking carts, conversations on the road—to surround the main character's concerns over whether she might disappear. Recording technologies allowed Beckett to penetrate an individual's psyche, using tape recordings (*Krapp's Last Tape*), radio (*All that Fall, Embers*), television (*Eh Joe, Ghost Trio*) film (*Film* [with Buster Keaton]), and video (*Quad*) as extensions of more primitive stage forms. In his television plays, Beckett experiments with the claustrophobia of the (then small) television screen. In *Eh, Joe* (1966), the titular character is framed—trapped—by the camera's monocular perspective, (and pursued by an unseen accusatory voice). It follows him around his narrow room as he attempts to convince himself that he is alone.

My primary example, *Krapp's Last Tape* (1958), fuses this technology to the problem of aging by using a reel-to-reel tape recorder as one of the play's main characters. Along with *Happy Days* and *Play* (1963) *Krapp's Last Tape* is one of Beckett's "middle period" plays featuring a single voice speaking, unlike the more obviously dialogic *Godot* and *Endgame*. But the voice is never strictly monologic. We hear Krapp's voice on a tape recorder from his earlier life quoting lines from an even earlier tape, thus allowing us access to three stages as he ages. The premise of the play is an allegory of the life course: a man on his 69th birthday listens to a tape recording made when he was 39 describing himself as "Sound as a bell" in earlier life. On that tape he describes listening to yet another birthday tape from ten or twelve years earlier, admitting to his 39-year-old self, "Hard to believe I was ever that young whelp" (58). Listening to his earlier life through two prior stages allows him to assess his current predicament as a person who has failed in his literary career, his magnum opus never gaining him the reputation he desired ("17 copies sold, of which 11 at trade price..." [62]). He has become alcoholic and is hard of hearing, nearsighted, and lives with stomach and mobility ailments. By listening to tapes composed on prior birthdays he recognizes the paucity of his accomplishments. By making a new tape on this birthday, he hopes to summarize the year's key events, based on notes jotted on an envelope. But the earlier tape mocks those attempts. He gives up and throws the tape aside. *Krapp's* last tape, then, becomes the one we are watching.

Although Krapp sits throughout most of the play, he occasionally punctuates his monologues by leaving the table and retiring to a back room behind him. We hear him uncorking a bottle, taking a swig, and see him returning with a ledger that lists the dates and numbers of his tapes and a dictionary that he uses to assist his failing memory. His monologue is constantly interrupted as he turns the tape back to hear a repetition of a passage, leaves the room, or unlocks a drawer in his table to retrieve a banana. Speaking of the play, Beckett noted that Krapp's "whole life has been an interruption," and indeed the play is very much about life as a series of interruptions, a retrospective rather than progressive life (Qtd. in Lawley 2005: 90). Temporalities become confused; the older Krapp reviews his earlier life via a young man's construction of a future. It is curious that when Beckett wrote the play, he had never seen or heard a tape recorder and so could only imagine the aesthetic uses to which it could be put. Stage direction for the play, "[A] late evening in the future" (1984: 55) refers to the fact that the portable tape recorder did not exist prior to the 1950s and thus could not have been used by the earlier Krapp. The failed writer, marking and storing his various tape boxes, playing and re-playing sequences, becomes an editor of his life.

At times old Krapp and younger Krapp share a laugh together, bringing the two identities together at a single moment, although this gives the source of the laugh a different valence. At 39 he laughs at his resolution to stop drinking ("And the resolutions!"). Hearing that remark at 69, the alcoholic Krapp laughs at the presumption he once had. We hear the aging process in their different voices, one youthful ("*Strong voice, rather pompous*" [1984: 58]), the other weathered. At 39 he is confident "full of fire;" at 69 he has become cynical and depressed. Alcohol has taken its toll on his voice and body; whatever sex life he once had—and it is prominently described on the earlier tapes—has been transformed to the tape recorder as a surrogate body.

We watch his gradual frustration and anger, fueled by his frequent taking of drams in the back room, as he realizes moments of loss. A visionary moment on a pier in which everything seemed possible, now seems a satire of failed hopes. An erotic moment with a young woman in a boat is reenacted as he moves physically to hover over the tape recorder:

Lie down across her. [Long pause. He suddenly bends over machine, switches off, wrenches off tape, throws it away, puts on the other,

winds it forward to the passage he wants, switches on, listens staring
front.] (1984: 63)

Not only is the tape recorder a mnemonic aid for a fading memory, it
is also a prosthesis for the other's body, a vehicle of affective relations
across time. Like Molloy's sucking stones that provide a sense of order to
his otherwise disordered progress towards his mother, these prosthetic
devices are emotionally charged. If they extend the decrepit body and
mind, they keep the conversation going. The portable tape recorder, mar-
keted for the first time in the early 1950s, is a device for capturing a voice,
but that voice, when heard later, becomes a rebuke and scold. Yet it permits Krapp, by a curious inversion of its dark content to "go on," to fill
time while sitting in an empty room.

"how to dance / sitting down"

Krapp composes his virtual life while sitting down, a condition man-
dated by his limited physical mobility and age. His condition resonates
with my title, which comes from "Tyrian Business," one of Charles Olson's
Maximus Poems. Olson is thinking of Martha Graham, and how the primitive violence of her dance embodies a certain American cult of action
and energy. Speaking elsewhere of Graham, Olson says, "It is as though
we [Americans] thought to slay the Dragon we had to be as violent and
thrashing as he is.... They don't even know how to sit down, how to dance
sitting down" (1971: 14). For Olson, dance becomes a model for poetry,
a "dance of the intellect" as Pound described one aspect of poetry. It is
worth thinking of this line in the context of Graham's most famous pro-
tégé, Merce Cunningham, who late in his life did dance sitting down.[15]
As he aged and became more disabled by arthritis, Cunningham reduced
his movements gradually until, by the end of his life, his choreography
was restricted to complicated hand gestures. Nevertheless, he remained

---

15   Olson had been influenced by contact with Cunningham while at Black Mountain College during the 1950s and participated himself in at least one of the
school's famous "Happenings," organized by John Cage.

an active director of his company, attending rehearsals daily and appearing in the company's performances. Where he had once been a vigorous and athletic member of the ensemble, he gradually detached himself, as Marcia Siegel says, hovering "in the background like an anxious chaperone" (1977: 252) He would occasionally enter into the ensemble to "tap someone on the shoulder to break up the sequence, or [pace] a difficult metre by clapping out the time" (252).

In *Loops*, which Cunningham choreographed as a solo work in 1971 and performed throughout his later life, the dancer's hands become the dancers. Although it was first designed as a full body dance, he gradually refined his movements to his hands while sitting in a chair.[16] Cunningham's face remained impassive while his hands performed a series of increasingly busy arabesques, loops and fidgets. His gestures might resemble manual sign language, but there was no semantic content to individual gestures. Or rather, the semantic content of these gestures was tied to movements in his long choreographic memory. Olson's trope of dancing while sitting down describes, for Cunningham, a form of choreographic intellection, acted out by hands and fingers and arms. And having watched a number of Cunningham performances throughout the 1970s and 80s, I recognize these gestures as those he introduced into his ensemble pieces, either by himself or other dancers.

The OpenEnded Group, a digital collective, collaborated with Cunningham on a digitized realization of *Loops* that was commissioned by the MIT Digital Lab in 2001.[17] Members of OpenEnded attached reflective markers to Cunningham's hands and had him perform "Loops" in front of infrared cameras, which recorded the markers' positions over

---

16   A rough cut from a film of Cunningham performing *Loops* can be seen on a You Tube video: https://www.youtube.com/watch?v=6snBoOfyypo. Accessed 20 November, 2020. I am grateful to Carrie Noland for her advice on Cunningham's late choreography.

17   The OpenEnded Group's film of *Loops* can be seen on YouTube: https://player.vimeo.com/video/25509279?title=0&byline=0&portrait=0. Accessed 20, November, 2020.

time using a form of digitalization called "motion capture." The resulting film fuses Cunningham's hand movements, stringing one hand to the
next, so that movement in the left hand blends into the same movement
in the right hand. The film resembles a galactic dance of shooting stars,
fireworks, cells dividing, webs forming and disappearing, tracers shooting into space, explosions and tentacular linkages between various digits and hand movements. Imposed over the video is Cunningham's voice
reading from his early diaries when he was a teenager, as well as selec-
tions from the composer John Cage's prepared piano works. It is a work
that, although modest in scale, hints at ("loops" over) vast temporal and
spatial distances, and whose intimacy recalls his long life with Cage, his
now deceased lover and collaborator. Cunningham's late choreography
derives from his increasing physical weakness, but out of that precarity
emerges a kind of retrospective novelty, dance that builds on a lifetime
of experimentation and curiosity about what the body can do and about
hands as an expressive element in movement.

I have attempted to redefine the "true gerontology" that Adorno
identifies with Beckett's aged characters to speak of the capabilities of
old age. Disability and gerontology studies have not always coincided,
the former focused around removing barriers and the limits of "compulsory ableism," and the latter focused on the aging process and its
institutional meanings.[18] Critical disability studies has introduced an
intersectional approach to disability, seeing it as the site through which
race, gender, sexuality, and national origin are lived, but it has not had
much to say about the intersection of disability and aging. If it did, the
"graying" of disability studies might describe disability through one's
life course and the various stages in which disability is experienced
as one ages. And the graying of disability studies might offer a way of
describing "late style" through impairments and limits that not only

---

18   On the differences between critical gerontology and disability studies, see
      Hailee Gibbons, "Engaging with Aging."

impacted that style but offered new ways of thinking about capability in general.[19]

I want to conclude on a personal note. My father lived to the age of 102. By the end he was almost blind from macular degeneration, crippled with arthritis, hard-of-hearing, and physically reliant on a wheelchair to get around. Fortunately, his mental faculties were pretty good, and when I told him I was working on disability issues, he wondered why that would be of interest to anyone. I pointed out that lots of people live with a disability, including him, but he rejected the idea, saying "I'm not disabled; I'm just old." I suspect that many people make the same distinction—that being old is a natural end of a continuum but having a disability is a tragic interruption or deviation. For a male of his generation, the necessity of hiring a full-time caregiver presented a disturbing challenge to his sense of masculine agency. He complained mightily about having to pay for such services, and yet he developed personal relationships with his caregiver that were probably as close and intimate as any he had with anyone, including my mother. My father's resistance to being defined as disabled suggests that the distinction between aging and disability is hard wired into our national psyche, at least in the U.S. When disability is seen a state of exception to the "good life," then we are indeed living in a state of perpetual debility.

The arts of disability offer an alternative set of scenarios and ways of thinking—what disability theorists call "cripistemology"—about futurity beyond the biocultural and that imagine other forms of kinship and association beyond the cult of independence and autonomy. Recent disability scholarship has focused on how nontraditional forms of embodiment—crip, cyborg, trans, queer—challenge the Vitruvian image of bodily perfection. What formalists call "experimentation" or "innovation" might be another word for capability—ways of living in the body we have, instead of the body we wish were better. It's hard thinking outside the narrative of ableism, but artists and writers who feature disability in their work show us a partially open side door. That way is to

---

19   The phrase, "graying of disability studies" is taken from Hailee Gibbons's "Engaging with Aging." I am grateful to her for her advice in writing this essay.

acknowledge our interdependency, our distributed subjectivity. As Clov is about to leave the room in *Endgame*, he and Hamm perform a little ritual of farewell that we know they will never complete. "I'm obliged to you, Clov. For your services," says Hamm, to which Clov responds, "Ah pardon, it's I am obliged to you." Hamm answers "It's we are obliged to each other" (1958: 81). If our worries about isolating aging persons from COVID-19 is any example, such mutuality might signal a truer gerontology.

Works Cited

Adorno, Theodor (1988): "Trying to Understand Endgame." In: Harold Bloom (ed.), *Samuel Beckett's Endgame*, New York: Chelsea House, pp. 9–40.

Bauman, H. Dirksen, and Joseph J. Murray (2013): "Deaf Studies in the 21st Century: 'Deaf-Gain' and the Future of Human Diversity." In: Lennard J. Davis (ed.), *The Disability Studies Reader* 4th edition, New York: Routledge. pp. 246–60.

Beckett, Samuel (1958): *Endgame*, New York: Grove Press.

Beckett, Samuel (1984): *The Collected Shorter Plays of Samuel Beckett*, New York: Grove Press.

Beckett, Samuel (1989): *Happy Days*, New York: Grove Press.

Bella, Timothy (2020): "'It affects virtually nobody': Trump incorrectly claims covid-19 isn't a risk for young people." In *Washington Post* September 22, 2020. https://www.washingtonpost.com/nation/2020/09/22/trump-coronavirus-young-people. Accessed September 25. 2020.

Berlant, Lauren (2007): "Slow Death Sovereignty, Obesity, Lateral Agency." In: *Critical Inquiry* 33/4, pp. 754–80.

Campbell, Sarah (2008): "The Man Who Talked Like a Book, Wrote Like He Spoke." In: *Interval(le)s*, II.2-III.1, Fall 2008 / Winter 2009, n. pag. labos.ulg.ac.be/cipa/wpcontent/uploads/sites/22/2015/07/18_campbell.pdf. Accessed April 2, 2020.

Davidson, Michael (2019): *Invalid Modernism: Disability and the Missing Body of the Aesthetic*, Oxford: Oxford University Press.

Duncan, Robert (2014): "Poem Beginning with a Line by Pindar." In: Peter Quartermain (ed.), *The Collected Later Poems and Plays of Robert Duncan*, Berkeley: University of California Press, pp. 56–63.

Edel, Leon (1969): *Henry James a Biography: The Treacherous Years, 1895–1900*, London: Rupert Hart-Davis.

Gallop, Jane (2019): *Sexuality, Disability and Aging: Queer Temporalities of the Phallus*, Durham: Duke University Press.

Gibbons, Hailee M. (2016): "Compulsory Youthfulness: Intersections of Ableism and Ageism in 'Successful Aging' Discourses." In: *Review of Disability Studies: An International Journal*, 12/2-3. https://rdsjournal.org/index.php/journal/issue/view/V12i2%263. Accessed May 1, 2020.

Gibbons, Hailee M. (2019): "Engaging with Aging: A Call for the Graying of Critical Disability Studies." In: Katie Ellis et al. (eds.), *Manifestos for the Future of Critical Disability Studies*. Vol. 1, New York: Routledge.

Gilleard, Chris (2018): "Old Age and Samuel Beckett's Late Works." In: *Age Culture Humanities: An Interdisciplinary Journal 3*, 33–56. https://doi.org/10.7146/ageculturehumanities.v3i.130154.

Gullette, Margaret Morganroth (1997): *Declining to Decline: Cultural Combat and the Politics of the Midlife*, Charlottesville: University Press of Virginia.

Hamraie, Aimee (2015): "Inclusive Design: Cultivating Accountability toward the Intersections of Race, Aging, and Disability." In: *Age Culture Humanities: An Interdisciplinary Journal 2*, pp. 337–46.

Herring, Scott (2015): "Djuna Barnes and the Geriatric Avant-Garde." In: *PMLA* 130/1, pp. 69–91.

Jain, Sarah Lochlann (2007): "Living in Prognosis: Toward an Elegiac Politics. In: *Representations* 98/1, pp. 77–92.

James, Henry (2009): *The Golden Bowl*. Ruth Bernard Yeazell (ed). New York: Penguin Classics.

Lawley, Paul (2005): "Stages of Identity: from *Krapp's Last Tape* to *Play*." In: John Pilling (ed.), *The Cambridge Companion to Beckett*, Cambridge: Cambridge University Press, pp. 88–105.

Linett, Maren Tova (2020): *Literary Bioethics: Animality, Disability, and the Human*, New York: New York University Press.

MacIntyre, Alasdair (1999): *Dependent Rational Animals: Why Human Beings Need the Virtues*, Chicago: Open Court.

Mitchell, David and Sharon L. Snyder (2015): *The Biopolitics of Disability; Neoliberalims, Ablenationalism, and Peripheral Embodiment*, Ann Arbor: University of Michigan Press.

Nguyen, Viet Thanh (2020): "The Ideas That Won't Survive the Coronavirus." In: *New York Times*. April 19,pp. 10–11.

Olson, Charles (1971): "A Syllabary for a Dancer." In: *Maps* 4, pp. 9–15.

Olson, Charles (1983): *The Maximus Poems*. George Butterick (ed.), Berkeley: Universisty of California Press.

Puar, Jasbir K. (2017): *The Right to Maim: Debility, Capacity, Disability*, Durham: Duke University Press.

Rodriguez, Adrianna (2020): "Texas' lieutenant governor suggests grandparents are willing to die for US economy." In: *USA Today*, 24 March. https://www.usatoday.com/story/news/nation/2020/03/24/covid-19-texas-official-suggests-elderly-willing-die-economy/2905990001/. Accessed April 2, 2020.

Said, Edward (2008): *On Late Style: Music and Literature Against the Grain*, New York: Vintage.

Shell, Marc (2005): *Stutter*, Cambridge: Harvard Universisty Press.

Shildrick, Margaret (2015): "living on; not getting better." In: *Feminist Review*, 111, pp. 10–24.

Siebers, Tobin (2008): *Disability Theory*, Ann Arbor: University of Michigan Press.

Siebers, Tobin (2010): *Disability Aesthetics*, Ann Arbor: University of Michigan Press.

Siegel, Marcia B. (1977): "Growing Old in the Land of the Young." In: *The Hudson Review* 29/2, pp. 249–54.

Straus, Joseph (2008): "Disability and 'Late Style' in Music." In: *The Journal of Musicology*, 25/1, Winter, pp. 3–45.

Wallace, Robin (2018): *Hearing Beethoven: A Story of Musical Loss and Discovery*, Chicago: University of Chicago Press.

Woodward, Kathleen (2015): "Feeling Frail and National Statistical Panic: Joan Didion in *Blue Nights* and the American Economy at Risk." In *Age Culture Humanities: An Interdisciplinary Journal*, 2. https://agecult urehumanities.org/WP/feeling-frail-and-national-statistical-pani c-joan-didion-in-blue-nights-and-the-american-economy-at-risk. Accessed 10 Sept. 2020.

Woodward, Kathleen (2020): "Aging in the Anthropocene: The View From and Beyond Margaret Drabble's *The Dark Flood Rises*." In: Elizabeth Barry and Margery Vibe Skagen (eds.), *Literature and Ageing*, Rochester: Boydell and Brewer.

Acknowledgements

A version of this paper was presented at the "Aging / Innovations" conference sponsored by University College Dublin, 26 September 2020. I am grateful to Joao Guimaraes for organizing this conference and for editing the current volume. I am also grateful to Peter Middleton and Kathleen Woodward for their comments on early drafts of this paper. An earlier version of this essay was published in *Journal of Modern Literature* 45.1. Thanks to the editors of JML and to Indiana University Press for granting permission to reprint.

Dancing Relational Bodyhood
Older Disabled Artist-Activist Tuuli Helkky Helle (1933-2018)

Heunjung Lee[1]

Abstract: *Being contrasted to the idea of disability-free aging as positive and successful aging, ill, impaired, older persons who are 'dependent' (physically, socially, economically) are often devalued and stigmatized in ageist and ableist societies. Tracing the extraordinary life course and artistic practices of Tuuli Helkky Helle (1933–2018), an older Finnish dancer who lived with cerebral palsy, this paper highlights how she had reclaimed 'dependency' in a positive term and had visualized the beauty and power of the interconnected, interrelated, and caring relationships in her arts and life. From her 60s until her 80s, as an artist and activist, she participated in various dance pieces, radical nude photography series, and activist performances for older adults with disability. This article is the first academic article that documents her remarkable works and examines her dancing body. Drawing on the theoretical perspective of Ann Cooper Bright (2017; 2019) about gravity, interconnectedness, and disabled and aged bodies and Pia Kontos's notion of "relational citizenship" (2017), this paper illuminates on the alternative danceability of aged-disabled body.*

Keywords: *Integrated Dance; Relationality; Dependency; Disabled Bodies; Crip Futurity*

---

1   University of Alberta.

Aging with Disability: Tuuli Helkky Helle's Extraordinary Life Course

Organized around chronological age and stage-based transitions, the idealized heteronormative model of the life course is primarily linear and "views individuals as progressing through normative notions or stages along a relatively linear structure, with life events occurring at particular times" (Grenier and McGrath 2016: 1–2). The age-based expectations frame the later period of life through "the master narrative of decline" (Gullette 2004), which equates aging with the loss and decline (e.g., loss or decline of physical and mental ability, beauty and sexuality, cultural activity and productivity, etc.). While this narrative of decline feeds the cultural anxiety of aging, the rhetoric such as 'successful/healthy/productive aging' and 'ageless life' promote aging without illness and disability as the ideal and exclude those who age *with and into* disability from the desirable future. The notions such as 'the third age' and 'fourth age' further demarcate the boundaries of normal and abnormal aging (Higgs and Gilleard 2014). From this perspective, both the old and disabled become a 'problem' against what Elizabeth Freeman (2010) calls "chrononormativity" that normalizes the notion of time for maximum productivity. Instead of revealing the problem within social and physical environments that are based on able-bodied values and standards, this perspective configures the older people and disabled people as an economic and social burden. Being contrasted to the idea of disability-free aging as positive and successful aging, ill, impaired, older, and frail bodies are configured as those who are 'dependent' (physical, social, economical) and cannot participate fully in the process of production. Following the work of Robert McRuer (2006) and Alison Kafer (2013), scholars in Critical Disability Studies have tackled the "curative imaginary" where the idea of a future is only be conceived through solving or curing disability and have advanced the crip notion of futurity which include "the widest array of bodies and minds" (McRuer 2014: 532).

To get one step closer to realize the "crip futurity' Kafer (2013) has advocated for, we need to unsettle the negative implications of 'dependency' that stigmatize and devalue older adults and disabled individuals and develop new understandings of dependency (cf. Fine and Glendinning 2005; Townsend 2007; Gilleard and Higgs 2005; Phillipson 2013). Fine and Glendinning (2005) write:

> "Sociologists have scrutinized the social construction of dependency; politicians have ascribed negative connotations of passivity; while medical and social policy discourse employs the term in a positivist sense as a measure of physical need for professional intervention. Autonomy and independence, in contrast, are promoted as universal and largely unproblematic goals" (601).

Refuting the traditional understanding that equates autonomy with independence, many philosophers and scholars across multiple disciplines (Kittay 1999; Fineman 2004; Sherwin and Minsby 2011; Kontos et al. 2017) have expanded more relational views of human ontology and reconfigured that "the inevitable primary dependency on others" as "a condition of embodied human existence" (Dodds 181). Relational perspectives consider the ways familial, community, institutional connections and interdependence enable one's agency and autonomy, and acknowledge dependency as "an indissoluble part of autonomy" (Scully 212–213). Negative attitudes and assumptions towards dependence have particularly marginalized and devalued people with serious disabilities and older adults. Theatre and Performance Studies also revisit the concept of care, interrelational mode of being, dependency; Fisher (2020) have argued that relational perspective can open up new ways of reading disability theatre by "acknowledging the hidden mutual dependencies and attitudes of care" (86).

Following this relational turn, this paper discusses the relationality that are foregrounded in the dance and artistic photography of older disabled Finnish dancer Tuuli Helkky Helle (1933–2018). This paper uncovers the extraordinary aging path of Tuuli and explores how her vigorous engagements in visual arts, performance, and activism in her later life offer counter-images and counter-narratives to the cultural assumptions that link "feebleness and helplessness" to people with disabilities and older people (Tarvainen 296). Aging, illnesses, and disability are intertwined and conflated in complex ways, and narratives that celebrate aging or the lives of older adults often coalesce with an ableist concept that emphasizes a triumph over the limits of human bodies and minds (Aubrecht and Rice 2020: 3–4). Tuuli Helkky Helle's life does not suggest the ableist narrative of 'the triumph over disability' or 'overcoming rhetoric' (cf. Linton 1998) nor the ageist narrative of 'ageless self' (cf. McHugh 2000) although it was intended to correct the negative stereotypes of old age. I argue that Tuuli had reclaimed 'dependency' in a positive term, and had visualized the beauty and power of the interconnected, interrelated, and caring relationships in her arts and life. She shows how one can embrace and celebrate disability and old age, instead of overcoming them.

Tuuli Helkky Helle was well aware that arts and performance are cultural spaces in which "disability and aging are created and experienced [...] [and] where taken-for-granted meanings and materiality of disability and aging may become exposed, frayed, and unraveled" (Aubrecht and Rice 5). She was a rare older woman who has performed in contemporary stage while living with a severe disability; her various art practices are testimony that she perceived her double-marginalized subjectivity–old and disabled–as the site for research and activism against the ageist and ableist social gazes and perspectives. She was born with cerebral palsy, which seriously impacted her mobility and verbal communication. In a short film about Tuuli, *Muuten menee katu-uskottavuus (Otherwise, You Lose the Street-Credibility*, 2016)[2] created by disabled artist Jenni-Juulia Wallinheimo-Heimonen,[3] Tuuli says she

---

2   The information on this film can be found on Jenni-Juulia Wallinheimo-Heimonen's website http://www.kolumbus.fi/jenni_juulia/muuten-menee-katu-u skottavuus-or-you-loose-the-street-credibility/index.html The full video of the film is available on YouTube https://youtube.com/watch?v=ah2yAx_1Miw&fea ture=shares.

3   For information of her works, see this interview with Jenni-Juulia Wallinheimo-Heimonen https://no-niin.com/issue-12/accessibility-is-not-static-a-conversat ion-with-jenni-juulia-wallinheimo-heimonen/ One of her artistic films on disability, *Squirrel* (2017) is featured as the cover image of *Routledge Handbook of Disability Studies 2nd Edition* (2019). http://www.kolumbus.fi/jenni_juulia/auth ority-and-resources/index.html.

lived with her parents until she was 40 years old and her life was extremely protected in her expression despite her desires for social life and adventure. She was self-educated – in her words, she was "mercifully released from compulsory education" (Helle 3), and she could communicate with people mostly through emails and written formats by using a communication assistive device.

However, after her father's passing, she decides to live on her own after living in a care home for a year. Although she struggled for a few years to be on her own, she states that her life becomes "wild" at this time (*Otherwise, You Lose the Street-Credibility*, 2016). She began to connect with other women living with severe disabilities and engage with dance, painting, writing, and photography. Freed from the normative life course, she began her artistic career at the age of 60 – according to the neoliberal idea of the life course, the period of 'third age' when someone retires from their profession and begins to enjoy new leisure lifestyle until they hit the 'fourth age' which is accentuated with the ideas of decline, frailty, and "unbecoming" (Higgs and Gilleard 2014: 13). Her life course and aging story and view of life radically refuse the stigmatized narratives of aging with disability. I argue that she permits us to see "disabled and aging futures as livable and even desirable" (Changefoot and Rice 174). Without trying to 'fit into' the idealized, normalized life course that is constructed through chronological age and institutions (e.g., school, family, work, retirement) (Hockey and James 2017: 91).

It may be 'late' to the standards of the normalized life course, yet she had engaged with diverse forms of arts for more than twenty years in her later life. From 2000 to 2009, at her age 67–77, she toured multiple countries as the central dancer in *Olotila (State of Being)*[4], a profes-

---

4   The premiere of *Olotila* was performed at the Zodiak Centre for New Dance, in Helsinki, Finland, September 13, 2000. Following its premiere, it was also invited to the Full Moon Dancer Festival (Pyhäjärvi, Finland), Theatre Festival (Tampere, Finland), Kulturhuset (Stockholm, Sweden), Dansstationen (Malmö, Sweden), Hebbel-am-Ufer HAUS (Berlin, Germany), Bergen International Festival (Bergen, Norway), Théâtre de l'Aquarium (Paris, France), and Hong Kong Mime Festival (HongKong) (https://www.yumpu.com/en/document/read/2510 2143/zustand-state-of-being-tomi-paasonen).

sional integrated dance-theatre piece of Rajat'on (Limit'less) ensemble[5], choreographed and directed by Tomi Paasonen[6]. After its premiere in Helsinki in 2000, *Olotila (State of Being)* was awarded with the "Theatre Event of the Year 2000," which is annually given by the Theatre Centre in Finland (Paasonen, "Olotila – State of Being"). According to Tomi Paasonen[7], Tuuli once mentioned that she had an idea about creating a nude photo series with a disabled body; she had long thought of finding a beautiful 'model' for it, but through conversation and discussion with Tomi, she became the model herself at the age of 70. Over multiple years of collaboration, the radical and experimental work called *Gala Dress* (2002), featuring collections of nude photographs of Tuuli's aged and disabled body, was created, and the collection was exhibited at Fort Mason Center in San Francisco, Lasipalatsi Galleria in Helkinki, City Gallery of Forssa, Full moon Dance Festival in Pyhäjärvi, Finland, and Rise Berlin in Germany. She was also one of the founders of DanceAbility Finland, and in her 70s, she danced in Kaaos Company, one of the most significant integrated dance companies in Finland. Notable dance pieces

---

5   Rajat'on ensemble is a Finnish dance collective, consisting of both disabled and non-disabled performers (Karhunen 2014: 11).

6   Tomi Paasonen, born in Helsinki in 1970, is a Berlin-based director, choreographer, and visual artist. After dancing as a soloist in Hamburg Ballet, the Lines Ballet, and the Joffrey Ballet, he founded KUNST-STOFF in 1998, a San Francisco-based interdisciplinary physical theatre and arts-event production company. However, Paasonen's dance career was prematurely interrupted in 1999 when a piece of the ceiling in a Chicago theatre fell on him during rehearsal and injured his spine. The accident changed his artistic direction, and he began working under the name Public Artistic Affairs (PAA) in Berlin and started to work with dancers with diverse backgrounds and abilities. In 2013, Paasonen was appointed as the new artistic curator of the ITAK Regional Dance Center of Eastern Finland, an organization which supports the visibility and development of dance in Eastern Finland, and he is currently working internationally producing his dance pieces (Kunst-Stoff, "Tomi Paasonen, Choreographer." Kunst-Stoff Wepsite http://www.kunst-stoff.org/artists/Tomi-Paasonen; Maija Karhunen, "Tomi Paasonen: A Maximalist with All My Heart," *Finnish Dance in Focus: 2013–2014* volume fifteen, pp. 11–12).

7   T. Paasonen. Personal communication. December 21, 2022.

she participated in are *Kaleidoscope – the Unbearable Beauty of Difference* (2010) and *Aurora Borealis* (2012), both choreographed by Sally Davison. Tuuli performed in multiple dance pieces until she was 83 years old when she passed away, and she had explored and foregrounded her own experience and views of aging and disability, and the beauty, power, and vulnerability of her unique body.

In addition, Tuuli always painted and produced many visual arts from late 1980s to 2000s; and the subjects of her paintings range from her childhood memories, portraits of people around her, self-portrait. In her 60s, she self-published two books of poetry: *Elämä on oivaltamista* (*Life is Understanding*, 1996) and *Palvelukseen halutaan* (*Looking for an Assistnat*, 1996) which address her lived experiences with disability, her dreams and desires, the ageist gaze imposed on her body.[8] Tuuli was not only an artist, but also an activist who passionately fought for disability justice and against ageism and ableism. Most remarkably, two years before her passing, Tuuli made a short activist film, *Muuten menee katuuskottavuus* (*Otherwise, You Lose the Street-Credibility*, 2016) with Jenni-Juulia Wallinheimo-Heimonen. This film, which captures Tuuli writing a petition letter to the minister of Family Affairs and Social Services in Finland and her rap song called "Granny Rap," had a huge political impact against the disability service legislation reformation which suggested removing personal assistance for older people with age-related disabilities (cf. Era 2021). Shortly after this film, Tuuli also participated in another activist performance that was documented as a short film *Method for Better Service* (2016)[9]. Created by Jenni-Juulia Wallinheimo-Heimonen, *Method for Better Service* (2016) gathered five aging female

---

8   The English titles of these books were included in the short film, *Or, You Lose Street Credibility* (2016), made by Tuuli Helle Helkky and Jenni-Juulia Wallinheimo-Heimonen. Further information about the books can be found here: https://www.lounakirjailijat.net/lounakirjailijat/kirjailijat/?authorid=41&newstitle=Helle+Tuuli+Helkky.

9   Full video of the film is available on YouTube https://youtube.com/watch?v=uLyMzTbygmo&feature=shares Further information on the film can be found on Jenni-Juuli's website http://www.kolumbus.fi/jenni_juulia/method-for-better-service/index.html.

activists including Tuuli who live with long-term disabilities; in this activist performance they go around the small streets of Finland on wheelchair, naked, and raise awareness of accessibility and different bodies. While other activists were middle-aged, Tuuli was 83 years old when she participated in this performance and needed to wear an adult diaper; yet, nothing stopped her and she led the radical march from the center of the group.

Tuuli Helkky Helle's *extraordinary* life-course, arts, and activism counter "the accepted notions of physical disability" and aging as "an absolute, inferior state and a personal misfortune" (Thomson 1996: 6). Her unique life story and bold acts reconfigure the old and the disabled as figures of desire, power, and subjectivity, and counter "the normate's frequent assumption that a disability cancels out other qualities, reducing the complex person to a single attribute" (ibid: 12). Tuuli's extraordinary life course gives us an insight into the inclusive model of crip futurity which does not project the idea that disability-free or ageless life is ideal and successful. In this essay, I illuminate how Tuuli uses her aged-disabled body as a political and artistic site to reveal and challenge the ableist and ageist gaze, expectations, and prejudices. Despite her artworks which urges us to rethink the definition of body's capacity and beauty that are based on ageism and ableism, Tuuli did not receive much academic attention from both Age Studies and Disability Studies in her lifetime. Tracing more than 20 years of active engagements in arts in her later life, this paper will shed light on how her arts fervently unsettle the various norms and assumptions applied to old-disabled bodies, as well as, to the narratives of aging with disability.

Methodology and Theoretical Frameworks

A major part of this research consists of tracing and documenting her artistic works by examining multiple archival materials such as video recordings of her dances, photographs, and poems. Although her traces scarcely exist online, I could obtain hard copies of her poem collections and a photobook, *Tuuli Helkky Helle 80 Years* (2013), which Sirppa Kinos

(Tuuli's niece) created to celebrate Tuuli's 80th birthday and her life. This photobook is an invaluable source as it contains Tuuli's paintings, photos of her dances, conversations Sirppa had with Tuuli in the summer of 2012, and include excerpts of studies discussing disability policies and justice in Finland. In addition, the artists such as Jenni-Juulia Wallinheimo-Heimonen, Tomi Paasonnen, Sally Davison who dearly remembered their works with Tuuli shared the video recordings of her dance works and other related materials for this research. My discussions of Tuuli's dance and body are based on the full video recording of 2009 Hong Kong production of *Olotila*, which is 100 minutes long; I draw on this particular production because it was performed in English while other productions were performed in Finnish. I also draw on the photos of *Gala Dress* (2002) to discuss the performance of her aged-disabled body. Only short video clips were available for more recent works such as *Kaleidoscope – the Unbearable Beauty of Difference* (2010) and *Aurora Borealis* (2012) by DanceAbility; so, this paper only briefly discusses Tuuli's performance in these performances.

As most materials are only available in Finnish, the author employed translation tools such as DeepL and Google Translate. While the biographical materials offer important insight into Tuuli's approach to her life and arts, my analysis of her dance and body focuses on the phenomenological and aesthetic aspects that are evident in these archives. From a performance studies perspective, I draw on phenomenological approaches and analyze her aged-disabled body performed in multiple dance pieces and photography, and discuss her body's corporeality, physicality, presence, movements, costumes, and relationships to the other bodies and beings. My study is mostly guided by the theoretical perspectives of Ann Cooper Bright (2017; 2019) about gravity, interconnectedness, and disabled and aged bodies. Drawing on their discussions on the "alternative danceability" (Nakajima and Brandstetter 2017: 61) offered by aging and disability, I examine Tuuli's dancing body and how her body pushes back against the typical meanings of dance, beauty, mastery, and virtuosity.

To articulate the ways in which Tuuli's dancing body reconfigures the ableist notion of dance(r), I bridge these theoretical discussions on

disabled dances with the theory of "relational citizenship" advanced by
Pia Kontos (2017) in her research about persons living with dementia.
Through an analysis of her body in dance and photography, this paper
asserts that Tuuli's performance allows us to reimagine a dancer's body
through *relationality* and *dependence*. I conceptualize her aged-disabled
body as a possibility of *relational bodyhood*. Furthermore, I argue that the
relational bodyhood Tuuli has foregrounded through her arts gives an insight into the crip futurity which both people age with and into disability
can have their full participation in life. I will also contemplate on how her
artistic engagements at the last stage of her life challenge both ableism
and ageism, and how her activism disrupts the stereotypical narratives
of older persons with disability, making them a burden of society and
invisible through the politics of concealment.

Reconfiguration of Dancer's Body: Relational Bodyhood

Olotila (*State of Being*, 2000–2009) stages seven dancers – five of them are
disabled (four dancers are wheelchair users and one dancer is blind) and
two of them are non-disabled. More precisely, there are nine performers including a dog and a robot who appear onstage in *Olotila*.[10] In this
piece, the central figure is Tuuli even though one might say she has the
'least' movements. The performance starts with Tuuli's voice and her poems are woven through the performance. In the first scene, the audience
sees her small body–approximately three to four feet in height, bent and
curled up both due to her disability and old age–laid against an able-
bodied younger male dancer, Stephane Hisler. Looking directly into the
audience with a subtle smile, she speaks, however, her words are inde-
cipherable; therefore, the male dancer translates her words sentence by
sentence:

---

10   The performers are Tuuli Helkky Helle, Stephane Hisler, Riikka Kekäläinen, Tom
      Leidenius, Dog: Ninnu, Riita Pasanen, Kalle-Antti Raunu, Sari Salovaara, and
      Eeva Simons. (Original order listed by Public Artistic Affairs, https://www.yump
      u.com/en/document/read/25102143/zustand-state-of-being-tomi-paasonen).

Today begins an adventure. A huge, exciting, and fascinating adventure.
It is beyond comparison, and it will make me a great free person.
Oh, my wonderful adventure.
You who could release me from the change of my everyday life.
But I am so small – too small to live up to you, today.
So, today, I will make you a doll and trivial incident.
Change to my habits. I cannot see the wonder of moments, today.
I can only expect the great adventure to occur tomorrow.
Not today.

What is powerful about *Olotila* is that this piece positions her as the main speaking subject, not a deviant object for the ableist and voyeuristic gazes. Instead of asking the disabled bodies to overcome their physical limits, this piece brings down the able-bodied to her height and her eyesight. The two dancers on the left side of the stage are lit from above with a pin light; there is a red rope hanging from the ceiling–the rope invokes the image of a noose and idea of suicide. When Stephane points to the rope, Tuuli shakes her head with a gentle smile. Behind them, the backdrop is a projection resembling a close-up X-ray image of a beating heart – in contrast to the rope and Tuuli's old body, it signifies both birth and death. While laying on the ground, Stephane gently lifts her off the floor and raises her body up with his arms; Tuuli's small body floats in the air while he continues to move with his back on the floor. Mirroring the idea of Pas de deux of a classical ballet, he supports Tuuli's body, lifts her up, turns her body, drags, and assists her to walk little by little. Being fully rested in his arms, Tuuli's arms are curled toward her torso and stiff legs are lifted upwards. Through these movements, her disabled body, which has always been "smaller," crips the normative idea of physical aging which assumes that a person's body becomes curled up and gets smaller as they grow old. Her body constantly communicates the irony and simultaneity between the newborn and the old age in *Olotila*, and this juxtaposition is also found in the photos of *Gala Dress*. But these representations are not in function of infantilizing her. I argue that her body becomes the site to question and critique the rhetoric and politics of (in)dependency that hunts many older adults and disabled individuals.

This slow intro without many typical dance movements takes about ten minutes—which is a significant length for a dance piece. As the sound of the heartbeat gets faster and mixes with the beeping sound of a heart rate monitor from a hospital, other dancers join the stage. The blind dancer Tom Leidenius and Sari Salovaara with a stiff spine from rheumatism navigates the stage while maintaining physical contact with each other; another duet dance of Eva Simons in wheelchair and able-bodied dancer Riikka Kekäläinen follows the next. Because all the dancers in this piece are wearing the same costume—white top and white tights—the bodies of dancers seem intertwined and expanded; sometimes they make one big amalgam. Another duet dance of Eva Simons in wheelchair and able-bodied dancer Riikka Kekäläinen follows the next.

During the remaining first half of the 100-minute-long performance, Tuuli remains seated on a giant white bean bag, in a white Tutu, holding a female doll also wearing a white Tutu. Nonetheless, she never recedes to the background. There is a scene where Tuuli dances a variation of classical ballet of *Don Quixote*; her dance is characterized with micro-scale movements [see Figure 1]. The movements of her foot and hand are so subtle and delicate, yet, they are moving at her best and exert tremendous energy and powerful presence. The micro-scale movements are barely visible in the video recording, and there is a high chance it could have been hard to notice from a far distance during live performance. Yet, as the prima ballerina, she is dancing her version of this classical ballet with other dancers surrounding her while sitting around her – these more able bodies do not override her and give her space while maintaining still. Holding a fan in one hand, her face is enlightened and gracefully expresses elegance and joy.

Fig. 1: Tuuli's solo dance in Olotila (2009), Hong Kong

Photo Credit: Tomi Paasonen

Tuuli's reflection on her body and her dream to be a dancer, documented in the photobook made by her niece, is worth quoting at length:

"When I told my parents at the age of 5–6 that I was going to be a dancer, I didn't understand at all why they were confused. My dearest dream above all has been to be able to dance. So, in the early 1990s, I applied to wheelchair dance, and got to know the Rajat'on dance community. I participated in the Unlimited Dance 2000 project, the goal of which was to create new cooperation between dance professionals and disabled dance enthusiasts. *Olotila* premiered in September 2000, and it was performed for the last time in Hong Kong in 2009. I was selected as the 'prima ballerina' of *Olotila*. And indeed, I danced – although I borrowed moves from other dancers. I performed my solo number lying on the floor on pillows. This is how the little girl finally came true after decades of waiting!" (Kinos 44).

Her dream, reflection, and actions disclose and confront the normative and ableist assumptions about dancing bodies—emphasizing "a traditionally virtuosic body", which not only present rigorous skills and technical mastery but also "sexual desirability" (Albright 2017: 64–65). For instance, in a traditional sense, dancing bodies are imagined as those who have excellent controls over their bodies and transcend the limits of our material body and present "a perfect body–one completely unhampered by sweat, pain, or the evidence of any physical negotiation with gravity" (ibid: 65). By many postmodern dancers, the narrow vision of dance has been challenged, however, as Anne Cooper Albright (2017) addresses, "this does not mean that we have sufficiently deconstructed the paradigm of the virtuosic dancer" (65).

Olotila enables Tuuli to dance on her own terms and celebrates her different bodily presence, without disguising her age and disability. This piece also does not suggest the common 'triumph' over disability narrative that are commonly found in disability dance (cf. Albright 64–68 for her critique of these examples that focus on the capacity of disabled bodies to overcome their physical limits and in turns, paradoxically reinforce the exclusionary practices that it was meant to dissemble). Tuuli's expression, 'borrowing moves from other dancers' (Kinos 44) is striking because she suggests a new idea of dance and dancing body. Her idea of dance suggests something greater than simply dancing with an assistant or help.

I argue that her statement counters the fundamental idea that a dancer's body or anyone's body should stand alone – the individualistic, autonomous, and independent understanding of the body. Throughout the performance of *Olotila*, the ideas of relational, interdependent, and interconnected bodies are explored and foregrounded. The dancers continue to support each other's body, move other's bodies, and even *become* each other's bodies. It is not only that; Tuuli's body that is rooted on the ground highlights our profound relationship to gravity. Her body that is always supported by something else (a pillow, other bodies, stage, wheelchair) underscores how our physical body is supported by nature, environment, and other beings including both humans and animals. In the first half of the production, the projected image of heart in the background implies a life; a frontal image of a fully-grown fetus appears in the last ten minutes of the performance [see Figure 2]. When Tuuli's old, disabled, and dependent body is paralleled with this image, it has a risk of infantilizing her–which often occurs in the narratives of elders and disabled persons; but instead, this image functions as a testimony about the inherent dependency all human beings and living creatures had experienced and still experiencing without realizing it. All of us grow in our mother's womb and are surrounded and protected by amniotic fluid; all of us first learn how to walk by holding onto other people or objects; all of us live by breathing air every second. But most of us, who do not experience an illness or disability, forget this, and assume that our body has always been autonomous and independent.

Fig. 2: An Image of Fetus at the Background of Olotila

Photo Credit: Tomi Paasonen

Scholars in Critical Disability Studies already have tackled the modernist idea that creates an illusion of autonomous, independent, and individualized self and an illusion of a clear distinction between self and other (cf. Goodley 2013; Goodley and Runswick-Cole 2016; Shildrick 2019). They have urged to shift the fundamental and ontological understanding of subjectivity to "the postmodernist contention that the self is always embodied, dependent on its others, unsettled, and always in progress" (Shildrick 2019: 37). Gibson et al. (2012) similarly discusses how the "self-as-individual" has been called into question by postmodern theorists, and proposes "viewing persons [with disability], their carers, and their assistive technologies as assemblages of bodies/technologies/subjectivities that together achieve a set of practices" while

refusing the view of the contained and sufficient self and negative
assumptions of dependency (10).

These ideas of assemblages, dependency, interconnectedness penetrate throughout the performance of *Olotila*. The dancers' bodies are often overlapped and interconnected; the beeping soundscape reminds us
of our dependency on medical machines (e.g., ventilator, heart monitor); our bodies' relationship to gravity are visible in the repeated actions
of disabled bodies falling from the wheelchair to the ground, climbing
back up, as well as other dancers moving by hanging onto the rope from
the ceiling. There is also a scene in which all disabled dancers are laid
down in a confined space (outlined by light), able-bodied dancers, representing either carers or parents, mechanically cut food, while a surgical
procedure description is typed onto the screen behind the performers.
It is followed by the scene where an able-bodied dancer feeding the food
to Tuuli sitting on the beanbag; a voice-over, representing Tuuli's voice,
says: "I had grilled meat and ice cream all at the same time. I had to because one was getting cold, and one was melting. ... Grilled meat and ice
cream all at the same time. Boy, interesting life." This is brought from Tuuli's poem. While *Olotila* remarks the interconnectivity and dependency
that are essential for our beings, in this scene, it reveals and critiques the
reality of dependency and care in ableist society which makes many disabled and older people to bear inhumane treatments. Later, a dog and a
robot also appear as performers; dogs are also casted as models who pose
together with Tuuli in *Gala Dress* [see Figure 3]. I interpret the inclusion
of animals or robots in these representations as a statement about the interconnectivity between disabled bodies with different living creatures
and non-living things such as assistive devices and technologies (e.g.,
prosthetic limb, wheelchair). The interconnected relationship with other
humans, animals, and technologies highlights the "embodied state of
connected identity" (Whitburn and Michalko 2019: 230) of many disabled
individuals. By including an image of fetus living inside mother's womb
and another Tuuli's poem about how dandelion gets its colors from the
brightness of the sun, *Olotila* reveals the inherent interconnectivity and
relationality among any living organism; therefore, disrupts the narrative which frames only disabled and old people as dependent.

Fig. 3: Tuuli and Two Dogs in Gala Dress (2002)

Photo Credit: Tomi Paasonen

In this piece, Tuuli reclaims dependency in her own terms and achieves her dream to be a dancer and to be freed. At the end of the piece, she comes out to the stage, carried by the young male dancer again. With his support, she walks little by little–a similar image to the opening scene is repeated. He lays her down to the ground and lifts Tuuli to the air by supporting her from below, and Tuuli reaches her hands towards the sky, making it appear as if she was floating. As the stage gets darker, we do not see Tuuli, but instead see a blurry image of a body in the same position as Tuuli flying and swinging while hanging on to the rope–I think Tuuli is borrowing another body to achieve the movement/dance she imagines and desires. In this image, the initial implication of the red rope that was drawn above Tuuli changes its meaning – from death or tragedy to freedom and dreaming.

I argue that Tuuli as an old and disabled dancer exemplify a mode of alternative danceability. Just like Joshua St. Pierre (2015)'s discussion on how the disabled speaker offers new modes of posthuman communication (331), Tuuli's dancing body eschews the autonomy and self-mastery of body and offers a new way to dance through relationality, reciprocity, and interconnectedness. Tuuli says in the opening: "I am too small to live up to you"; she does not try to overcome her disabled and aged body to perform the normative idea of dance. Instead, she focuses on the movements she can make, and her intention, physical and emotional feelings, facial expressions, energy, and perhaps breathing. The changing scenography in *Olotila* shows the dynamic movements of different organs such as heart, brain cells, and muscles; in front of these images, the audience are invited to see the *inside* of bodies. Dreaming to be a dancer for more than 60 years, on this stage, as prima ballerina, we can imagine her inner dance: the fast pumping of hearts, dancing muscles and bones, flows of air and heat, and tingling sensations at her fingertips and toes.

Furthermore, she shows her excellence in surrendering to the other's bodies, to the environment, and to the gravity – it is a special somatic skill to feel how the other body is and to completely entrust and to let go of one's control over their own body. I am using the word 'surrender' in a positive meaning, implying being able to entrust others including both other beings and environment. Tuuli's dance and her dancing body reminds me of Abright (2018)'s investigation and theorization of the act of falling, and how it teaches us to be responsiveness, resistance, and resilience to falls and failures literally, emotionally, and financially. Throughout the performance Tuuli never loses her agency and personality; and maintains her unique calmness, grace, and warmth without any signs of anxiety, tension, or fear. Her powerful presence, positive and playful energy, and calmness breaking through her small body are evident signs of the strong resilience that she had developed over seventy years of living with severe disabilities.

Anyone who has been onstage would understand how difficult it is to be present without many visible actions for the extended duration of time. Albright writes, "instead of nervously trying to avoid falling (metaphorically and literally in a world in which so many aspects of our social, political, and economic environment are being turned upside down, I believe we need to learn how to fall with grace, connecting with gravity to find a place to ground our impact" (Albright 2017: 70). In the Western world that foregrounds "the cultural hegemony of the vertical" (ibid: 71) and in the Western dance which "focuses on the virtuosity of the up," Tuuli showcases how one can "celebrate the down" and teaches us "to dwell on the floor, revel in the process of rolling, sinking, crawling, and pushing" (ibid: 71–72). Her dance, grounded in connectivity and relationality, "radically refigure the very category dance[r]" (ibid: 66).

Similarly, in the intimate photo collaboration *Gala Dress* (2002), Tuuli brilliantly demonstrates the ways in which her body navigates the world in deeper connectivity, interdependency, and kinship with other beings. In this photo series, she poses her naked, disabled, and old body in relation to animals and nature such as forest, stream, ice, and sand. In the photo book created by her niece, Tuuli says: "I have been dependent on the help of others since I was born. I haven't been able to choose who I've been naked in front of. But this nudity was my own choice" (Kinos 33).

By exposing her aged and disabled body through performative photography, Tuuli "reclaims her right to be seen naked" (Millett-Gallant 39) at the same time, she questions the social practices and values that render disability and aging both invisible and hypervisible. Tuuli's artistic self-exhibition was used by many disabled artists such as Mary Duffy, Susan Harbage Page, and Sandie Yi, who "confront[ed] stigma, manipulate[d] the gaze, and cleanse[d] shame" by performatively posing their disabled female bodies in nude (ibid: 40). While Tuuli shares this approach, her old age adds an extra layer to her photographs of naked bodies. Tuuli's exposed body–with saggy breasts and skin, winkles, white pubic hair, distorted legs–confront "the artistic and social traditions that have deemed [old and disabled female body] shameful and unacceptable" (ibid: 27). In addition, similarly to *Olotila*, the softness and vulnerability of her body, which simultaneously layer images of a young child and an old woman, create irony and unsettle the stigma around the dependency older or disabled bodies require. In most of these photographs, her body is laid on the ground; there are a few photos where her laid-down body is tilted via photoshop which makes her look like she is standing and dancing in water [see Figure 4]. In these photos, she as the speaking subject and active performer makes her aesthetic choices, shapes her bodies while laying down, and creates images full of dynamism and a wide range of affects.

Fig. 4: Tuuli in Gala Dress (2002)

Photo Credit: Tomi Paasonen

While making intentional and creative choices, Tuuli's body in these series of photography again display her mastery of relational engagement with other beings and environment. She comfortably surrenders or sinks into the surroundings, and therefore exemplifies *relational body-hood* that relinquishes control over one's body and exists in reciprocal trust, relationship, and engagement with others. In this way, I argue that this project not only challenges the ableist perception which frames disabled bodies and old bodies as non-desirable and asexual, but also re-marks disabled bodies as the critique of an autonomous, arrogant idea of the self. Her performances in both cases show her life-long lived experience of disability and dependent relationship with others gave her a gift that most able-bodied persons have lost. In both cases, Tuul's *relational bodyhood* shows a tactile and corporeal touch and contact with other beings and surroundings and offers critical insight into the possibility for human bodies to overcome the border of the self and exist more porously.

Conclusion: Living Relationally

I would like to conclude this paper by talking about Tuuli's incredible resilience that is exemplified throughout her artistic works and involvement in activism, which continued until the very last stage of her life. Tuuli's last artistic works are two activist short films, *Otherwise, You Lose the Street Credibility* (2016) and *Method for Better Service* (2016) that were collaboratively created with Finnish multidisciplinary artist Jenni-Juulia Wallinheimo-Heimonen. *Otherwise, You Lose the Street Credibility* (2016) is an activist work about the rights of older adults who age *with/into* disability but also is an autobiographical documentary of Tuuli; and the film was invited to multiple film festivals such as Serbia Film Festival: Seize the Film in 2017, Grand Rapids Feminist Film Festival (GRFFF) in Michigan in 2017, Bluenose Ability Arts and Film Festival (BAAFF) in Canada in 2018, Art Color Digital Cinema International Film Festival in Montreal in 2018. This work was a response to the Finnish government's announcement that from 2018 they will remove the rights to personal assistance for people older than 75 years old. In 2016 when this was announced, Tuuli was 83 years old, and she wrote a rap song called "Granny Rap" to fight against the governmental disability service legislation reform. Although the policies of disabilities and older adults vary in different countries, this is an obvious example that reveals the complexity surrounding aging and disability and indicates the socio-political frame that tries to demarcate and contrast *aging into disability* from *aging with disability*.

In the film, she says: "I would like to ask Mr. Rehula (Minister of Family Affairs and Social Services in Finland). Ten years from now, are you going to sit in a rocking chair and just stay at home? We all should come up with something to do, otherwise we will lose the street-credibility." Then, clips of Tuuli follow with her rap song (sung by a younger volunteer performer): Tuuli on her electric wheelchair with a personal assistant taking the elevator, crossing road, sending mails, doing grocery shopping. It is followed by the video where Tuuli writes a petition to the minister by using a communication device that translates her spoken words and types in written languages. The film mixes Tuuli going around the neighborhood; her talk on her life journey and artistic works; young person singing the rap song, and the process of growing beans which is an artistic installation by Jenni-Juulia. 83 years old Tuuli not only subverts the ageist assumptions about older persons by choosing 'rap,' but also the lyric humorously and critically reveals the ageism, elder abuse, and generational conflicts by talking about old women from an ageist perspective:

> "Grandmas slosh around on the road [...] [with] care services–paid by my tax money! Why don't they stay home? [...] Grannies don't need supportive services. Such don't delight old bones. So, let's pack the grannies nicely into paper envelopes!"

At the end of the film, she says: "I am privileged. ... I'm probably just a slowly growing individual. There is always something fun waiting to be found." It is evident in her works that Tuuli was always open to new and radical ideas, and always appreciated and cared about people around her. *Method for Better Service* (2016) is a similar short film about a middle-aged disabled woman who acquired dystonia later in her life; the film questions if disabled people would get better service from carers if they could see one's personality and their life history. This film includes a clip of street performance-protest about accessibility in Finland. According to Jenni-Juulia[11], when she asked her friends and activists who live with disabilities to join this sort of radical performance, only five people came along and Tuuli was one of them. Covering their face with a thin fabric mask, five aging disabled women on wheelchair go through a busy street of Helsinki behind Finnish National Gallery Ateneum; they pass through the crowd until they encounter the stairs at the end of the street, turn back to where they started, and put their clothes back on and take off their masks [See Figure 5]. Similar to the strategy of *Gala Dress* (2002), the nudity/nakedness of older and disabled bodies in public addresses

---

11   J.J. Wallinheimo-Heimonen, personal communication, December 27, 2022.

the double state of old-disabled bodies which are invisible and hypervisible at the same time.

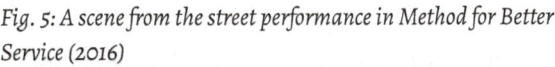

Fig. 5: A scene from the street performance in Method for Better Service (2016)

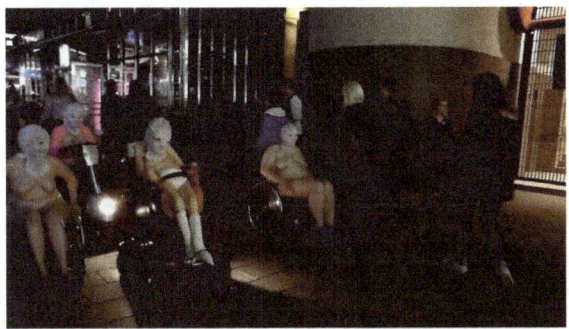

Photo Credit: Jenni-Juulia Wallinheimo-Heimonen

Even though I do not know Tuuli personally nor met her in person, I feel honored to learn about her unique and daring life journey and arts that underscore relationality, dependency, and care between beings and environment. Perhaps, her life-long embodied experience of falling in everyday life and in dance practices has trained her to be resilient (Albright 2018: 20). As an activist and artist, Tuuli raised her voice for others until the last stage of her life, and her works communicate her extraordinary mind which is characterized with extensive creativity, wonder, passion, openness, and compassion for others. In 2017, she was awarded "the Kunnia-Vimma (the honor-Vimma)" by Kynnys ry (The Threshold Association)[12] for her "versatile, irreplaceable life-long works where her

---

12   The Threshold Association (or Kynnys ry in Finnish) is a cross-disability organization, which focuses on the basic and human rights of persons with disabilities. https://enil.eu/meet-kynnys-ry-the-threshold-association-our-members-from-finland/.

contribution to the development of integrated dance in Finland is central" which is given to people who has been promoting disability arts in Finland (Purhonen 2018: 4). Her life journey and aging story reconfigure aging as an ongoing process of becoming and living with disability as a chance to exist more relationally to others, and therefore, exemplify an alternative crip aging future that are enabled through enhanced embodied connections and relationships.

Works Cited

Albright, Ann Cooper (2017): "The perverse satisfaction of gravity." In Nanako Nakajima/Gabriele Brandstetter (eds.), The Aging Body in Dance, London: Routledge, pp. 77–86.

Albright, Ann Cooper (2018): How to Land: Finding Ground in an Unstable World. Oxford: Oxford University Press.

Aubrecht, Katie/Christine, Kelly/Rice, Carla (2020): The Aging–Disability Nexus. Vancouver: UBC Press, 2020.

Berchtold, Nicole C/Cotman, Carl W (1998): "Evolution in the conceptualization of dementia and Alzheimer's disease: Greco-Roman period to the 1960s." In Neurobiology of Aging 19/3, pp. 173–189.

Changfoot, Nadine/Rice, Carla (2020): "Aging with and into Disability." In Aubrecht, Katie/Christine, Kelly/Rice, Carla (eds), The Aging–Disability Nexus, Vancouver: UBC Press, pp. 163–180.

Dodds, Susan (2014): "Dependence, Care, and Vulnerability." In Mackenzie, Catriona/Rogers, Wendy/Dodds, Susan (eds). Vulnerability: New essays in ethics and feminist philosophy, OUP USA, pp. 181–203.

Era, Salla (2021): "Equality according to whom? Debating an age-related restriction in the upcoming disability legislation reform in Finland." In Journal of Aging Studies 58/100953, pp. 1–9.

Fine, Michael/Glendinning, Caroline (2005): "Dependence, Independence or Inter-dependence? Revisiting the Concepts of 'Care'and 'Dependency'." In Ageing & society 25/4, pp. 601–621.

Fineman, Martha Albertson (2004): The Autonomy: Myth a Theory of Dependency, New York City: New Press.

Fisher, Amanda Stuart (2020): "Introduction: Caring Performance, Performing Care." In Fisher, Amanda Stuart/Thompson, James (eds). Performing Care: New Perspectives on Socially Engaged Performance. Manchester University Press, pp. 1–18.

Freeman, Elizabeth (2010): Time Binds. Durham: Duke University Press.

Gibson, Barbara E/Carnevale, Franco A/King,Gillian (2012): "'This is my way': reimagining disability, in/dependence and interconnectedness of persons and assistive technologies." In Disability and Rehabilitation 34/22, pp. 1894–1899.

Gilleard, Chris/ Higgs, Paul (2005): Contexts of Ageing: Class, Cohort and Community. Cambridge: Polity.

Goodley, Dan (2013): "Dis/entangling critical disability studies." In Disability & Society 28/5, pp. 631–644.

Goodley, Daniel/Runswick-Cole, Katherine (2016): "Becoming dishuman: Thinking about the human through dis/ability." In Discourse: Studies in the Cultural Politics of Education 37/1, pp. 1–15.

Grenier, Amanda/Griffin, Meredith/McGrath, Colleen (2016): "Aging and disability: The Paradoxical Positions of the Chronological Life Course." In Review of Disability Studies: An International Journal 12/2&3, pp. 1–17.

Gullette, Margaret Morganroth (2004): Aged by Culture, Chicago: University of Chicago Press.

Higgs, Paul/Gilleard,Chris (2014): "Frailty, Abjection and the 'Othering'of the Fourth Age." In Health Sociology Review 23/1, pp. 10–19.

Hockey, Jenny/ James, Allison (2017): Social Identities Across Life Course. London: Bloomsbury Publishing.

Kafer, Alison (2013): Feminist, Queer, Crip. Bloomington: Indiana University Press.

Kittay, Eva Feder (2013): Love's labor: Essays on Women, Equality and Dependency. London: Routledge.

Linton, Simi (1998): *Claiming Disability: Knowledge and Identity*. New York: NYU Press.

McHugh, Kevin E (2000): "The 'Ageless Self'? Emplacement of identities in sun belt retirement communities." In Journal of Aging Studies 14/1, pp. 103–115.

McRuer, Robert (2006): Crip theory: Cultural Signs of Queerness and Disability. New York: NYU Press.

McRuer, Robert (2014): "The then and there of crip futurity." In GLQ: A Journal of Lesbian and Gay Studies 20/4, pp. 532–534.

Millett-Gallant, Ann (2010): The Disabled Body in Contemporary Art. New York: Springer.

Nakajima, Nanako/Brandstetter (2017): The Aging Body in Dance. London: Routledge.

Phillipson, Christopher (2013): Ageing. Hoboken: John Wiley & Sons.

Purhonen, Sanni (2018): "Kynnys ry:n Vimma-kulttuuripalkinto Kaisa Lekalle." In Kynnys, p. 4.

Scully, Jackie Leach (2014): "Disability and Vulnerability: On Bodies, Dependence, and Power." In Mackenzie, Catriona/Rogers, Wendy/Dodds, Susan (eds). Vulnerability: New essays in ethics and feminist philosophy, OUP USA, pp. 204–21.

Sherwin, Susan/Windsby, Meghan (2011): "A Relational Perspective on Autonomy for Older Adults Residing in Nursing Homes." In Health Expectations 14/2, pp. 182–190.

Shildrick, Margrit (2019): "Critical Disability Studies: Rethinking the Conventions for the Age of Postmodernity." In Watson, Nick/Roulstone, Alan/Thomas, Carol (eds.) Routledge Handbook of Disability Studies. London: Routledge, pp. 32–44.

St. Pierre, Joshua (2015): "Cripping Communication: Speech, Disability, and Exclusion in Liberal Humanist and Posthumanist Discourse." In Communication Theory 25/3, pp. 330–348.

Tarvainen, Merja (2019): "Ableism and the Life Stories of People with Disabilities." In Scandinavian Journal of Disability Research 21/1, pp. 291–299.

Thomson, Rosemarie Garland (2017): Extraordinary bodies: Figuring physical disability in American culture and literature. New York: Columbia University Press.

Townsend, Peter (2007): "Using Human Rights to Defeat Ageism: Dealing with Policy-Induced 'structured dependency.'" In Bernard, Miriam/Scharf, Thomas (eds). Critical Perspectives on Ageing Societies, pp. 27–44.

Whitburn, Ben/Michalko, Rod (2019): "Blindness/Sightedness: Disability Studies and the Defiance of Di-vision." In Watson, Nick/Roulstone, Alan/Thomas, Carol (eds.) Routledge Handbook of Disability Studies. London: Routledge, pp. 219–233's.

A Recognition of Certain Realities
Keith Rowe's *Absence*

Ryan Bell[1]

Abstract: *British experimental musician and free improviser Keith Rowe suffered from Parkinson's for roughly a year before he decided, mid-performance, to retire from guitar-based solo improvisations. A recording of that performance was released as Absence in 2021, and his liner notes direct listeners to the precise moments when he decided to retire – an eleven-second window during which his Parkinson's tremor can be heard, marking the set as both a final performance and a self-conscious performance of finality. In "Shibboleth: For Paul Celan," Jacques Derrida shows that dates function precisely by promising readable repetitions of the supposedly-unrepeatable – the final, the only-once – while simultaneously flattening the uniqueness of their referents through that repetition. While sound recording is generally seen as antithetical to the performance philosophies of Rowe and the free improvisers and experimental composers of his milieu, it here serves to date, temporarily bearing witness to Rowe's contributions to music against the all-forgetting tide of history. This chapter examines Rowe's decision to retire and its subsequent documentation and distribution in the context of his performance philosophy, his relationship to tradition, and the dynamics between intention, nonintention, improvisation, and indeterminacy in British experimental music.*

Keywords: *experimental music; improvisation; Keith Rowe; Jacques Derrida; recording*

---

1   University at Buffalo.

On November 6, 2015, British experimental musician Keith Rowe, then 75, performed his final guitar-based set as a soloist[2]. This detail was not announced or planned beforehand, and it's unlikely that anything appeared out of the ordinary for those in attendance, or at least for those already accustomed to Rowe's work. Equipped with a Lapstick guitar placed horizontally on a table, radios, contact microphones, a few effects pedals, a six-band equalizer, and a metal strip, Rowe began with silence, a pivotal element of his sonic language since the 1960s. From this space of silence, captured on the 2021 album *Absence*, we soon hear the trace of a presence, a marking: nothing obviously musical, but a violent scrape, a tear, the sound of a contact microphone dragged across a surface. And then: absence. This pattern continues over the next minute, with each noisy gesture answering the call of its preceding silence. Though still uncompromisingly textural, Rowe's sounds soon begin to take on broader dynamics; we hear crumpling, gentle brushing, and other unseen tinkerings. Snippets of radio intermittently enter the field before eventually taking a more prominent role, with Rowe allowing beamed-in music and other transmissions into his improvisation for extended periods of time.

At the time of performance, Rowe had been suffering from Parkinson's disease for over a year[3]. Writing in the online liner notes to *Absence*, he identifies the window of time when he decided to retire from solo performance, directing listeners to an eleven-second section from 12:10 to 12:21 during which his Parkinson's tremor can be heard (Rowe 2021b). While even the ears of the most devoted and attentive listeners would likely fail to register this section as particularly atypical without prior conditioning, for Rowe, it marked the passing of a decisive threshold. Before even considering the specifics of his reasoning, it is clear that, following these moments, we are no longer listening to merely a final performance, but to *a performance of finality*.

---

2   The performance was part of Christian Kobi's 2008 »zoom in« festival in Bern, Switzerland.

3   Biographer Brian Olewnick reports noticing Rowe's tremor as early as summer 2014. cp. Olewnick 2018: p. 379.

What does a performance of finality amount to, especially in the context of aging performers, and how does this performance complicate the finality it seeks to inaugurate? In popular music, we are most familiar with the farewell tour, a well-worn trope that most would uncontroversially acknowledge as mere theatrical spectacle, pointing to countless instances of supposedly-departing musicians breaking their contracts of disappearance, returning years later – sometimes only a few – to perform yet again, resurrected from self-imposed retirement. There are, of course, other kinds of final performances: the final performance of a particular piece, or the final performance of a program or event. All the more tragic are unplanned final performances, retroactively dictated by the death of the performer. Yet Rowe's finality is of a different kind, not merely performed according to an existing plan, but emerging *from* performance and shaping both the remainder of the set and all performances thereafter; it is, to borrow his description of retirement from the liner notes of *Absence*, a "recognition of certain realities" (ibid) captured on record. It was not, however, his final performance. In addition to three guitarless solo sets, Rowe would also perform with Kjell Bjørgeengen and pianist John Tilbury before eventually rejoining Tilbury and percussionist Eddie Prévost in AMM, the free improvisation group that he founded with Prévost and members of the Mike Westbrook band in 1965 before leaving twice, first in the early 1970s and later in 2004. Rowe reunited with AMM once again in 2015, and this reconciliation would culminate in *that group's* final performance, which took place at London's Cafe Oto on Saturday, July 30, 2022 in the absence of John Tilbury, who could not make it for medical reasons (Grundy 2022). Clearly lacking the calculated profitability of the zombified pop star's post-farewell resurrection tour, Rowe's "returns" reflect an artist coming to terms with changing limitations and circumstances beyond his control, negotiating his relationship to tradition through his ability to perform.

* * *

Rowe first picked up the guitar in 1957 while studying painting at the Plymouth College of Arts and Crafts, inspired by big band jazz, modern abstract art, and the ephemerality of sound as a medium (Olewnick 2018: 26). He recalls in a 2001 interview with Dan Warburton: "With music, I didn't have the commodity. I didn't have the luggage of the canvas. I hit the guitar and made a note, and the note disappeared into air, I didn't have anything. It was completely fluid." (Rowe 2001) He soon joined a band led by Mike Westbrook, a jazz enthusiast and self-taught pianist who also attended Plymouth; initially composed of amateur musicians, the Westbrook band played relatively-conventional jazz influenced by Duke Ellington and Count Basie. However, Rowe's penchant for unconventional approaches was already on full display, even in this early phase: trumpeter Henry Lowther compares hearing Rowe's Westbrook-era solos to "hearing three minutes of Stockhausen in the middle of a Mozart symphony" (Olewnick 2018: 64), while the band's other guitarist, Malcolm Le Grice, recalls that Rowe "did not seem to bother to learn the guitar before he started playing in public – he learned on the stage and so his style was very wild and quite disruptive, but a challenge. I knew more about chords and sequences than Keith, but he was doing something more committed and dangerous." (ibid: 31) His methods would only get more radical: by the end of his tenure with the group, he made a New Year's resolution to stop tuning his guitar and was beginning to experiment with unconventional notation, pasting images from magazines and pop culture onto Westbrook's scores (ibid: 62). Naturally, the group splintered: Rowe and saxophonist Lou Gare began to play with Prévost, who Gare knew from outside of the band. They would soon be joined by multi-instrumentalist Lawrence Sheaff, a Westbrook alum, and Cornelius Cardew, the British experimental composer who, having worked under Karlheinz Stockhausen, John Cage, Morton Feldman, and more, brought a transatlantic perspective on avant-garde art music to the group's experiments in improvisation. This was the beginning of AMM.

Inspired by the explosive free jazz coming out of America and exemplified by Ornette Coleman and late-period John Coltrane, early AMM opted to continue in the creative spirit of these musicians rather than superficially replicating their sounds; without a repertoire, they not only dispensed with composition and jazz conventions, but also with soloing and constant rhythm (ibid: 73). As Brian Olewnick acknowledges in his biography of Rowe, prior to the addition of Cardew, AMM independently arrived at something akin to American experimental composer John Cage's attitude towards jazz improvisation, believing that established patterns and lexicons inhibit the proclaimed freedoms of the practice. In place of improvisation, Cage valued indeterminacy of composition and performance, utilizing chance operations and emphasizing non-intention to create works whose manifestations vary greatly from performance to performance. Of course, for the performer, this too is a type of improvisation, if with additional constraints. Identifying this contradiction, George E. Lewis argues that the prevalent use of 'indeterminacy' over 'improvisation' in the discourses surrounding New York School composition denies the influence of jazz and other African-American traditions on the development of experimental music; however, in 1960s Britain, where both free jazz and Cagean aleatory musics were essentially American imports, these traditions were often viewed as complementary, as if free improvisation was the natural culmination of modern composition (cf. Lewis 2004; cf. Piekut 2014). By the time of AMM's first record (*AMMMusic*, 1967), Rowe was performing with his guitar laid horizontally on a table – inspired by Jackson Pollock's action painting and recalling the materially-altered lexicons of Cage's prepared pianos – and manipulating radios as instruments in live improvisation. Perhaps epitomized by his use of radio, his work with AMM and beyond could be said to use 'classical' indeterminacy for the purposes of improvisation. In the liner notes to 2003's *Duos for Doris* (with John Tilbury), he revised his position on the above issues, arguing that the term 'improvisation' is "in need of a radical overhaul" because "what is far more crucial is being aware of the decisive moment." (Rowe 2003). Retaining intention and locating it in discrete moments of decision, Rowe offers a music structured by and existing *between* decisions, always colored by the possibility that the performer will decide to *stop*.

* * *

Mortality and aging had already informed much of his 21st-century work before *Absence*. *Duos For Doris* was recorded in memory of Tilbury's late mother, who died shortly before the recording session; eight years later, the duo would record for the first time since Rowe's 2004 departure from AMM, this time in memory of Rowe's late mother, for *E.E. Tension and Circumstance*. Of that album's handwritten notes, Rowe once remarked that they were meant to "recall a trace of old age and an increasing lack of facility": "I wanted it to look shoddy, with errors, away from those slick images of conceit." (Warburton 2012: 64). Rowe's aversion to "slick images of conceit" is here indicative of an unabashedly frank attitude towards mortality that we also see in 2016's *The Room Extended*, a 4-CD set that continues Rowe's engagement with what might be called composition as opposed to improvisation[4]: recorded in the years surrounding *Absence*'s November 2015 performance, its cover is disarmingly minimal, featuring only an x-ray scan of Rowe's skull taken on March 5, 2015.

The image of the skull would reappear in Rowe's later description of the development of Parkinson's, captured in the 2021 documentary *What Is Man And What Is Guitar?: Keith Rowe*:

> In the skull we have these peepholes which are kind of conduits for communicating with the rest of the world, and as the Parkinson's develops, the peepholes become more constricted, they kind of close down, their aperture is lessened. Very slowly, year by year, week by week, month by month, minute by minute, second by second, it is contracting. (Burnett/Jones 2021)

He continues, tying this gradual reduction of perception to a philosophy of performance: "But it's about you inside the skull, not able to do all of the things that you want to do, but just doing the things you can do." Later on, he reframes the statement: "So the performance becomes a performance of what I cannot do and a recognition of my own vulnerability." With Parkinson's functioning as an embodied constraint, Rowe con-

---

4   Like its 2007 predecessor, *The Room*, *The Room Extended* was deliberately assembled at Rowe's home rather than emerging through live improvisation. cp. Brian Olewnick, *Keith Rowe: The Room Extended*, pp. 371–373 and 380–385.

fronts the limits of improvisation, staging his negotiations of the possible with each performance.

In the same documentary, he discusses his reasoning for deciding to retire from solos: "If I had a contact mic in my right hand, I would want to manipulate that with the utmost sensitivity, as if I was playing a piece of Mozart. I lost the ability to do that." The evocation of Mozart may initially seem odd coming from a guitarist who famously vowed to stop tuning his guitar ("Comparing your work with Mozart seems pretentious, but that's the way I'm going to do it," he continues), and there is indeed an appeal to cultural capital here – if not to demand the reverent listening typically reserved for one of Europe's most beloved composers, then at least to combat common dismissals of free improvisation, noise, and other sonic experimentalisms as being undisciplined or even non-musical. However, anyone familiar with his work from the last twenty years knows that the European classical tradition is central to his practice and self-conception. Rowe biographer Brian Olewnick recalls a mid-2000s lecture at the Columbia University Computer Music Studio during which the guitarist began by simply playing a recording of a Jean-Joseph de Mondoville piece; after pausing playback, he questioned the students: "OK. What is the question?" (Olewnick 2018: 362) When they failed to deliver what he deemed to be an adequate response, he provided one for them: "How can I, as a contemporary electronic musician, achieve the level of probity heard in that work by Mondonville?" For Rowe, this probity seems to largely be a matter of intentionality and discipline, as if there is a moral imperative to the aforementioned "sensitivity." In a 2007 interview, he discussed the experience of seeing classical music in a live setting in terms of audience expectations: "When you go to hear a Haydn string quartet, there are no surprises, are there? In terms of newness. People listen for the exquisite exposition of the quartet." (2007) Compared to the perpetual unknowability of improvisation and aleatory music, this proposition may appear comforting, even easy: the performers and audience both know what they are getting into. Freed from the promise of the unknown, audiences can listen to the excellence of the performance itself, the "exquisite exposition of the quartet." Perhaps this quality of exquisiteness is what Rowe is getting at when he evokes the sensitivity required to perform Mozart: a haptic responsiveness that is divorced from the music proper, mediating between the space of the room and the transcendent ideal of the score.

As indicated in his comments to his solo performance at 2008's AMPLIFY: light festival (recorded and released as *Cultural Templates*), questions of mortality also underlie his investment in this tradition. Being the only non-Japanese musician present at the festival, Rowe decided to prepare a performance that would foreground his own cultural and musical backgrounds (Olewnick 2018: 366–367). The resulting piece, organized into a series of "templates," utilizes long and untampered recordings of pieces from the European art music tradition alongside Rowe's usual electronics. Each template serves a specific conceptual and personal function, with many framed as a question. Ending with a selection from Henry Purcell's *Dido and Aenas*, the piece thematizes death, the movement of history, and the longevity of art. Rowe explains: "All of these sounds are foreshadowing the end, the Dido, I know it's coming. It's about death. It goes away and comes back. What I'm saying with this death motif going, is that that's what will become of our music, and us all, in 100 years probably." (ibid: 370) The loss of music over time is invoked through its opposite, music yet to be lost: "I wanted pieces that survived" (ibid), he explained regarding his selection of sampled material, notably chosen beforehand rather than grabbed from the air. "That's making art, trying to become eternal, resisting loss." (ibid). His apocalyptic foreshadowing – "death [...] that's what will become of our music, and us all" – asserts the futility of art's apparent goal, suggesting a performance of finality not on the scale of an isolated individual, but on that of humanity and history, resituating his relatively-niche contributions in relation to not just a tradition, but to that-which-was-tradition, to an after-music when not even Purcell is remembered – music swallowed by its primary material, the passing of time.

Rowe foreshadows and thematizes both physical death and death by collective forgetting, but he is also concerned with death by *remembering*, or more specifically, death by *misremembering* – death by canon. The third template features a section of Jean-Philippe Rameau's opera *Castor and Pollux,* whose horns, Rowe tells us, are heard three centuries later "as beautiful writing, not as revolutionary" (Rowe 2009):

> This template represents the idea that no matter how different, how revolutionary and new we think our creations are, they will become a part of the mainstream, they will become absorbed. Duchamp's urinal, no matter what observers thought at the time, 100 years later it will be a part of the history of the plastic arts. Picasso's Les Demoiselles d'Avignon (1907) and Matisse's Dance (1909) were both regarded as ugly anti-art and without merit at the time, but are now thought of as possibly the most important and greatest paintings of all time. (ibid)

One can read in this an acknowledgment of the significant delay between the creation of innovative or important works of art and their popular and/or critical appreciation, if such appreciation ever surfaces. "Will our abstract scratching rubbings noise metallic scraping electronic interference glitches need to be placed alongside Haydn?" (ibid) he asks in an explanation of the template. Rowe seems to suggest that this process changes something of the artwork itself, presenting the process of [art] history as the slow neutralization of the then-avant-garde. We may encounter a Duchamp or listen to Rameau, and we may even appreciate their provocations in their historical contexts; however, if they still provoke at all, their provocations are not the same, serving to reinforce the tradition they once challenged. Even that which is remembered and etched into tradition – and only for so long – is remembered as a false memory, divested of the qualities that admitted it to the canon in the first place in order to make it accessible to future audiences; the artwork may still exist, but what and how it signifies has been irrevocably altered.

* * *

In "Shibboleth: For Paul Celan," Jacques Derrida inquires, via Celan's poetry and thought, into the nature of the unrepeatable, the only-once[5].

---

5   I would like to thank James M. Kopf, who thoughtfully directed me to Derrida's essay when I first expressed interest in the ideas of this chapter.

For Derrida, that which marks itself as final – that is to say, that which performs finality – can be most simply called a *date* (2005: 2). He is not merely interested in the singularity of dates, but also in their self-effacement and the seemingly-contradictory nature of their revenant repetitions: "How can one date what does not repeat if dating also calls for some form of return, if it recalls in the readability of a repetition? But how can one date anything other than that which never repeats itself?" (ibid). While each date marks a period of time wholly unique in its ephemerality, one that will never again come to pass, its designation *as* date requires its entry into recognizable systems of language and measurement that depend upon repetition for their cohesion, promising it in the forms of readability and anniversary if nothing else. A date can certainly be written, spoken, recalled, or implied; however, it is because of this, Derrida tells us, that the same date can also be "transcribed, exported, deported, expropriated, reappropriated, repeated in its absolute singularity" (ibid: 6), and in the process, risk losing itself *through* readability, collapsing its sublime totality of phenomena and experiences into a single sign. Encountering markings which profess uniqueness – readable dates – one faces *shibboleth*, signified asignification:"It shows that there is something not shown, that there is ciphered singularity: irreducible to any concept, to any knowledge, even to a history or tradition." (ibid: 33) Marking that-which-was, the date professes to signify a concentration of events as well as its inability to sufficiently do so.

Dating hence follows a circular logic and forms a *ring*, simultaneously announcing the unrepeatable and its [im]possible repetition; while the English phrase "one time" alludes to time itself, Derrida shows that its roughly-equivalent translations in Romance languages emphasize a *turn*, as in the Italian idiom *una volta* (ibid: 2). Turning and returning, the date is in essence a *record* – or, in the case of *Absence*, a CD. Perhaps this is why it is common when discussing jazz and free improvisation to refer to recording sessions (and metonymically, records themselves) as "dates." However, as David Grubbs has shown in *Records Ruin The Land-*

scape: John Cage, The Sixties, and Sound Recording[6], this very characteristic of dating is why many free improvisers and experimental composers alike oppose commercial recordings of their work – and for some, like Cage and guitarist Derek Bailey, records of anyone; while philosophies of improvisation and indeterminacy stress an ephemeral music that is enacted through the choices and actions of its performers, the act of recording flattens the fleeting moment to readable and repeatable data. In an interview with Grubbs, Rowe notes that AMM took seriously the idea that "recordings were really undesirable" (Grubbs 2014: 109), echoing statements published elsewhere by the band, such as the statement published in the notes to The Crypt – 12th June 1968: "This music is apparently unsuited to mechanical reproduction." (ibid: 120) Yet there it was, taking the commodity form that Rowe had hoped to escape *through* music. The Crypt was released thirteen years after its recording, suggesting that its function was at least partially intended to be archival, preserving for posterity not just a single performance, but a document of a long-departed era of AMM and, beyond that, of a particular epoch of British experimental music (cf. Born 2005). Mechanical reproduction may not be ideal for a music like AMM's – a music that certainly cannot be preserved with standard notation – but it is nearly a necessity for contemporary musicians if their goal is indeed "trying to become eternal, resisting loss."

Absence, like any live recording, directs us to a specific date. What is concentrated within November 6th, 2015 other than Rowe's performance, whose recorded double, testifying to the former's existence, is also our primary entrypoint *to* the date? Rowe's use of radios in improvisation, a "calibration of the everyday" (Grubbs 2014: 120), could be said to make the date's concentration audible, overlaying not only multiple experiences of the *same* time, but also multiple temporalities; he creates a space in which musics from multiple centuries can coexist and speak to each other, pointing to different dates of writing and recording while

---

6   Grubbs dedicates the fourth chapter to an analysis of British free improvisation and experimentalism, specifically AMM and guitarist Derek Bailey. cp. "The Antiques Trade: Free Improvisation and Record Culture," pp. 105–134.

simultaneously accompanying him in one concentrated present. He also begins his liner notes to the record by describing his experience of the day, presumably to highlight its importance to his performance, his *reading of the room*. For Rowe, "the room" is a highly-loaded concept. Even with early AMM, he often tried to make music that sounded and functioned as a direct outgrowth of its surroundings. However, the term would later grow to encompass "an altogether larger imaginary conceptual space" (2004) that includes his thoughts, relationships with collaborators, and anything else that might influence performance, such as a situated awareness of politics, history, and global conflict.

In the liner notes for *Absence*, he recalls his experience of November 6th, 2015, as if to provide us with a sketch of the room. He describes a visit to the Kunst Museum, focusing on an exhibition that paired the work of Henri de Toulouse-Lautrec with contemporaneous photography – "Lautrec's Photographic Eye": "What struck me was how the fashion of the day became aged, yet the TL paintings stayed fresh, and that his drawings were fantastic." (2021b) Echoing the themes of artistic longevity explored in *Cultural Templates*, he seems to find in Toulouse-Lautrec an artistic model for resisting loss and pursuing the eternal, measured against the unflinching verisimilitude of the exhibit's accompanying photographs. Though Rowe mentions other exhibitions, only that of Toulouse-Lautrec is granted any substantial comment, and we can reasonably infer that it was a major presence in the room at the time of performance, bringing with it to the stage interrelated concerns of aging and longevity.

While artifacts can announce themselves as dated through the usual codes – month, day, year – they are also more subtly dated through what Derrida calls the cuts and incisions in poetic language, the singular markings that distinguish a text as being *of a time*, of *its* time, caught in between language and history:"Wherever a signature has cut into an idiom, leaving in language the trace of an incision, the memory of an incision *at once* unique and iterable, cryptic and readable, there is date." (2005: 48) We can say that the fashion depicted at the Toulouse-Lautrec exhibit, "aged" as it seemed to Rowe, bears the idiomatic cuts of an aesthetic language long departed. But what does it mean for Toulouse-

Lautrec's work to remain "fresh"? Surely it, too, is dated, bearing the cuts of its language and time. Unlike the fashion Rowe mentions, Toulouse-Lautrec has been made canonical, which is to say both remembered and etched into the visual language of 'tradition.' Yet something escapes this codification into history, and it is precisely that which marks its uniqueness and which Rowe experiences as an otherwise inarticulable freshness.

Let us return to the quality of sensitivity Rowe mentions in *What is Man*. It too is *of a time*, linked more to our own than to Mozart's: it is the level of sensitivity generally expected for a performance of Mozart in the 21st century. It is shibboleth: can we perceive its presence when it accompanies performance? Can we perceive its absence, such as when it is overtaken by Rowe's Parkinson's tremor? If we cannot, we fail to hear Rowe experimenting *within* a tradition. It is not simply a question of whether Rowe's contributions to tradition are made intelligible through performance, but if his performance makes tradition intelligible and audible. Do we hear Mozart in and through Rowe's instruments and objects, passing through him and in time? If we do, do we hear the ineffable Mozart, that which has escaped canonical and institutional codification, only expressible through the abstraction of the shibboleth? Do we hear the layered and spectral temporality of the classical tradition amidst the gathered concentration of November 6th, 2015, or is the contemporary world *too* concentrated for us to make out anything but noise? "[...] it's a world without focus, the sound is overprocessed, distorted and overwhelmed by its overprocessing," (2009) Rowe wrote of the world in the online notes to *Cultural Templates*. Time moves on; from 12:10 to 12:21 in *Absence*, we hear him decisively acknowledge this reality, or we at least know to listen for it. He writes of this towards the end of his liner notes:

> Retirement, or stepping away, is difficult and painful. It requires a recognition of certain realities, that you are not important, that the world does not care that you have stopped performing solos, actually the world does not notice that you have stopped, life outside your bubble continues, get used to it, you are not at the centre of anything. A part of the reality is to try not to leave a big mess for others to tidy up

> after you have left the departure lounge, retirement is an opportunity
> where you are able to discard all the junk you've accumulated. (2021b)

In the first two sentences, Rowe addresses himself and other, himself *as* other, through persistent second-person address. Piling on top of each other like thoughts-in-motion, the clauses culminate in dour Beckettian deadpan: "get used to it, you are not at the centre of anything." With the final sentence, Rowe appears to offer somewhat standard advice for the elderly, but beyond its literal implications, its relationship to his practice is unclear. What "junk" is accumulated? He seems to provide an answer at the start of the subsequent paragraph: "I want to share with you a recording of that 33 mins solo from Bern before it too departs for the dustbin." (ibid) *It too departs.* Performance, recording, memory: all to be discarded. The recording testifies to what was there, allowing us to listen for Rowe's performance, his Mozart-worthy sensitivity, and the latter's absence. It is its own shibboleth, marking a unique and unrepeatable event while making the latter legible through the literal repetition of playback, turning and returning between 200 and 500 rpm. But like anything else, it too will disappear through and beyond memory.

Thirty minutes in, *Absence* ends with roughly two uninterrupted minutes of Haydn's Symphony No. 80 in D minor, starkly juxtaposed with the pop song that precedes and briefly overlays it. We hear little else but its triumphant glory until Rowe slowly fades out the piece, leaving only the hollowed sound of the room, silence made audible. Shifting. Coughing. Applause. After music.

Works Cited

AMM (1981): The Crypt – 12th June 1968. Recorded June 12 1968. Matchless Recordings, MR5, box set of two vinyl records and printed materials.
Born, Georgia (2005): "On Musical Mediation: Ontology, Technology and Creativity." In: Twentieth-Century Music 2, no. 1, pp. 7–36.

Burnett, Bob / Jones, Alan H (2021): What Is Man And What Is Guitar? Keith Rowe. Filmed October 2018, short film (https://vimeo.com/721 484964).

Derrida, Jacques (2005 [1986]): "Shibboleth: For Paul Celan," trans. Joshua Wilner. In: Thomas Dutoit/Outi Pasanen (eds.), Sovereignties in Question: The Poetics of Paul Celan: Fordham University Press, pp. 1–64.

Grubbs, David (2014): Records Ruin The Landscape: John Cage, the Sixties, and Sound Recording: Duke University Press.

Grundy, David (2021): "Nowhere Band: AMM says farewell, keeps its secrets." In: Art Forum (https://www.artforum.com/music/amm-says -farewell-and-keeps-its-secrets-88873).

Lewis, George E (2004): "Improvised Music after 1950: Afrological and Eurological Perspectives." In: Daniel Fischlin and Ajay Heble (eds.), The Other Side of Nowhere: Jazz, Improvisation, and Communities in Dialogue: Wesleyan University Press, pp. 131–62. Originally published in 1996.

Olewnick, Brian (2018): Keith Rowe: The Room Extended. powerHouse Books.

Piekut, Benjamin (2014): "Indeterminacy, Free Improvisation, and the Mixed Avant-Garde: Experimental Music in London, 1965–1975." In: Journal of the American Musicological Society, Vol. 67, No. 3 (Fall 2014), pp. 769–824.

Rowe, Keith (2001): Interview conducted by Dan Warburton. In: Paris Transatlantic, January 2001 (http://www.paristransatlantic.com/ma gazine/interviews/rowe.html).

Rowe, Keith (2003): Liner notes to Duos For Doris (with John Tilbury). Printed with the compact disc (Erstwhile Records, 030–2).

Rowe, Keith (2007): Interview conducted by Josh Ronsen. In: monk mink pink punk (http://www.ronsen.org/monkminkpinkpunk/12/rowe.h tml).

Rowe, Keith (2008): Cultural Templates. Recorded September 20th 2008. Erstwhile Records, ErstLive 007, compact disc.

Rowe, Keith (2009): "EL007." Online liner notes for Cultural Templates. erstwords, blog entry (http://erstwords.blogspot.com/2009/01/el007.html).

Rowe, Keith (2016): *The Room Extended*. Recorded 2014–2016. Erstwhile Records, ErstSolo 004–4, 2016, four compact discs.

Rowe, Keith (2021a): *Absence*. Recorded November 6th 2015. Erstwhile Records, ErstLive 014, compact disc.

Rowe, Keith (2021b): Online liner notes to *Absence* (https://www.erstwhilerecords.com/store/p268/Keith_Rowe_-_Absence_%28CD%29.html).

Rowe, Keith/Tilbury, John (2003). Duos For Doris. Recorded January 7th 2003. Erstwhile Records, 030–2, compact disc.

Rowe, Keith/Tilbury, John (2011): E.E. Tension and Circumstance. Recorded December 17th, 2010. Potlatch Records, P311, compact disc.

Warburton, Dan (2012): Review of E.E. Tension and Circumstance. In: The Wire, Issue 336: February 2012, p. 64.

A Measure of Dignity?
Age & the Abject Body in Clarice Lispector's Short Fiction

Patrícia Silva[1]

Abstract: *This essay examines Clarice Lispector's experimentation with focalization, through stream of consciousness, with characterisation and with modal devices – ranging from the naturalistic to the incongruous and uncanny – to explore alternative representations of aging and old age; notably, adverse ones, which foreground both risk, vulnerability, and empowerment. It does so by analysing fictional representations of the unsettling experiences of ageing in short-stories from her 1974 collection, Onde estivestes de noite (Where Were You at Night), namely "A Procura de uma dignidade" (The Search for a Dignity) and "A partida do trem" (The Train's Departure). Drawing on Julia Kristeva's delineation of abjection in Powers of Horror: An Essay on Abjection, I argue that in these works the Brazilian author engages with the binomial association between old age and the abject body – playing on the received notion of abject as "a person, or their behaviour, completely without pride or dignity" (OED) – to redress the dichotomy between dignity and abjection and test their semiotic limits in positing an embodied sublime. Lispector's treatment of these questions will be explored partly with reference to correlative modernist experiments in ageing by W.B. Yeats – notably, in the "Crazy Jane" poems – and Virginia Woolf.*

Keywords: *Clarice Lispector; Women; Aging/Old Age; Abject Body; Embodied Sublime*

---

1   University of Coimbra (CES).

A Measure of Dignity? Age & the Abject Body
in Clarice Lispector's Short Fiction

Critically acclaimed Brazilian writer Clarice Lispector (1920–1977) is known for articulating a woman's experience in her fiction. This essay examines her depiction of aged women and the representation of aging and old age in two short-stories from the collection *Onde estivestes de noite* [Where were you last night], published in 1974, three years before her early death from ovarian cancer. Lispector's biographer, Benjamin Moser, claims that the author refers to this short-story collection as being "light" and "direct", thereby differing from the weightier tone and hermetic style characteristic of her fiction (2009: 357). He also underscores the autobiographical overlap with female characters in some of the stories, namely the woman writer in the story that entitles the collection, and the middle-aged woman featuring in one of the stories who would become the author's avatar in a subsequent fictional work (Moser 2009: 76). Therefore, these short-stories can be seen as case studies of the writer's stylistic experimentation in her late short-fiction, arguably combining semi-autobiographical self-inquiry with imaginative projection, and ranging from a realistic to an incongruous register, occasionally bordering on the uncanny and on parody.

My analysis will center on the two short-stories that open the collection, "A procura de uma dignidade" [The Search for a Dignity] and "A partida do trem" [The Train's Departure], which the author identified as the most accomplished of the collection (Moser 2009: 342). It focuses on Lispector's use of narrative devices such as characterization and focalization to portray the unsettling effects of diminished mental and bodily capacities in old age and to convey the female protagonists' perplexity and dismay over the process of aging. The women's self-perceptions and their perception of others, notably their feelings of self-doubt, abasement and deprecation, perceived uselessness and marginalization is conveyed through stream-of-consciousness narration and free indirect discourse. In doing so, I argue, she aims to convey a multifaceted representation of aging and old age as seen from the perspective of the protagonists, through internal focalization, and that of other characters and narrators.

Additionally, in these stories Lispector troubles the conventional association between old age and the abject body, questions the dichotomy between dignity and abjection, and ultimately proposes their synthesis in an embodied sublime. In arguing this, I draw on Julia Kristeva's delineation of abjection in *Powers of Horror: An Essay on Abjection* (1982). My critical engagement with Kristeva is akin to that of Jane Duran who draws on this critic's conceptualization in her analysis of Virginia Woolf's fiction, claiming that "one of the most appropriate theoretical stances for reading Woolf is Kristeva's notion of abjection", notably with regard to "the dissociative states that Woolf is so gifted at depicting" (2007: 82). In similarly fashion, the liminal states of being and consciousness experienced by the characters in the aforesaid short-stories by Lispector can also be productively examined in the light of Kristeva's understanding of abjection as the feeling of horror or disgust brought on by the perception of self-dissonance, underscoring its relation to processes of evolving identity fashioning and perception over time, with which Lispector, like Woolf, is concerned in her fiction.

"The Search for a Dignity": Which Dignity in Old Age?

Evoking the received notion of abject as "a person, or their behavior, completely without pride or dignity" (OED) in its title "The Search for a Dignity" and theme, the opening short-story of the collection addresses the association between abjection and old age. The plot centers on the misadventures experienced by the protagonist – Mrs. Jorge B. Xavier, an elderly woman of high social standing – during the course of a day, which lead up to her realization of the lack of dignity brought upon her by her old age. According to Moser – for whom the fact that the protagonist "doesn't even have her own name" and is referred to by that of her husband, attests to her social insignificance –

the story's title also signals the woman's attempt to find a new life for herself beyond her role as wife and mother (2009: 341). Through free indirect speech, which conveys Mrs. Jorge B. Xavier's stream of consciousness, the reader finds that she

> made an effort not to miss anything *cultural* because that was how she
> kept herself young inside, since even on the outside nobody imagined
> that she was almost 70, everyone guessed she was around 57. (Moser
> 2009: 341)[2]

However, on her way to attend a conference near the Maracanã Stadium she finds herself "lost in the internal and obscure meanders of the Maracanã" (Lispector 1990: 8).[3] The narrator's choice of adjectives to describe the corridors of the famous stadium in Rio de Janeiro suggests that her ordeal has a psychological quality, and the choice of the term meanders points to her bewildered state of mind, which is equated to being lost in a labyrinth. Hence, the expected (and initially suggested) naturalistic register suited to a realistic portrayal of a well-to-do aged woman's routine of attendance of cultural events to socialize and try and delay mental aging, is subverted by an incongruous register which betrays the deterioration of her mental condition, as the narration closely follows the stream of consciousness of her confused thoughts.

Mrs. Xavier's perception of the deteriorating effects of aging encompasses her physical condition. Hence, though she thinks herself younger-looking than her age, as the excerpt above shows, when she loses her way in the Maracanã, she finds herself "shuffling her heavy feet of old woman" (Lispector 1990: 8). Her ordeal gains a symbolic *pathos* when, in a stream of consciousness free indirect speech mode, the narrator claims "her physical health now already destroyed, for she shuffled the feet of many years of walking through the labyrinth. Her *via*

---

2   Translation of excerpt from *Onde estivestes de noite* quoted in Benjamin Moser's
    biography, *Why this world: a biography of Clarice Lispector*. The emphasis in this
    passage is in the original text and, by highlighting the term "cultural", seeks to
    convey the stress ascribed to it in the character's mental reflections so as to un
    derline the importance she ostensibly assigns to that facet of existence.

3   My translation of excerpt from *Onde estivestes de noite*. Unless otherwise stated,
    henceforth all translations from the short-story collection are mine, based on
    the Portuguese edition, entitled *Onde estiveste de noite: contos* (1990).

crucis." (Lispector 1990: 9–10). The latter expression draws an allegorical parallel with the passion of Christ, heretically comparing with it the aged woman's physical and emotional suffering. As a metaphor for the hardships experienced over the course of a long life it prolongs the process of aging, ascribing it a metaphysical scope which is reinforced by the allusion to the labyrinth, another metaphor for a lifespan's perplexing progression in non-Christian classical culture. The dissociation felt between her idealized self-perception and her realization of her actual physical, mental and emotional deterioration leads into a growing self-estrangement which is analogous to the sense of being "radically separate" which, according to Kristeva, "harries" the subject following a "massive and sudden emergence of uncanniness" (1982: 2).

The eruption of the uncanny in Mrs. Xavier's life is described as "the black magic of the corridors of Maracanã" (Lispector 1990:12). She eventually escapes them, though not without being taken for "mad", "not well in the head" (Lispector 1990: 9), by a stranger she meets there, who eventually guides her out of the stadium. To this humiliation, a set of others follow, such as forgetting the address of the lecture hall when she boards a taxi (Lispector 1990: 10). Even when she accidentally finds the lecture hall, she feels like an outsider and cannot concentrate on the lecture, concluding that "she didn't much care for culture" (Lispector 1990: 11). These mishaps and her feelings and reactions can result from her confused state, to an extent, but can also be seen as effects of her old age condition, displaying signs of senility such as forgetfulness, lack of concentration, especially regarding more abstract activities, and of patience for social gatherings.

Her self-abasement is complete when, already at home, she gets on her knees to look for a misplaced financial bond her husband had given her, which leads the narrator to make the following remark: "Mrs. Xavier was tired of being a human being. She was being a bitch on all fours. Without any nobility, with the last haughtiness lost" (Lispector 1990: 13), in a scene that ends with the old lady crying. This passage, which evokes the grotesque image of the dog-woman, displays a radical otherness akin to Kristeva's configuration of abjection as that which is "Not me", and which she characterizes as "loathsome" (1982: 2). The recognition of Mrs.

Xavier's lessened condition, therefore, takes on a self-deprecatory tone. Examining herself in the mirror, she describes her facial appearance as ridiculous: an inexpressive "mask of a 70-year-old woman" which "with light make-up, seemed to her that of a clown" (Lispector 1990: 14). In effect, her self-perception seems to concur with and corroborate Simone Beauvoir's claim that "Old age is life's parody" in *La vieillesse* [Old Age] (1970: 565).

However, despite this apparent emotional numbness and her advanced age, Mrs. Xavier is overcome with sexual desire upon seeing her music idol, Roberto Carlos, on a TV show – "*That*, now without any modesty, was the painful hunger of her entrails, a hunger to be possessed by the unattainable TV idol" (Lispector 1990: 14) – and its strength is such that it produces a powerful, ostensive effect of self-dissociation:

> Outwardly – she saw in the mirror – she was a dried thing like a *dried fig*. But inwardly she was not dry. On the contrary. Inwardly, she seemed a *damp gum*, soft like a toothless gum. [...] And all out of season, an out of season fruit? Why hadn't other old women warned her that it could happen until the end? She'd seen lusty glances in old men. But not in old women. Out of season. And she *alive* as if she were somebody, she who was nobody. Mrs Jorge B. Xavier was nobody.'
> (Lispector 1990: 15, my emphasis)

The vivid imagery in this passage, with its dichotomy of dryness and moistness to signify lack and abundance of desire, eloquently shows the extent to which giving into the body, to bodily desires and sensations can be enlivening, liberating and empowering in old age, countering the misogynous myth of the frigid elderly woman. It recalls the "transgressive female desire" conveyed in W.B. Yeats's "Crazy Jane" poems and in the sequence "A Woman Young and Old", which, as noted by Heather Ingman, "run directly counter to the Victorian emphasis on mastering old age through self-discipline and self-control" (2018: 41, 38). This fully embodied version of Mrs Xavier, liberated from the taboos of a false morality, is a stark contrast to the self-effacement that she is made to acknowledge at the end of this excerpt, through stream of consciousness, and an ostensibly more effective, rewarding response to the growing limitations of old age.

The code of conduct of the Victorians remained to a great extent in Christian societies up to the twentieth century, and had also been that of the prude and conventional Mrs. Xavier, who was fairly unfamiliar with the instinctual and regarded all things to do with the body as abject and potentially dangerous. But the ironic lusting she experiences in her old age has her infatuated with a popular romantic crooner, for whom she feels uncontrollable lasciviousness, even while perceiving it as a damnation:

> And because of Roberto Carlos she was enmeshed in the darkness of matter where she was profoundly anonymous. Standing in the bathroom, she was as anonymous as a chicken. [...] And now she was enmeshed in that deep and mortal well, in the revolution of the body. Body whose depth was unfathomable and the malignant darkness of her live instincts like lizards and mice. [...] Then she wanted to have beautiful and romantic feelings in relation to the delicacy of Roberto Carlos's face. But she couldn't: his delicacy only took her to the dark corridor of sensuality. And the damnation was lasciviousness. It was lowly hunger: she wanted to eat Roberto Carlos's mouth. She wasn't romantic, she was lewd with regard to love. There in the bathroom, in front of the washbasin mirror.
>
> With her age indelibly soiled. Without even one sublime thought to guide her and render her existence noble. (Lispector 1990: 15)

The reference to the fact that her age is "indelibly soiled" shows that she regards her infatuation with Roberto Carlos as abject, which is underscored through the epithet's association with lack of cleanliness. However, this soiling affects her morality, as the reference to the "revolution of the body" suggests, causing a profound moral crisis which is analogous to that described by Kristeva when she argues that abjection "disturbs identity, system, order" (1982: 4). This account attests to a state of being which, through the lens of her Christian morality, is perceived as a fall from grace into the hellish domain of the instinctual and described through a series of images of disgust reinforced by grotesque imagery, namely through association between the Body and repellant animals, such as lizards and mice.

Furthermore, as the claim of absence of "even one sublime thought" suggests, succumbing to carnal desire leads her to question the received concept of old age as a gradual refinement of emotions and, given its proximity to eternity, the advent of a state of blessedness, enlightenment and exultation often referred to as the spiritual sublime. Conversely, rather than these intimations of the soul's salvation after death, according to Christian belief, Mrs Xavier experiences a soiling of her emotions and puzzlement, dismay and desolation, which she associates with the soul's fall and damnation:

> There she was, trapped in an out-of-season desire just like the summer day in the middle of winter. Trapped in the tangle of the halls of the Maracanã. Trapped in the mortal secret of old women. She wasn't used to being almost seventy years old, she lacked practice and didn't have any experience at all. (Moser 2009: 341)

Her bewildered condition ultimately leads to the revelation of what she terms "the mortal secret of old women" – that of experiencing lust, with its youthful urgency to quench the pressing call of nature, and realizing that it cannot be quenched due to the taboo of old age. This extreme dissociative state is accompanied by disgust over the deterioration of her body due to the aging process – as conveyed in the passage, "Were her lightly rouged lips still kissable? Or was it by chance disgusting to kiss an old woman's mouth?" (Moser 2009: 341) – corresponding to Kristeva's understanding of abjection as the feeling of disgust brought on by the perception of self-dissonance.

Therefore, Mrs Xavier's epiphany can be regarded as the intimation of an embodied sublime, whose poignancy is presented by Lispector as a distinguishing feature of a woman's experience of aging and old age, precisely due to the onus of beauty and desirability placed on women. In ascribing an essentiality to the body, this category of sublime subverts the teleological Christian narrative of the soul's salvation. Hence, the life-shattering effect it has on the story's protagonist, leading to a startling denouement which is the story's climax:

It was then that Mrs Jorge B. Xavier bent brusquely over the sink as if she was going to vomit out her insides and interrupted her life with a shattering muteness: there has! to! be! an! exiiiiit! (Moser 2009: 341).

The narrator's choice of words suggests that she committed suicide, but (in)conclusive though her actions may be, nonetheless, the sense of despair they convey have a horrific, tragic quality comparable to that evinced by the notions of abjection and of the terrible sublime proposed and discussed by Kristeva in *Powers of Horror*.

"The Train's Departure": a Variation on the Theme of Aging

"A partida do trem" resumes the same theme as "A procura de uma dignidade", which it immediately follows in the collection, and also features as main character a woman in her seventies. Dona Maria Rita is described as a "dignified old lady" (Lispector 1990: 26), an epithet that echoes the theme of dignity central to the previous short story, with which it establishes several intertextual links, not least in her characterization, which resembles that of Mrs Jorge B. Xavier both physical and psychologically:

> The well-dressed old woman with jewelry. The fine shape of an ageless nose, and a mouth that would have once been full and sensitive, cropped out of the wrinkles that disguised her. But what does that matter. You get to a certain stage and what was does not matter. A new race begins. An old woman is unable to express herself. (Lispector 1990: 17)

As this excerpt shows, despite addressing similar issues to the previous story, regarding the trials and limitations of old age, they are complexified through narratorial devices such as dual focalization, whereby the narrative voice is shared by the two female protagonists, Dona Maria Rita and Ângela Pralini, a woman in her late thirties traveling on the same carriage of the train leaving from São Paulo's Central Station. Evoking a scene from the previous story, this passage underscores the ravages of time and aging upon Dona Maria Rita's face, ostensibly conveying the musings of the younger woman seating across from her, while scrutinizing the old woman. However, this third-person narratorial voice shifts to a subjective focalization which follows the old woman's stream of consciousness through free indirect speech, conveying her perception of old age as a separate racial category that sets the aged apart from other individuals, not only isolating them but also rendering them unintelligible to others. This claim introduces the main theme of the story, which centers on the abyssal communication gap between old and younger aged people, illustrated by the misunderstandings experienced by the characters, especially the two female protagonists, for the duration of the train trip.

Dona Maria Rita's abased self-perception likely derives from her feelings of rejection over having to leave her daughter – who is cold towards her and makes no accommodation for her mother in her life – to live with her son in the countryside. Distraught, she is startled by Ângela's offer, when the train starts, to swap seats with her so she can face forward and, surprised by the younger woman's act of kindness towards her, Dona Maria Rita fails to express herself clearly and blunders an attempt to thank her. Puzzled by the old woman's odd reaction, Ângela has trouble understanding her and deciphering the meaning of her facial expressions, as her face is so heavily wrinkled that it is transformed into an expressionless rictus – "While she laughed, the wrinkles had gained some meaning, thought Ângela. Now they were again incomprehensible, overlaid in a face again untraceable" (Lispector 1990: 18). In turn, from Dona Maria Rita's perspective, she can only communicate effectively if she assumes a stereotypical old person's tone and appearance that render her intelligible to her interlocutor:

> She seemed to think and think, and find with tenderness a fully-fledged thought to which she could barely fit her feeling. With the care and wisdom of an elder, as if she had to take on that air to speak like an old woman, she said: Youth. Kind youth. (Lispector 1990: 21)

Once she does so, she is able to express herself and the two women warm to each other. Hence, this episode addresses ageist preconceptions and prejudices on the part of the younger aged about and towards the old aged, which are responsible for the so-called generation gap. The extent to which old age misconceptions affect communication between people of different ages is apparent in the misunderstandings that mark the women's exchanges, initially preventing them from communicating and bonding.

Overall, "A partida do trem" offers a fairly realistic social comment on the limitations of aging and old age as perceived by women at different stages in life. It does so by using consecutive focalization to alternate the narratorial perspective between the two women and by interweaving each woman's stream of consciousness to follow particular chains of thought that reveal their contrasting views and concerns, seamlessly shifting between third person and first person free indirect speech. The story's experimental quality in terms of narrative technique is best exemplified by the intertextual allusion to the protagonist of "A procura de uma dignidade" and meta-textual allusion to the author of both stories in the following passage:

> The old woman was as anonymous as a hen, as a certain *Clarice* had said on the subject of a shameless old woman who was in love with Roberto Carlos. *That Clarice* made people uncomfortable. She made the old woman shout: there! has! to! be! an! exiiiiit! And there was. For example, that old woman's exit was the husband who would be back the next day, it was the people she knew, it was her maid, it was an intense and fruitful prayer when faced with despair. Angela said to herself as if biting herself in rage: there has to be an exit. For me as for Maria Rita. (Moser 2009: 342, my emphasis)

By alluding directly to the plot of the previous story, namely its abrupt ending, and questioning the old woman's suicide, suggested by the expression "interrupted her life", Ângela proposes alternative endings as plausible exit doors not only out of Mrs Jorge B. Xavier's desperation, but also of Dona Maria Rita's and her own existential dilemmas. This story's denouement, in turn, thwarts the expectations set at the beginning in that neither of the two women are as alone as it would seem (nor is Mrs Jorge B. Xavier in Ângela's rewrite), since Dona Maria Rita is travelling to be with her son and Ângela is returning to the farm of the loving uncle and aunt, and leaving an unfulfilling amorous relationship she reviews during the course of the trip. The life-changing travels of the two protagonists of this story is a characteristic plot device of the so-called *Reifungsroman*, a fictional genre that focuses mostly on the female experiences of aging which, as noted by Barbara Frey Waxman,

> defy the outmoded social expectation of passive senescence by taking charge of their lives, making changes, and traveling – inward, backward, forward into fuller, more intense lives and richer, philosophical deaths. (1990: 183)

However, the characters' ability to empower themselves and change their destinies is ostensibly sabotaged by the author, as suggested by the opening remarks of the passage quoted above: "The old woman was as anonymous as a hen, as a certain *Clarice* had said on the subject of a shameless old woman who was in love with Roberto Carlos. *That Clarice* made people uncomfortable." (Moser 2009: 342, my emphasis) This statement revisits the grotesque imagery of the previous story by associating the old woman with a chicken, a metaphor used in this collection (and in other instances of Lispector's fiction) as a symbol of the anonymity and lack of self-worth experienced by women – in this instance due to old age. Ângela, the character who assumes the narratorial voice in this passage, conveys precisely as much, adding:

> The old woman was nothing. She looked at the air as you look at God. She was made of God. That is: all or nothing. The old woman, thought Ângela, was vulnerable. Vulnerable to love, love for her son. (Lispector 1990: 32)

And indeed, the old woman's vulnerable condition leads her to feel love for and loved by her son, as the following free indirect rendering of her musings shows, "The old woman thought: her son was so kind, so warm hearted, so tender!" (Lispector 1990: 30). Not only is she able to express and elicit tender feelings as a mother, but she also displays warm feelings towards Ângela in appreciation for her display of concern. Hence, despite being a diminishing feature, the physical and emotional vulnerability of the aged can also elicit sympathy and empathy towards oneself and from others, be it from loving relatives, like the son Dona Maria Rita is travelling to live with, be it from strangers met on a train, like Ângela. This realization is the younger woman's epiphany:

> And the result was that she had to disguise the tears that came to her eyes. [...] Ângela was loving the old woman who was nothing, the mother she lacked. Sweet, naïve and suffering mother. Her mother who had died when she turned nine years old. Even ill but with life she had some worth. Even paralyzed. (Lispector 1990: 32)

In effect, her empathy with the old woman gains a further layer in ostensibly being motivated not just by the sympathetic treatment of elders encouraged by social norm, but also by psychological factors, namely Ângela's association of the old woman with her mother. The subsequent emotional transfer and evocation of her loss due to her mother's fatal illness causes her to project her strong emotional response onto Dona Maria Rita. However, the reference to Ângela's mother being paralytic also establishes a bond of identity between this character and the author, since the biographical details reported in this passage are those pertaining to Lispector's life and mother. This projective characterization, alongside the imbrication of narratorial voices in this story and the imagery and thematic linking of the two stories, reinforce the emotional communion between the characters and constitute formal strategies to underscore the sense of inquiry into shared experiments in aging among women, including the author. The communal identification between these characters, particularly Ângela, and the author is overtly established through the ironic reference to *Clarice*, which entangles the author in her own fictional web and, by extension, enmeshed in the same bewildering experience of living and aging as her female characters, namely Ângela who, as noted earlier, became the author's avatar in another fictional work, *Um sopro de vida* [*A Breath of Life*], which was Lispector's last work of fiction, published posthumously.

As I hope to have shown, in "A procura de uma dignidade" [The Search for a Dignity] and "A partida do trem" [The Train's Departure] Lispector fictionally addresses the dichotomy between dignity and abjection underpinning conventional representations of aging, challenging and subverting it by equating the vulnerability of old age with self-empowerment, compassion and empathy. This analysis of the stories has underscored the role of expressive characterization in representing unsettling experiences associated with aging and old age. It also examined the way in which inner and outwardly oriented focalization is used as a means of conveying both experienced and imagined sensations and emotions from different standpoints. The multi-perspective effect produced, I argue, enhances the readers' appreciation of the complexity of the process of aging and of its implications and effects, and facilitates their empathetic identification with the aged protagonists. Hence, through these devices, Lispector dramatizes and problematizes established prejudices about old age, offering a critique of ageism from a distinctly feminine standpoint, while exploring alternative representations of old age by deploying the *reifungsroman* mode in her short-fiction.

Works Cited

Beauvoir, Simone (1970): *La vieillesse*, Paris: Gallimard.

Duran, Jane (2007): *Women, Philosophy and Literature*, Aldershot: Ashgate.

Ingman, Heather (2018): *Ageing in Irish Writing: Strangers to Themselves*, New York: Palgrave Macmillan.

Kristeva, Julia (1982): *Powers of Horror: An Essay on Abjection*, trans. Leon S. Roudiezup, New York: Columbia UP.

Lispector, Clarice (1990): *Onde estiveste de noite: contos* (Where Were You at Night: Short-stories), Lisbon: Relógio d'Água.

Moser, Benjamin (2009): *Why this world: a biography of Clarice Lispector*, Oxford: OUP.

Crones, Care Homes, and Crises
'the material culture of growing older'
in Leonora Carrington's *The Hearing Trumpet* (1977)

Jade Elizabeth French[1]

Abstract: *This chapter examines the titular hearing trumpet of Leonora Carrington's novella as a crucial yet under-explored object in her surreal narrative. Turning to the 'material cultures of growing older', this chapter examines the more-than-human objects and spaces at play in Carrington's novella in relation to her fantastical representations of older age. To address the materiality of the hearing trumpet, this chapter is broken into three sections exploring the themes of self-identity, institutionalism, and hybridity as mediated through material objects. By exploring the material-spatial arrangements in the novella a new perspective emerges on how Marian, as narrator, circumvents the chronological life span: her journey suggests that time passing is not to be feared but rather represents an opportunity for growth and futurity enhanced by the material cultures of growing older. Overall, I suggest that in Carrington's novella, the hearing trumpet not only changes Marian's life as an assistive technology but also, in the end, takes her beyond cultural inscriptions of older age, offering readers a vision of a proto-posthuman figure whose task is to rebuild a post-apocalyptic earth.*

Keywords: *Leonora Carrington; material culture; Surrealism; post-humanism; care*

---

1   Loughborough University.

Introduction

The titular hearing trumpet of Leonora Carrington's novella is a crucial yet under-explored object in her surreal narrative, which follows nonagenarian Marian Leatherby as she moves into a mysterious care home. Marian, as the narrator of *The Hearing Trumpet* (1977), relays the strange events that unfold at Lightsome Hall, a care institution for older women that becomes a site of mysterious happenings, presided over by a cult-like figure head and a portrait of a winking nun. From here, a diverse group of older women go on a quest to reclaim the Holy Grail and, in turn, save the world from ecological disasters with the help of a magic parallel realm, a swarm of bees, and a majestic wolf-woman. Work has been done in restoring the crone and old age as symbolically important in Carrington's work (Chadwick, 1993; Smith, 2005; Wallraven, 2015) but in this chapter, I propose using the material cultures of growing older (Lovatt, 2021; Höppner and Urban, 2019; Alftberg, 2018) to examine the more-than-human objects and spaces at play in Carrington's novella in relation to her fantastical representations of older age. I examine how the material-spatial arrangements in the novella allows for a new perspective on how Marian, as narrator, circumvents the chronological life span: her journey suggests that time passing is not to be feared but rather represents an opportunity for growth and futurity enhanced by the material cultures of growing older.

As we age, material objects might "compensate or replace parts of the ageing body and its altered abilities" (Alftberg, 2018: 23). From in-home camera surveillance (Cozza et al, 2021), to walking frames (Alftberg, 2018) and Viagra (Joyce and Mamo, 2006) a multitude of technological and biological supplements have been developed in the twenty-first century to support the ageing process, which, in turn, prompt questions about the role and place of objects in care relationships. A new materialism approach demonstrates how physical *things* are active agents in the complex relationships enacted between people, objects, technologies, social organisations and more (Fox, 2016; Lovatt, 2018; Cozza et al, 2021). Scholars interested in the materialities of ageing are alert to the meanings of objects for older adults' construction of identity and the emotional exchange between bodies and non-human materialities (Wanka and Gallistl, 2018; Twigg, 2007). A material approach helps researchers "define aging not as linear courses, but as co-formations taking place within relational processes that constantly re-shape the experience of age and ageing" (Höppner and Urban, 2018: 8). Introduced in the opening pages, the hearing trumpet might be symbolically considered as a more-than-human technology that highlights the active role that *things* play in constructing an identity for older adults (Cozza et al, 2021) as Marian begins an intense search for the self in increasingly surreal surroundings. In relation to the novella, a material perspective allows a focus on the more commonplace aspects of Marian's experience of ageing, refocusing a perspective on how an everyday object puts her both in conversation with embodied realities of ageing as well as the magical and esoteric turns the novella takes.

For Joyce and Mamo (2006), technology and science act at ever more complex interactions in the relationship between ageing and care, where an increasing desire to live beyond the body creates a "graying [of] the cyborg" (99). The posthuman cyborg, as defined by Donna Haraway (1985), acts as a hybrid symbol that connects animals, organisms, machines, and technology. Carrington's art and literature often embraces liminal and fluid connection between the human and non-human, and in *The Hearing Trumpet* hybridity becomes a crucial tool for circumnavigating the tyranny of the institution. For Lyon (2017), Carrington's work "makes posthuman thinking possible" (168) as her worlds embrace a diverse multiplicity that takes the hybridity of organic life, technology, animality as a given.

Starting from a place of hybridity, the more-than-human objects in *The Hearing Trumpet* take on qualities beyond their expected capabilities, it is in no small part influenced in part by Carrington's commitment to the transformative potential of feminist, avant-garde writing and the carnivalesque mode she embraces (Suleiman, 1990). An interest in transformation runs throughout Carrington's career: from her long-standing interest in Celtic mythology (see: Barber, 2018) and her early career alongside Surrealists such as Max Ernst, to her move to Mexico in the 1940s, which brought her into contact with magical realism and the marvellous alongside comrades such as Remedios Varo. Even so, within Carrington's fantastical and surreal symbolism, there remains a grounding in the ordinary, particularly in her fiction, which "resists the very flight into fantasy to which its absurdities beckon" (Eburne and McAra, 2017: 4). The everyday nature of the hearing trumpet also speaks to Surrealist concerns such as Marcel Duchamp's concept of the 'ready-made' and general interest in the *objet d'art*, which asked viewers to reimagine the normative function of any given found object (Ades, 2021). These objects – from Duchamp's famous *Fountain* (1917) to Joseph Cornell's assemblage works that pieced together found bottles, trinkets, and photographs – confirmed "the reality of other dimensions: dream, desire, imagination, or memory" (Ades, 2021: 270). That the hearing trumpet is found in a flea market by Marian's friend, Carmella, imbues it with an everyday surrealism that Carrington riffs on through a feminist and fantastical lens.

To address the materiality of the hearing trumpet, this chapter is broken into three sections exploring the themes of self-identity, institutionalism, and hybridity as mediated through material objects. First, I examine how Carrington presents the hearing trumpet as a subversive everyday object of empowerment, as she uses it as a potent tool to counteract the ageist perspectives of her family. Second, I explore the care home setting as an institution that has the potential to destroy Marian's identity, as well as a site that holds the secrets to her spiritual self. Third, I suggest by the end of the novel, ageing has become a building block for the future through a hybrid post-human perspective, reinscribing the older body with cultural power and social visibility in the face of crisis. In Carrington's novella, the hearing trumpet not only changes Marian's life as an assistive technology but also, in the end, takes her beyond cultural inscriptions of older age, offering readers a vision of a proto-post-human figure whose task is to rebuild a post-apocalyptic earth.

The Hearing Trumpet as More-than-Human Technology

The novella opens with the gifting of a hearing trumpet to Marian by her loyal friend, Carmella, who prophetically proclaims from the first page: "Your life will be changed" (3). Marian's life is *practically* changed as the hearing trumpet is an object with a specific use as a hearing aid device. Hearing trumpets are a funnel-shaped devices that collect sound waves to channel the sound into the ear, providing directionality towards the sounds the user most wants to hear (Verwaal, 2021). Marian's trumpet magnifies her hearing to supernatural proportions, picking up 'a cricket chrip[ing]' (Ochoa, 2010: 76) in the distance. Alongside it's enhanced qualities, the hearing trumpet is also described as being "encrusted with silver and mother o'pearl motives and grandly curved like a buffalo's horn" (1). The decorative nature of the trumpet suggests a traditional item, highly visible with its shining exterior and grand curves. The old-fashioned design of the trumpet indicates certain associations. By the late 19th century, hidden hearing aids were becoming the norm, and Sweet (2017) outlines how women, in particular, had begun to regard medical prosthetics as an invisible intervention that should be hidden from view. In contrast, Marian enjoys using an object that draws more attention to her ageing status, revelling in the "aesthetic presence" of such an "exceptionally pretty" item (3). The trumpet may be ostentatious, but it is not merely decorative, as Marian notes that the trumpet "magnified sound to such a degree that ordinary conversation became quite audible even to my ears" (3). Artner (2019) suggests that although Material Culture Studies often emphasise the ambiguous nature of things, the symbolic or metaphorical properties of material objects should not be overlooked, particularly pertaining to objects that might reproduce specific ideas about being older. Carrington deploys the metaphorical associations of the hearing trumpet in order to subvert them, using the connotations of the hidden nineteenth-century hearing aid to embrace the ornamental visibility of her hearing aid device. Carrington's subversive use of the hearing trumpet suggests that the symbolic meaning emphasised by the object – making visible an older woman with altered abilities – is a central aim of the novella. Furthermore, in a novella interested in the comedic voice of its narrator, the hearing trumpet offer light relief: despite being an ostentatious object it often goes unnoticed by those around Marian. In one illustration, as the family gather to talk about Marian, the trumpet intrudes into the frame allowing her access to a space usually kept from her. The family, however, fail to notice and continue with their conversation.

The failure of Marian's family to notice and listen to her triggers a series of events, as they discuss sending her to a care home. Her son, Galahad, is passively convinced "it seems the sort of place to send her, she will be quite well cared for there" (15). His wife, Muriel, more forcefully feels "[s]he ought to have been put away long ago", whilst her grandson, Robert, can't wait to "pack her off" (15). The language used by the family turns Marian herself into a type of object, to be packed and put away. They do not suspect that Marian has the agency or ability to listen in. As Natalya Lusty (2017) suggests, the act of eavesdropping is a crucial theme in the novella, and the hearing trumpet is the key object that empowers Marian to overhear people speaking about her. Lusty argues that Carrington is interested in recasting "the roles of storyteller and listener [...] a relationship constructed around the objectification of the passive other" (2017:pg). From her position as narrator, Carrington gives Marian the power to debunk presuppositions about her experiences and the trumpet is a key tool for her advocating for herself, as she subverts and challenges the expectations that others have about her age. When Galahad tells her "you are going away on a nice holiday", Marian is forewarned and able to reply "My dear Galahad, don't tell me such silly lies. You are sending me away to a home for senile females" (23). The family's vague language – the "sort of place" to be "put away" – is spoken in crude terms by Marian, who brings to light that which the family would rather allude to.

Indeed, Marian's view of herself sits in stark contrast to her family, as she says to them: "you all think I am a repulsive old bag and I dare say you are right from your own point of view" (23). Living in the space of the paradox of ageing– seen as abject but unseen as a social agent (Woodward, 2006) – Marian uses the hearing trumpet as a way of regaining power in the novella's opening. In the face of her family's condescension, Marian declares her individuality and sets up a riposte to the social invisibility of older people by claiming that she is happy as she is. Marian is consistently framed as a *thing*, as she further overhears her grandson describing her as a "drooling sack of decomposing flesh" (15). In this comment, her grandson reduces Marian to an object who "can hardly be classified as a human being" (10). Rosina, the maid, also ignores Marian, who says "'I do not believe that she puts me in a human category'" (4). Marian cannot be "classified" or categorised in her grandson or Rosina's eyes as 'human'. However, just as the hearing trumpet is reinvigorated from a decorative "specimen" to useful technology, so too does Marian take a stance for her own worth from the very first page: "Here I may add that I consider that I am still a useful member of society and I believe still capable of being pleasant and amusing when the occasion seems fit" (1). As Suleiman (1990) suggests, there is a dynamic of empowerment in the novella, as Carrington rewrites and shifts expectations of old age: "Only by having the old 'senile' crone tell her own story is the contradictory effect achieved. Marian's sharp wit counteracts her 'decomposing flesh' and her dependent status is belied by her narrative mastery" (169–170). This narrative mastery is facilitated by the hearing trumpet, allowing her to overhear and respond to the reductive, ageist perspective of her family and advocate for herself as a useful person.

In Carrington's novella, the tension "between *being in* the body (a material, biophysical state) and imagining or culturally constructing the limits, desires, and possibilities of the body" (Joyce and Mamo, 2006: 104) is bridged in the opening pages by the fantastical hearing trumpet. Her family view Marian as inhabiting an abject body but she pushes at these limits and reframes the possibilities of her embodiment: she shares how although her "rheumatics have bent [her] skeleton somewhat" this does not prevent her from taking walks or sweeping her rooms. She has no teeth and refuses to wear dentures but reasons "I don't have to bite anybody and there are all sorts of soft edible foods easy to procure and digestible to the stomach" (3). It is in these first pages that we see how Marian's sense of self – a confident, practical, funny, engaged older woman – is set at odds against her family's perspective. Marian might bear symbolic markers of older age but is far from defined by them. As she arrives at the care home, a further search for the self allows Marian to imagine new possibilities set against the restricting impulses of the institution.

Objects in the Fantasy Care Home: Search for the Self

Carrington was alert to the ways in which space and place impact on the search for the self, having documented her own experience of institutionalisation at a Santander asylum in *Down Below* (1944). In *The Hearing Trumpet*, Marian is faced with the potential damage of such an institution to her individual self. In Goffman's (1961) study of the "total institution" he defined spaces such as asylums, prisons and even care homes as "a place of residence and work where a large number of like-situated individuals, cut off from the wider society for an appreciable period of time, together lead an enclosed, formally administered round of life' (xiii).[2] A prolonged stay in a "total institution" may have the effect of effacing personal identity, as control is exerted in a number of ways, including the confiscation of personal possessions (Jones and Fowles, 2008). Indeed, Carmella notes to Marian that she will not be allowed to bring her cats as "[i]nstitutions, in fact, are not allowed to like anything" personal, "[t]hey don't have time" (21). The imposing austerity of the institution is emphasised as Marian arrives, noting the "front door was a massive lump of wood studded with iron lumps that might once have been heads" giving the effect "more like a medieval castle than the hospital or the prison I had expected" (28–29). The lumpy door, with its indiscriminate and weathered iron heads, suggests those that enter will be worn down into homogeneity. Before her arrival, Marian imagines Lightsome Hall as a violent place of "police hounds, grey walls, machine guns" (20). The care home is presented as even more imposing than an institution: it is an impenetrable fortress. Dr Gambit's ethos follows "the grim knowledge of what is better for other people and the iron determination to better them whether

---

2   Find reference to care home

they like it or not" (16). Carrington riffs on the Lightsome Hall as a potential prison, fortress, and religious order: a "total institution" thrice over as Carmella worries it is a "morally sinister" (17) place.

The pathway between personal development and institutional destruction is emphasised when Marian is allotted a tower to live in, reminiscent of a lighthouse or watchtower. She finds that the only real furniture she has been given is a wicker chair and small table and "[a]ll the rest was painted" (30). Marian tries to open a painted wardrobe and take a book off the painted bookcase to no avail. The *trompe l'oeil*, another artistic technique embraced by Surrealists, makes it seems as if the furniture is three-dimensional when, in fact, it is painted onto the wall. The psychological effect of the "one-dimensional furniture" on Marian has "a strangely depressing effect, like banging one's nose against a glass door" (29). In this care home room, objects are strangely absent: there are no personal touches to suggests this is Marian's new home, nor any assistive technologies. The lack of materiality suggests Marian will need to trust her own intuition in the institution, divining what is real and fake and which senses to trust. So, too, must the reader decide what is real and what is fantasy. Narrative instability is a feature of Surreal fiction, and the novel encourages the reader to be as alert as Marian to the "multiple voices and possible imaginaries, undermining any hierarchy of reality.' (O'Rawe, 2017: 199). What appears on the surface to be a strange setting begins to open up a series of personal signs and symbols for Marian, as Byatt notes "[t]hese walled placed are internalized, becoming maps with signposts pointing towards a spiritual goal" (Byatt, 1996: xi). The tower takes us beyond the medical, spiritual, or social settings usually associated with care for older people and, radically, become the site of a fulfilling agency for the older women who live there.

When faced with the fear of institutional life, characters in other "care home stories" (Chivers and Kriebernegg, 2017) might seek to get away, telling "fantastical stories of escape" (Life, 2017). Early in the novel, Carmella advises "[in] case they lock you up in a tenth-storey room" that Marian "take a lot of those ropes you weave, and escape. I could be waiting down below with a machine gun and an automobile" (26). Marian soon finds fault with such an escapade, as Carmella imagines their final destination as "join[ing] a gang at an expensive seaside resort and go on tapping telephone writes for horse race winners" (29). Carmella's fantasy could almost be the type of care home narrative Chivers (2015) describes, an "escape narrative" (136) where the older residents become fugitives and offer a satisfying possibility of adventure. In care home narratives such as this, Goffman's "total institution" is subverted, as characters "challenge ageist stereotypes and decline narratives fervently" (Kriebernegg, 2017).

A similar subversion of the "total institution" (Goffman, 1961) takes place in *The Hearing Trumpet*. If the "total institution" is marked mainly by its uniformity, the care facilities provided at Lightsome Hall are marked by their randomness. In sociological studies, researchers have found that nursing homes were "rarely described in detail" and instead became "associated with physical and mental incapacity" (Biggs et al, 2001: 660). Carrington offers an abundance of surreal details: the older women's houses are made up of "incongruous shapes" that emerge as "Pixielike dwellings shaped like toadstools, Swiss chalets, railway carriages, one or two ordinary bungalows, something shaped like a boot, another like what I took to be an outsize Egyptian mummy." At first, Marian intuits a threatening undertone to these fantasy home, worrying that "[a]ll those eccentric huts outside began to take on a sinister meaning. Nursery rhyme bungalows to trick the old ladies' families into thinking we led a childish and peaceful life" (34). Towards the end of the novella, it is revealed that an even more sinister reasoning undergirds the foundations of Lightsome Hall, as Dr. Gambit has chosen each bungalow's design based on "what he calls the azimuth vibrations from the lower nature" so that residents can "watch the workings of our own nasty nature" (143). Dr. Gambit has designed the fantasy bungalows as a method of self-policing. However, although he seeks to create a "community overinterested in manipulating its inmates" (Byatt, 1996: xiii), the wardens consistently underestimate the older women's autonomy.

With Carmella's warnings in play, Marian begins to pack for Lightsome Hall as if readying for an escape or an adventure. Previously, Marian has mentioned that she always wanted to travel to Lapland and so she decides to take:

"[…] a screwdriver, hammer, nails, birdseed, a lot of ropes that I have woven myself, some strips of leather, part of an alarm clock, needles and thread, a bag of sugar, matches, coloured beads, sea shells and so on. Finally […] a few clothes to prevent things rattling about inside the trunk". (26)

These seemingly random objects are brought together as "something seemingly useless might become essential under specific circumstance" (1) and later Marian advocates "one never can know what might be useful, I never throw anything away" (25). A dilemma many older adults face when leaving for care facilities outside of the domestic home. Goffman (1961) defines an institutional "identity kit" as a "set of the individual's possessions that has a special relation to the self". For Goffman

"The individual ordinarily expects to exert some control over the guise in which he appears before others. For this he needs cosmetic and clothing supplies, tools for applying, arranging, and repairing them, and an accessible, secure place to store these supplies and tools – in short, the individual will need an 'identity kit' for the management of his personal front" (27).

For Marian, control over her fate is exerted by packing for Lapland, and she takes "cosmetic and clothing supplies" in the form of coloured beads, strips of leather, and clothes; "tools for applying, arranging, and repairing them" comes in the form of the needle and thread, screwdriver, hammers and nails, and the "accessible, secure place to store these supplies and tools" "a practical tin trunk" (25). There are also, of course, items that have no practical use (seemingly) such as the strips of leather, part of an alarm clock, and birdseed. Indeed, Marian has lots of items that others might not deem 'useful' but for her are important to her sense of self. As she packs for the institute, she notes "[o]ne has to be very careful what one takes when one goes away forever" (26). For Cruz (2022), Marian's decision to pack the items she would have taken to Lapland reframes the care home as a potentially utopian space, a setting she might "reimagine and rebuild with the use of her own hands" to create an "object of her most profound desires" (6). As the next section suggests, Carrington's 'care home story' works against temporalities of decline, loss, and abjection often associated with the care home setting (Gilleard and Higgs, 2011; Gullette, 2011). Instead, the revolutionary possibilities of Marian's identity kit find a new context in the crisis that unfolds towards the end of the novella.

Post-human Hybridity and Objects in a Crisis

The opening of the novella refers to the trumpet as a "fatal" (25) instrument and further calamitous connotations are alluded to when Marian compares the trumpet to the Angel Gabriel's although, Marian recalls, "I believe he is supposed to blow his and not listen through it, that is, according to the bible, on the last day when humanity rises to ultimate catastrophe." (25). Marian's survival kit takes on a more literal meaning at the end of the novella, when a "New Ice Age" is visited upon the older women. The link between Lightsome Hall and Lapland is stronger than Marian first suspects. One key plot point (if anything so linear can be applied to Carrington's work) is a search for the Holy Grail that is undertaken midway through the action. Marian's narrative is superseded by a short-story-within-a-short-story that follows the action of a winking nun: Dona Rosalinda Alvarez Cruz della Cueva. The nun loses the holy grail as it is taken on a route through Dublin to London, via underground bunkers that shelter only the wealthy, passing through the hands of religious clergy and witches alike. We are told the grail holds "the elixir of life [that] belonged to the Goddess Venus" (114). Recovering the grail leads to a series of events that brings ecological destruction to Lightsome Hall, as the poles shift to bring an eternal winter.

Marian's search for the self and the grail moves forward when she comes face to face with an alternative version of herself in a liminal chamber below the ground. Here, she comes face to face with a version of herself. At first, she writes her alter-ego "may have been a hundred years older or younger, she had no age" in contrast Marian feels "my age upon me like a load of stones" (172). Marian is told to jump into the broth to be boiled alive but as she steps into the cauldron, she cannot tell which version she really is. After she steps out of the broth, Marian is reinvigorated "climbing to the upperworld as spry as a mountain goat" (176). Avoiding death, Marian's exchange with her alternative self removes age as a "load of stones" and casts chronological time out. The women become ageless as an indiscriminate amount of time passes where "[d]ays and nights were distributed unevenly" (178). Orenstein reads the final section of the novella as a feminist retelling of the grail quest, one where women "wrestle the grail from the hands of patriarchy" (182). The grail quest might also be read as an anti-ageist quest. *The Hearing Trumpet* situates the eternally older women as the only people capable of rebuilding the world after the apocalyptic breakdown. Finding the grail does not dispel the ice age immediately, nor does it grant eternal life to those who find it but rather, it seems to signal an ongoing late life for the women. Metamorphosis and cyclical change are central components of Carrington's concept of ageing. Moorhead (2017) also gestures to Carrington's portrayal of ageing: "Later-life women combine female intuition, lived wisdom and insightful logic: they are perhaps the only human creatures to bring these elements together" (230). In bringing the elements of intuition, wisdom and logic together, though, Marian suggests that an intergenerational shift will occur to give power to non-human life, as the New Ice Age will pass "till the planet is peopled with cats, werewolves, bees and goats. We all fervently hope that this will be an improvement on humanity" (199). In *The Hearing Trumpet*, we see this ethos come together as Carrington navigates the chronological limitations of the human body by extending Marian and the other older women's lifespans in the face of ecological disaster and bestowing future power to the natural world.

The shifting stories-within-stories allows Carrington to open up more post-human possibilities, particularly as the New Ice Age works as an opportunity for a more equal relationship across species lines. In one of Carrington's most well-known pieces 'Portrait of Max Ernst' (c.1939) she explores biomorphic transformations, depicting Ernst as a furry mammal with curled fin, where one stockinged foot emerges from the burgundy pelt. Behind him is an icy world, where a horse (a symbol often acting as a representation of Carrington) stands frozen. In the novella,

Carrington introduces Anubeth, a similar hybrid creature who exists in the icy world, a "wolf-headed woman" whose "tall body was finely proportioned and, apart from the head, entirely human" (190). Arriving on an ark, Anubeth's arrival does not see animals traipse in two-by-two but rather arrive in a fully formed duality, signalling a departure from the binaries of human/animal. As Cruz suggests, the dehumanisation of Marian earlier in the narrative could be read as a form of "ageism and speciesism" displayed in "hierarchical views of the biosphere that connect animals and the older population on the lower level of the same power structure" (2). The shift towards an apocalypse ironically offers hope, and as Cruz further suggests, it allows the older women to find freedom in "a posthuman community, where animals and people, mostly women, coexist peacefully" (7). The New Ice Age signals a time where human and non-human become fully integrated, allowing the older women to take charge of their surroundings, vanquishing both the ageist attitudes and the institutional control that characterised the opening of the novella.

The integration of Marian with the hearing trumpet also occurs at the end of the novella. By fusing a more-than-human technology with the older body, Carrington's novella celebrates the cyborg's hybrid form. As Lee and Sowerby (2020) note, Marian is a character "who refuses to conform to any of the social norms, who finds happiness in regression, who moves forward by eschewing action, who refuses progress in material terms". As such, Marian's status as an unclassifiable 'thing' might be reframed as representing the more-than-human power she holds, as "a prophetic model for [the...] posthuman" (Lee and Sowerby, 2020: 123). A post-human integration of body and technology is further implied by the illustrations that accompany the novel, drawn by Carrington's son, Pablo Weisz Carrington. The illustrations depict the trumpet as a part of Marian's body. The hearing trumpet is fused with Marian, and she becomes a cyborg, as Haraway (1985) defines: "[a] hybrid of machine and organism, a creature of social reality as well as a creature of fiction" (5).The exaggerated size of the trumpet is in proportion to Marian's height, her arm fitting perfectly into the curvature of the trumpet as if it was an extension of herself. As Marian becomes fused with hearing trumpet she finds she no longer needs it to function as the useful-decorative object it entered the narrative as, instead she develops "a premonition of sound which I could translate afterwards through the trumpet" (148). Entering into a symbiotic relationship with the trumpet that turns sound waves into experiences, where howling becomes "a new sound... strangely reminiscent of mince pies" (187). Marian has assembled mind, body, and spirit as one experience, facilitated by, but not dependent on, her trumpet.

It is in this final section of the novella that the importance of a materiality of ageing through seemingly random objects becomes clearer. As the care home collapses around them, the older women are tasked with rebuilding the earth. Carmella reappears at the end of the novella to help the care home rebuild in the face of the New Ice Age. The objects she brings to help include:

> "[...] sheepskin cloaks, top books, oil lamps, oil, umbrellas, caps, jerseys, flower pots with plants, and twelve agitated cats amongst which I recognised my own rejoicing" (163–164)
> [Also:]
> "[...] 'Mushroom spore. Beans, lentils, dried peas and rice. Grass seed, biscuits, tinned fish, miscellaneous sweet wines, sugar, chocolates, marshmallows, tinned cat food, face cream, tea, coffee, medicine chest, flour, violet capsules, tinned soup, sack of wheat, work basket, pickaxe, tobacco, cocoa, nail polish, etc, etc.' There were enough provisions to face a siege" (165)

That Carrington takes time to list such an array of objects suggests their importance. The list juxtaposes the ostensibly useful items (oil lamps, sheepskin coats, dried foots) with the seemingly frivolous (nail polish, marshmallows, twelve agitated cats). Just as Marian's initial packing seemed like random assemblage of odds and ends, Carmella's objects become important items in the context of world re-building. To repeat Marian's practical assertion in the opening page: "one never can know what might be useful" (25). The playful array of objects suggests that a 'materiality of older age' can include any *thing*. Carmella and Marian's surrealist kit bags reject a view of older age as a time of stagnation, where an individual might stop "acquiring new objects... or replacing old things because life is near its end" (Ranadaa and Hagbergb, 2014: 111). Carrington deploys the apocalyptic action of *The Hearing Trumpet* to ultimately question what a 'useful object' (and by extension, the 'useful user') might look like. The ending of the novel opens up an alternative vision of utopia and world re-building that begins from the position of a post humanist older age.

Conclusion

The hearing trumpet – as a symbolic material object – helps Marian to subvert the cultural construction of the older body by reshaping her embodied experience of ageing. The trumpet empowers Marian to be able to speak up and challenge her family's ageist views when they will only use euphemisms. As an assistive technology, the hearing trumpet allows Marian the chance to plan and question the care home setting she moves into. In Lightsome Hall, Carrington sets the homogenous institution against the rebellious non-conformity of its residents. At first, Marian and Carmella are wary of the institution, thinking of it in terms of a prison or cult that must be escaped. As Marian begins to explore, however, she finds that the one-dimensionality of the setting belies a deeper more esoteric secret. In an ironic twist, Marian's survival kit – modelled on her imagined freedom in Lapland – proves to be precisely the most useful things she could have brought, as the novel ends with the coming of a New Ice Age. Marian's search for the Holy Grail – ostensibly for everlasting life – suggests a critique of anti-ageing temporalities by making a dystopian trope – the apocalypse – a moment of progress and opportunity that suspends chronological time. Carrington reformulates older age as a site of feminist commune and ecological stewardship, rebuilt with the help of hybrid humans and an assortment of random objects. The 'materiality of older age' in this novel, then, takes us beyond the assistive technologies and personal items often focused on and into the realm of fantastical, post-human possibilities. The culmination of the novella embraces a more-than-human world populated with wolf women, bee goddesses and winking nuns that exists symbiotically and relationally alongside the older women at the core of its narrative.

Works Cited

"Experiencing Ear Trumpets in the Enlightenment", October 26 2021 (ht tps://wellcomecollection.org/events/YVSCyRAAAEGADThi).

Ades, Dawn (2021): "The Poetic Object". In: Stephanie D'Alessandro/Matthew Gale (eds.), Surrealism Beyond Borders, New York: Metropolitan Museum of Art, pp. 270–279.

Alftberg, Åsa (2018): "New Objects, Old Age. The Material Culture of Growing Old." In: Ethnologia Fennica 44, pp. 23–34.

Artner Lucia (2019): "Materialities in and of Institutional Care for Elderly People." In: Frontiers in Sociology 3, pp. 1–12.

Barber, Fionna (2018): "Surrealist Ireland: the Archaic, theModern and the Marvellous." In: Pam Meecham (ed.), A Companion to Modern Art, New York: Wiley-Blackwell, pp. 109–124.

Biggs, Simon/ Bernard, Miriam/ Kingston, Paul/Nettleton, Hilary (2001): "Lifestyles of belief: Narrative and culture in a retirement community". In: Ageing and Society 20, pp. 649–672.

Byatt, Helen (1996): "Introduction". In: The Hearing Trumpet, Boston: Exact Change. pp. v-xix.

Chadwick, Whitney (1985): Women Artists and the Surrealist Movement, Hampshire: Thames and Hudson.

Chivers (2015): "'Blind people don't run': Escaping the 'nursing home specter' in Children of Nature and Cloudburst." In: Journal of Aging Studies 34, pp. 134–141.

Chivers Sally/Kriebernegg Ulla (2017): Care Home Stories: Aging, Disability, and Long-Term Residential Care, Bielefeld: transcript Verlag.

Cozza, Michela/ Bruzzone, Silvia/ Crevani, Lucia (2021): "Materialities of care for older people: caring together/apart in the political economy of caring apparatus." In: Health Sociology Review 30/3, pp. 308–322.

Cruz Mariana (2022): "Of Cats and Crones: Hope and Ecofeminist Utopianism in Leonora Carrington's The Hearing Trumpet." In: Anglo Saxonica 20/1, p. 1–11.

Eburne, Johanthan P/McAra, Catriona (2017), Leonora Carrington and the international avant-garde. Manchester: Manchester University Press.

Fox Nick (2016): "Health sociology from post-structuralism to the new materialisms." Health 20/1, pp. 62–74.

Gilleard, Chris/Higgs, Paul (2011): "Frailty, disability and old age: a re-appraisal." In: Health 15/2, pp. 475–490.

Goffman Erving (1961): Asylums; essays on the social situation of mental patients and other inmates, New York: Anchor Books.

Gullette, Margaret Morganroth (2011): Agewise: Fighting the New Ageism in America, Chicago: University of Chicago Press.

Haraway Donna (1985/2016): A Cyborg Manifesto: Science, Technology and Socialist-Feminism in the Late Twentieth Century, Minneapolis: University of Minnesota Press.

Höppner Girt/Urban Monika (2018): "Where and How Do Aging Processes Take Place in Everyday Life? Answers From a New Materialist Perspective." Frontiers in Sociology 2/7, pp. 1–10.

Jones Kathleen/Fowles A. J. (2008) "Total Institutions." In: Julia Johnson/ Corinne DeSouza, (eds.) Understanding Health and Social Care: An Introductory Reader, London: Sage, pp. 103–106.

Joyce Kelly/Mamo Laura (2006): "Graying the cyborg: New Directions in Feminist Analyses of Aging, Science and Technology." In: Toni Calasanti and Kathleen Slevin (eds.) Age Matters, New York: Routledge, pp. 99–121

Kriebernegg, Ulla (2017): "Putting Age in Its Place. Representations of Institutional Eldercare in Contemporary North American Film and Fiction." Virus 16, pp. 251–271.

Lee Jon/Sowerby Georgina (2020): "Alchemical Adaptations: Performing Leonora Carrington's The Hearing Trumpet." In: Michelle Mann (ed.) Living Legacies: Leonora Carrington, Delaware: Vernon Press, pp. 101–126.

Life, Patricia (2017): "Outside the Nursing-Home Narrative: Race and Gender Exclusions in Green Grass, Running Water". In: Sally Chivers and Ulla Kriebernegg (ed.) Care Home Stories, Bielefeld: transcript Verlag, pp. 191–202.

Lovatt, Melanie (2018): "Relationships and material culture in a residential home for older people." In: Ageing & Society 41/12, pp. 2953–2970.

Lusty, Natalya (2017): Surrealism, Feminism, Psychoanalysis, Oxfordshire: Routledge.

Lyon, Janet (2017): "Carrington's sensorium". In: Johanthan Eburne and Catriona McAra (ed.) Leonora Carrington and the international avant-garde. Manchester: Manchester University Press, pp. 163–176.

Moorhead Joanna (2017): The Surreal Life of Leonora Carrington, Boston: Little, Brown Book Group.

Ochoa, Gabriel García (2010): "The Hearing Trumpet: Leonora Carrington's Feminist Magical Realism." Colloquy 20, pp. 121–143. Ranadaa Åsa Larsson/Hagbergb Jan-Erik (2014): "All the things I have — Handling one's material room in old age." Journal of Aging Studies 31, pp. 110–118.

Orenstein, Gloria Feman (1990): The Reflowering of the Goddess, New York: Pergamon Press.

Smith, Ali (2005). "Introduction". In: The Hearing Trumpet, London: Penguin, p. xii.

Suleiman, Susan (1990). Subversive Intent Gender, Politics, and the Avant-garde, Massachusetts: Harvard University Press.

Sweet, Ryan (2017): "'Get the Best Article in the Market': Prostheses for Women in Nineteenth-Century Literature and Commerce". In: Claire L. Jones (ed.) Rethinking Modern Prostheses in Anglo-American Commodity Cultures, 1820–1939. Manchester: Manchester University Press, pp. 114–136.

Twigg, Julia (2007): "Clothing, age and the body: A critical review." In: Ageing and Society 27, pp. 285–305.

Wallraven, Miriam (2015): Women Writers and the Occult in Literature and Culture: Female Lucifers, Priestesses, and Witches", Oxfordshire: Routledge.

Wanka Anna/Gallistl Vera (2018): "Doing Age in a Digitized World—A Material Praxeology of Aging With Technology". In: Frontiers in Sociology 3:6, pp. 1–16.

Woodward, Kathleen (2006): "Performing Age, Performing Gender." In: NWSA Journal 18/1, pp. 162–189.

Eternity is Nothing but a Second
A Reflection

Sofia Matos Silva[1]

> Forever – is composed of Nows –
> *(Emily Dickinson)*

Abstract: *This reflection explores various approaches to immortality in science fiction. Toying with the literal meanings of immortality, eternity and timelessness, theoretical physics is used to acknowledge that, at some point on the universe's trajectory (an unfathomable number of years in the future) even matter itself will not be a possibility. Regardless of whether humanity manages to prolong its organic life by slowing senescence or finds a way to transfer itself to a digital counterpart, this is a deep time game. Just short of falling on gloomy or nihilistic thinking, the present reflection aims to provide an alternative to humanity's obsession with eternity as a life purpose by showing how our existence as a species is a wonder in itself and should be lived (and honoured) as such.*

Keywords: *Science Fiction; Immortality; Theoretical Physics; Rejuvenation; Trans-humanism*

"But what drives us to seek the timeless, to search for qualities that may last forever? Perhaps it all comes from our singular awareness that we are anything but timeless, that our lives are anything but forever" (Greene

---

1   University of Porto.

2020: xi). On *Until the End of Time: Mind, Matter, and Our Search for Meaning in an Evolving Universe*, Brian Greene (theoretical physicist and mathematician, with a special research focus on string theory) proposes that the awareness of our own aging and inevitable death plays a big part on keeping us moving forward, since most of what we do is an attempt to create something that will outlast us. Every single thing we strive to accomplish, he reflects, might as well have an underlying encompassing goal, which is to try to reach eternity.

We know we won't live forever. We are well aware of our own physical fragility, of our own ephemerality, of our own aging and impending death, as well as the unpredictably of everything and how little control we have over any of it. This awareness leads to two parallel and slightly paradoxical states. First, in order to lead normal lives and have the capability of going with our daily affairs, we have to let it go. To be human, especially an adult human, is to consciously ignore most of what we know to be truth to stay alive; otherwise, the constant wondering and worrying would crush us and drive us to a state of permanent immobile confusion. Second, while all that surface forgetting is happening, our minds still hold the truth and still inform all the choices we make. That "foreboding that quietly lives within us, one we learn to tamp down, to accept, to make light of" (ibid: 4), that almost forgotten but nonetheless always present knowledge, drives us to keep searching for something better, something that will outlast us, something that we hope will make sure our individual existence isn't forgotten the moment we are gone.

> "If high intelligence is the ability to hold two opposing ideas in our heads at the same time, then most of us are geniuses about aging a few times over. We think it will never come for us. We think it might come but it will stop before it reaches us. We think it's coming and there is absolutely nothing we can do about it",

writes Jonathan Weiner for *The MIT Technology Review* (2022). Mentioning the work of cultural anthropologist Ernest Becker, Brian Greene states that it's this "constant existential tension" – a life "pulled toward the sky by a consciousness that can soar to the heights of Shakespeare, Beethoven, and Einstein but tethered to earth by a physical form that will decay to dust" – that angles our lives: "we are impelled by such awareness to deny death the capacity to erase us" (2020: 4). As such,

> "Some soothe the existential yearning through commitment to family, a team, a movement, a religion, a nation – constructs that will outlast the individual's allotted time on earth. Others leave behind creative expressions, artifacts that extend the duration of their presence symbolically. [...] Others still seek to vanquish death by winning or conquering, as if stature, power, and wealth command an immunity unavailable to the common mortal." (ibid: 4)

"Across the millennia, one consequence has been a widespread fascination with all things, real or imagined, that touch on the timeless" (ibid: 4), he adds. Present society is no different. From Silicon Valley high-end tech companies' ongoing research to wellness and fitness post-newage obsessive anti-aging practices, copious human energy and time is dedicated to trying to find solutions for, not only how to make us live better, but also longer. And if something is central to fiction, that is the endless possibilities our minds can imagine and create. Immortality has been a theme in fiction since the *Epic of Gilgamesh* – which is to say, ever since the birth of fiction. Immortality and eternity have always played big roles on mythology and on the fantasy genre: vampires and (some) elves, plants, fountains and elixirs that grant immortality or endless youth, dark magic performed with obscure spells, rituals or sacrifices – these are all examples of how immortality is approached. And on science fiction... well, defying what is physically possible at present lies at the core of the genre, and defying aging and mortality are as essential to sci-fi as oxygen is to Earth's living creatures. Still, this poses an interesting question: we keep circling around the idea of eternity, but is there such a thing as eternity?

We'll get back to that later. For now, let us focus on the ways to reach immortality through sci-fi technologies – and all of them are ideas that have been around for decades. Notwithstanding their value, the specifics of both the narratives and the characters' affairs in the following examples pose little relevance to the purposes of this reflection – our main focus will be on the worldbuilding elements.

The *Altered Carbon* universe poses a magnificent case of study here, as Richard K. Morgan's books, along with the Netflix production (2018–2020), gather three of the usual suspects: uploaded consciousness, cryosleep and synthetic bodies. In the *Takeshi Kovacs* series – *Altered Carbon* (2002), *Broken Angels* (2003) and *Woken Furies* (2005) –, future Earth technology has evolved (with some extra-terrestrial help) so that most people have 'stacks', cortical devices where human consciousness is copied into. This is possible through 'DHF' (digital human freight) backup, the transformation of human neural consciousness into digital code, allowing people's memories, abilities, and identity (or their digital versions) to be independent from physical bodies, since upon physical death the stack can be removed and placed onto a new body. The information on the stacks in updated by the minute, and the wealthiest guarantee that several copies are safely guarded in different vaults, since stacks can also be irredeemably damaged.

Bodies are simply called 'sleeves', and can be biologically born, genetically or cybernetically modified, cloned, or artificially created (the 'synths'). Upon physical death, since sleeves are expensive, a lot of people's consciousness will be stored in a state of suspended animation. Victims of unfair deaths (like murder) will be attributed new sleeves by the state, but all others will have to wait until their families or friends can afford to buy a new one. The prison system follows a similar route: people's stacks will be placed on a much more painful degree of suspended animation, and their bodies will be stored on cryosleep until the likely event of being attributed to someone else's consciousness. Another possibility of the digitalization of consciousness and the creation of synthetic bodies also surfaces: 'needlecasting', a specific method of (unspecified but fairly quick) interstellar travel which allows consciousness to be transmitted off-world and transferred to sleeves on other habitable planets (one at a time, as 'double-sleeving' is illegal).

Cryosleep is a tech element largely employed in sci-fi when it comes to interplanetary travelling. Productions like *2001: A Space Odyssey* (1968), *Interstellar* (2014), *Passengers* (2016) and *Star Trek* depict variations of this. The same goes for *The 100* (the TV show, that run from 2014 to 2020 and surpassed by far the time frame and the technology involved in the book series), which encompassed, among many other future possibilities, centuries-long cryosleep, partial cyborg beings – minds enhanced by artificial intelligence (AI) devices that also store previous hosts' memories –, an entire digital city built and populated by AI, and a last stop on the transcendence ride that allows an ethereal (and eternal) existence made out of pure light. James Cameron's *Avatar* (2009) is a similarly good example as *Altered Carbon* for our purposes, given that interplanetary travel resorting to cryosleep ('cryostasis') and synthetic bodies ('avatars') are essential to the narrative. Plus, the long awaited second instalment, *Way of Water* (2022), adds a new technology to the franchise: the capacity to store human memories and 'recombine' them with Na'vi avatars.

The future reality depicted on a Ken Liu's sequence of stories and its recent adaptation – the AMC+ production *Pantheon* (2022) – brings a solution to immortality on a whole new level of innovation and (lack of?) ethics. "The Gods Will Not Be Chained", "The Gods Will Not Be Slain", and "The Gods Have Not Died in Vain" is a collection of short stories included on *The Apocalypse Triptych* books. These are three anthologies of apocalyptic and post-apocalyptic fiction edited by John Joseph Adams and Hugh Howey – *The End is Nigh* (2014), *The End is Now* (2014) and *The End Has Come* (2015). The three-time Hugo Awards' winner author Ken Liu has a story in each book, each narrative corresponding to a different stage of the apocalyptic process.

The 'gods' are uploaded intelligences (UI), a combination of human neural pathways' maps and artificial intelligence – "no longer quite human, and not entirely artificial, but something in-between" (Liu 2014b: 140). The process as depicted on *Pantheon* consists of the progressive reading of the brain with a laser, like if it were a scanner slicing through the organ and killing its owner in the process. Once the process is completed, the digital version of the person lives now on the 'cloud' and, once given connection to the web, has access to everything humankind has ever discovered. All that knowledge combined with AI unlimited processing, power, and access capabilities, plus the underlying self-awareness of digital immortality, makes of the UIs something similar to gods.

These divinities are very different from the ones of *Altered Carbon*. On Richard K. Morgan's world, the richest people, also known as Meths, see themselves as gods because their privilege allows them to easily 'resleeve' regularly into younger and stronger bodies (numerous times artificially enhanced with different features) or even to their own on-demand clones, while their multiple stack copies assure that they will most likely never die. However, they are still confined to more or less human brains and bodies, and limited to human intelligence – and this makes of them baby divinities when compared to what the UIs from Ken Liu's world are capable of doing. Since the UIs exist only in the digital world, they don't need to eat or sleep; they don't get sick, don't get tired and are not vulnerable to most of the things human bodies are. Their processing speed will never be reached by a human being, and the same goes for their information storage and for their universal and instantaneous reach. The digitalization of our era means that the UIs can get access to almost anything and control everything when and how they want it. Even so, the Meths do have something the UIs don't: human physical senses and sensations.

There are two other noteworthy elements in this UIs' world. First, from Liu's short stories, a 'being' entirely artificial, created by one of the UIs, mostly from his own code, as well as pieces from the other gods' lines and some new sections. Second, from the TV show, a clone created from the DNA of the genius that started it all, the man that is both the founder of Logorhythms (the primary company researching and developing the UIs) and the brain behind the UIs concept and execution. Having learned he was dying, he tirelessly tries to fix the flaw in the gods' base code that would later slowly erode them the more they used processing power, but to no avail. As such, before he dies, he and his team develop a plan B: to create a clone of him, and make sure the baby has a life path just like his, so that he can reach his full potential and figure the flaw out. Both of this pose interesting possible 'answers' to death. The completely digital 'human' mind could mean the next stage of humanity, eliminating problems like lack of resources from overexploitation of nature and overpopulation. The completely synthetic 'human' being could be an answer to individuals death, even if, unlike the Meths' clones, these allow more of a genetic reincarnation than an existence's continuation.

The last minutes of the first season of *1899* (2022), the latest creation of Jantje Friese and Baran bo Odar, reveal a new answer: human bodies placed on suspended animation inside a spaceship drifting through space, while their minds run a simulation again and again. Could life on a conscious simulation while the body is 'preserved' allow humans to both 'live' and delay aging? Of course, the bodies framed on those last minutes, which seemingly represent reality for those individuals, could also be on a simulation in itself; unless the creators choose the divulge what they had imagined for the show on their own, the answer will remain a mystery, since Netflix hasn't picked the show for a second season.

Ready Player Two (2020), an unexpected continuation to Ernest Cline's LitRPG *Ready Player One* (2011), also plays with these ideas but with a twist. Taking place on a future Earth badly devastated by climate change and populated by social inequality, the books' narrative focuses on a virtual reality game (world?) that eventuality becomes the default area for all aspects of life (save for keeping the physical body alive, naturally). Trying to prevent the looming possibility of human extinction, the main characters place their new AI counterparts (some UI siblings, one can imagine) on a data centre-like spaceship, along with dormant copies of every user that has ever logged onto the OASIS and frozen human embryos, and send it on the direction of Proxima Centauri with the purpose of finding another habitable planet. Cline plants the seed for "immortal beings of pure intellect, freed from our physical forms and set adrift in the vastness of outer space, possibly for all eternity" (2020: 363). The last book of Blake Crouch's *Wayward Pines* trilogy (2012–2014), *The Last Town*, proposed a similar idea to this, with a whole town (unwillingly) placed in suspended animation on a mountain stronghold to prevent human extinction.

All these pop culture examples pose an interesting question: the vulnerability of physicality. In none of these universes is the software able to exist without its hardware counterpart. And the quirkiest thing of all is that not even science fiction is getting (fictional) immortality quite right.

Any kind of suspended animation would be highly beneficial for humankind when it comes to space exploration (we're not on the interplanetary travel phase yet, obviously, at least not in the sense of periodic regulated travel between inhabited planets), since it would allow humans to endure the enormous duration of transit. Agencies like NASA and ESA have been testing both ways of reducing metabolic rates and different kinds of habitats or capsules for years now.

Somehow, cryonics are always presented as associated with immortality; however, suspended animation doesn't stop aging, it merely delays it – just like the dormancy periods observed in many organisms all over the world (like hibernation or diapause), where metabolic activity is reduced to a minimum to conserve energy. Plus, cryosleeping people wouldn't even be conscious – there is a reason why the concept was dubbed 'sleeping', after all –, so, while on that dormant state, individuals would be existing more than genuinely living.

Synthetic bodies can still die, and would have to be replaced again and again, until resources were no longer available. And bodies can still succumb to diseases and be destroyed by sudden accidents or natural disasters. Plus, uploaded consciousness devices can always be broken and wrecked. On *Altered Carbon*, stacks can and will be easily destroyed, both physically or though digital viruses' attacks, which can also destroy the cloud and remote copies. On *Pantheon*, it is far more complicated. The UIs require ever more storage and processing, which also imply more cooling units and electricity generators. They call themselves gods, but humans can cut parts of them by powering off servers or deleting them, and other UIs can throw them on cat-and-mouse deadly fights, killing them bit by bit. Plus, not even spreading parts of the code around the world and hiding multiple copies will save them once the electricity is out, which eventually happens on Ken Liu's post-apocalypse depiction (*Pantheon* managed to get to the lights-out phase on its last seconds but not any further, since the studio abruptly cancelled the show, even after having finalized production on its second season).

Aside from the vulnerability of physicality, another interesting concern arises from the obvious economic privilege implicated. The quest for immortality requires wealth (and not just wealth per se, but real wealth), as well as time (tricky, since, after all, this is a run against time), and manpower, which also allows for another concern to arise, that of will and agency. Liu and Morgan are both well aware of this, as are most of these worlds' creators. In *The Apocalypse Triptych* stories, the technology behind the UIs is created by the moguls of big tech companies in total secrecy, and, since they needed to test the process's efficiency first, most of the first people to be uploaded are nothing but lab-rats, chosen for their programming skills, submitted (and physically killed) to the proceeding without consent and, already as UIs, turned into digital slaves, forced to program 24/7 for the companies in controlled simulations and with limited access to their own codes.

Ironically – or perhaps predictably – the multibillionaires' ache to achieve immortality by any means necessary (while continuing to generate the highest possible profit figures) is what ends up causing the collapse of the whole human system, since, once the UIs break free from their 'chains', they seek vengeance and start breaking apart their creators, piece by piece. Vengeance turns into open war against humanity; their access to everything-digital allows them to launch nuclear missiles from countries' arsenals into other nations, provoking responses and, by so, setting the beginning of the end of civilization as we know it in motion.

To keep the UIs running? Money – large sums of it, for storage units, for cooling units, for processing units, for security and so on – and, most likely, (organic) people on the ground, which makes this digital immortality technology a possibility only to multibillionaires. This is also the truth for *Altered Carbon*'s stacks-fuelled immortality. In theory, the technology and the possibilities exist for everyone to be indefinitely immortal; in reality, most people have guaranteed only the life they are born with, with maybe one or two sleeves' extensions at best. The only ones who have something more within their reach are the Meths, not just rich, but insanely rich – a future version of our own multibillionaires. They are the ones with spare skins, clones and stack backups. They are the ones who get to live all the experiences available to humans, even death, with no fear of consequence. They regard most human lives as expandable, and dispose of people however they like. And, because the majority of the population is so poor, people have little agency over their own lives – and their own bodies (or skins), in many instances.

In *Ready Player One*, large segments of (digital) life inside the OASIS are accessible only to those with real money in the real world. However, since the main characters turn into billionaires overnight by the end of the book, everything is quite different in *Ready Player Two*. Individual will seems to evade their minds altogether, since they choose to make copies of every user (which, in Cline's world, pretty much equals creating a copy of the entirety of humankind), transfer them into a new OASIS and send them into outer space, without the idea of asking people for their permission ever crossing their minds. Worse, they have no near-future intentions of ever telling anyone outside of their circle what they've done.

Each of these economic privilege implications have roots in our current world order. Most of nowadays research on aging (or de-aging, or aging reversing, or rejuvenation) and immortality-ish are done by billionaires or funded by billionaires. Billionaires are, in fact, going about the oddest practices and methods to try to slow aging down, and they have no issues with stepping over everyone else to get there, whether it is taking medication from sick people (who actually need it to survive) or injecting younger people's blood. And, given that even immortal human beings would require a planet to live in if they were to stay organic, the 1% are desperately trying to bypass the collapse of civilization. Whether it comes from climate change-induced chaos, from nuclear extermination or from a space object impact, they will be ready. Over the last years, we've been witnessing a new space race, mostly driven by the super-rich, but an unimaginable number of well-hidden projects have been going on around the globe at the same time. Just like Douglas Rushkoff writes on his recent *Survival of the Richest: Escape Fantasies of the Tech Billionaires*,

> "Taking their cue from Tesla founder Elon Musk colonizing Mars, Palantir's Peter Thiel reversing the aging process, or artificial intelligence developers Sam Altman and Ray Kurzweil uploading their minds into supercomputers, they were preparing for a digital future that had less to do with making the world a better place than it did with transcending the human condition altogether. Their extreme

wealth and privilege served only to make them obsessed with insulat-
ing themselves from the very real and present danger [...]. For them,
the future of technology is about only one thing: escape from the rest
of us. These people once showered the world with madly optimistic
business plans for how technology might benefit human society. Now
they've reduced technological progress to a video game that one of
them wins by finding the escape hatch. Will it be Bezos migrating
to space, Thiel to his New Zealand compound, or Zuckerberg to his
virtual Metaverse?" (2022: 9–10).

It's somewhat impossible to comprehend how some people are so obsessed with immortality and, yet, can't seem to care about the future of
our planet. We, humanity as a whole, have driven – and haven't stopped
driving – our world's natural system to its edge with all our extracting
and building and consuming. The Earth has been around for some es-
timated 4.54 billion years, and our species the duration of a mere blink
of an eye – and still, we have managed to be the thing that throws the
planet off-balance like no other. At present, "These rising social and environmental changes point towards either a new configuration of human society or its collapse" (Lewis & Maslin 2018: 15). We seem to forget
how quickly we could be erased, if it came to it, and how much easier the
planet would have it without us.

In *What We Owe the Future*, William MacAskill defends his case for
longtermism, which essentially means "Future people count. There could
be a lot of them. We can make their lives go better" (2022: 16). The idea is
simple, and its ethics are strong. Also, if one wants to live forever, even if
forever means just a bit longer, one ought to care about both the future
of the planet and the future of humanity. Even so, MacAskill believes humanity is at its beginning, since the typical mammalian species has a
lifespan of one million years, pointing out that, in that case, some eighty
trillion people are still to live their lives. And, following a 'why not?' logic,
he argues that, since humanity has far more sophisticated tools than all
other species, we could live far beyond that, even beyond our planet's
habitability, around five billion years from now. MacAskill, just like Elon

Musk, another longtermism believer, are optimists and, if one were to be straightforward, both tech-dreamers and full of naïvety, because

> "The world is increasingly unthinkable – a world of planetary disasters, emerging pandemics, tectonic shifts, strange weather, oil-drenched seascapes, and the furtive, always-looming threat of extinction. In spite of our daily concerns, wants, and desires, it is increasingly difficult to comprehend the world in which we live and of which we are a part" (2011: 1),

like Eugene Thacker writes in his *In the Dust of This Planet* preface. Taking all this into account, "One can, perhaps, understand why a utopian treatment of the immortality theme might be viewed as carelessly, even dangerously idealistic, optimistic, and naïve", wrote Joseph V. Francavilla in 1984, adding "But isn't there an alternative to this pervasive version of the theme, this dystopian version which is necessarily realistic, pessimistic, and cynical?". Both extremes of the spectrum pose interesting reflexions; all the examples given in this text fall mostly into the dystopian version, although most of them could have the potential to reach the utopian level, if it weren't for some humans' greed and lack of empathy.

Transhumanists have been considering and revolving around matters like these for decades. Maybe we can't prevent most natural phenomena, but maybe we could eradicate disease and stop aging altogether. Aubrey de Grey's SENS, or Strategies for Engineered Negligible Senescence, are one of the examples. Cyborg solutions are another possibility, quite common among immortalism enthusiasts like Ray Kurzweil, with the replacement of parts of the body – organs, bones, members, eyes – or even the whole body except for the brain. Cryonics and resurrection are also central to the movement, although neither grant immortality.

Even with the ever-going advances on scientific, medical and engineering research, even if we could use bioengineering to modify part of our DNA to inform as many of our cells as possible to rejuvenate themselves, even if we could train nanorobots to detect and eliminate cancer cells, even if we could develop a machine capable of detecting all maladies on a body through a single exam, even if we could find cures and drugs and answers to most of our diseases, even if we managed to eat all the right things, even if we could prevent the climate crisis altogether and revert the drastic ecological changes that are affecting our collective health – even if, even if, even if...

If we're thinking on a short-term future, there are tectonic plates' movements (earthquakes, tsunamis, volcanoes' eruptions) to consider, as well as celestial bodies' collisions. On a long-term, deep time future, everything changes. On *Notes From Deep Time*, Helen Gordon reflects that entering a deep time scale "engenders a sort of temporal vertigo" (2021: 9). Later, she writes that

> "deep time is 'foundational to our full understanding of life's origin and diversification, it is a critical concept for understanding geology, physics, and astrophysics'. We need to grapple with deep time if we want to make sense of the world around us, the long march of evolution, the rapidly multiplying challenges of climate change that threaten life as we think we know it. Without deep time we cannot begin to answer the questions 'Why am I here?', 'Where have I come from?' and 'Where am I going?'". (ibid: 13)

There are more than a trillion atoms in a single cell. The human brain has ninety billion neurons that work on a network of one hundred trillion synaptic connections. There are more stars in the universe than grains of sand on our planet (Greene 2020). "If you compressed the whole of Earth's unimaginably long history into a single day, the first humans that look like us would appear at less than four seconds to midnight" (Lewis & Maslin 2018: 7). The universe has existed for 14 billion years, and will still exist for so many more that the number is unimaginable to us. How could we ever conceive of living forever, if our minds can't even hold the digits? What would longer lives do to the human consciousness? One can confidently assume a great ordeal would change. And what about purpose? Finality? Meaning? With indefinitely immortal lives, which is to say, without the single acknowledgement that, according to Greene, keeps us moving forward, how would life look like? Once the novelty run out, life would maybe be just a long, bleak, lonely and bored thing (as many science fiction characters are well aware of).

One could always consider, for the human timescale, that to reach something like a 500th anniversary would be like reaching eternity itself. Should we think of human immortality as a thousand years? A hundred thousand? A million? Even so, to reach that longevity and remain completely biological is still quite unlikely. Scientists predict that "the natural maximum human life span" is between 120 and 125 years (Smith 2022). Some also believe human biology "can be optimized for greater longevity", allowing more people to live longer lives, because very few "get anywhere close" that age (ibid).

So, our best shot at living lives on an upper timescale would be to transition either partially or completely to some sort of synthetic life, like those imagined by Richard K. Morgan and Ken Liu. And even those are tricky, since, as multiple scientists consider, to move the human mind to a digital alike wouldn't necessarily mean a continuation of the human life, but rather a copy of it that continues from that point onward. One thing we can almost know to be sure – even if all the things we don't know yet, and all the things we will never know, are far more than the things we do: human life as we know it will never be immortal. Genetic editing would likely change far more than expected, and synthetic life would be completely alien to the reality we perceive now. We could never be immortal and remain human. We cannot have both, something would have to give.

Furthermore, etymologically (and according to the *Merriam-Webster.com* dictionary), 'immortal' means "exempt from death" or "exempt from oblivion". 'Eternal' means "having infinite duration" or "continued without intermission", and 'timeless' means "having no beginning or end" or "not affected by time". And this brings us to the one thing our minds cannot possibly grasp: there might come a time when time doesn't exist and everything that is will no longer be.

"What's new in our age is the remarkable power of science to tell a lucid story not only of the past, back to the big bang, but also of the future. Eternity itself may forever lie beyond the reach of our equations, but our analyses have already revealed that the universe we have come to know is transitory. From planets to stars, solar systems to galaxies, black holes to swirling nebulae, nothing is everlasting. Indeed, as far as we can tell, not only is each individual life finite, but so too is life itself. Planet earth, which Carl Sagan described as a 'mote of dust suspended on a sunbeam', is an evanescent bloom in an exquisite cosmos that will ultimately be barren. Motes of dust, nearby or distant, dance on sunbeams for merely a moment" (2020: 4–5),

Brian Green writes. As the title suggests – let us recall, *Until the End of Time: Mind, Matter, and Our Search for Meaning in an Evolving Universe* – the physicist's book explores the various paths humanity has followed on the search for meaning, while also explaining how the mind and matter work, how time and space, and the universe and life, came to be, providing the reader with all the essential physics notions to understand his lines of thought along the way. The last chapters, though, are dedicated to the event that motivated all this: the end of time itself. On *Duration and Impermanence* (ibid: 244–279) and *The Twilight of Time* (ibid: 280–309), Greene takes the reader along the theories that try to foresee where the universe is headed and what it all means for life.

We, after all, are nothing but "a living, breathing, thinking, sensing, feeling collection of bone, tissue, and cells" that support "organic processes of energy transformation and waste excretion", and these rely "on atomic and molecular movements honed by billions of years of evolution on a planet forged from the detritus of supernova explosions scattered throughout a realm of space emerging from the big bang" (ibid: 6). There will come a day when the conditions for life won't be met, and this doesn't mean life on Earth only. Yes, life on Earth won't be possible some five billion years from now, when the sun's aging process moves to its final steps, but that's just thinking 'small'. The scientist draws the reader far beyond that, through the breakdown of stars, planets and into realms and timescales absolutely unfathomable to the human mind.

Greene makes the physics of all of it understandable, but it is complex enough to go over on this text, so let us skip to the theoretical big finale: the disintegration of matter itself. Could consciousness exist without matter? Could thought exist without life? Could intelligent life prevent the whole process early-on, directing the long-term fate of the cosmos as a whole? Could such intelligence shift entropy, or even have the capacity to create new universes? Could our universe go through seasons instead of a linear-like evolution? Could the universe have no beginning and no end, as Stephen Hawking once (probably humorously) suggested? Could there be other universes already?

Brian Greene asks all these questions and many more. Theoretical physics of this level is still way out of our league when it comes to reaching any kind of sure answers. Even so, since everything we know will eventually cease to exist (and since that is a certainty), it's certain that life cannot be immortal. This far into time, within the next 10^{50} years (and that is already a far-fetched prediction), not even some kind of abstract thought could be possible. And "as we hurtle toward a cold and barren cosmos, we must accept that there is no grand design. Particles are not endowed with purpose" (ibid: 325), he believes, reflecting that

> "We are ephemeral. We are evanescent. Yet our moment is rare and extraordinary, a recognition that allows us to make life's impermanence and the scarcity of self-reflective awareness the basis for value and a foundation for gratitude. While we may long for a perdurable legacy, the clarity we gain from exploring the cosmic timeline reveals that this is out of reach. But that very same clarity underscores how utterly wondrous it is that a small collection of the universe's particles can rise up, examine themselves and the reality they inhabit, determine just how transitory they are, and with a flitting burst of activity create beauty, establish connection, and illuminate mystery." (ibid: 322–323)

Becky Chambers, the author of the (probably) most soothing and feel-good science fiction, writes something interesting and along the same lines. The *Monk & Robot* series – which is a two-part novella, *A Psalm for the Wild-Built* (2021) and *A Prayer for the Crown-Shy* (2022) – is built out of the introspective conversations between a tea monk and a robot, and at on point, by the end of the first book, they reflect on their different understandings of 'purpose'. The monk is confused by how humans respected robots for having transcended their intended industrial purpose and having chosen something different for themselves, but kept insisting on a purpose for themselves, "one which you are desperate to find and miserable without" (2021: 94).

The robot reminds the monk that they are animals and, just like all other animals, they're not meant to have a purpose, adding that "Nothing has a purpose. The world simply is" (ibid: 95). If they "want to do things that are meaningful to others, fine! Good!", but they if they want to simply exist, "that would also be both fine and good" (ibid: 95) – "You keep asking why your work is not enough, and I don't know how to answer that, because it is enough to exist in the world and marvel at it. You don't need to justify that, or earn it. You are allowed to just live. That is all most animals do" (ibid: 96).

They keep going back and forth. The monk says that "Survival alone isn't enough for most people", and that "You can't just reduce something to its base components. We're more than that. We have wants and ambitions beyond physical needs. That's human nature as much as anything else", to which the robot replies with "I have wants and ambitions too, Sibling Dex. But if I fulfill none of them, that's okay" (ibid: 96). This leads to an exchange that fits perfectly in the present reflection:

> "'It doesn't bother you?' Dex said. 'The thought that your life might mean nothing in the end?'
> 'That's true for all life I've observed. Why would it bother me?' Moss-cap's eyes glowed brightly. 'Do you not find consciousness alone to be the most exhilarating thing? Here we are, in this incomprehensibly large universe, on this one tiny moon around this one incidental planet, and in all the time this entire scenario has existed, every component has been recycled over and over and over again into infinitely incredible configurations, and sometimes, those configurations are special enough to be able to see the world around them. You and I—we're just atoms that arranged themselves the right way, and we can understand that about ourselves. Is that not amazing?'
> 'Yes, but—but that's what scares me. My life is… it. There's nothing else, on either end of it. […] I don't know what my pieces were before they were me, and I don't know what they'll become after. All I have is right now, and at some point, I'll just end, and I can't predict when that

will be, and—and if I don't use this time for something, if I don't make the absolute most of it, then I'll have wasted something precious.' Dex rubbed their aching eyes. 'Your kind, you chose death. You didn't have to. You could live forever. But you chose this. You chose to be impermanent. People didn't, and we spend our whole lives trying to come to grips with that.'

'I didn't choose impermanence', Mosscap said. 'The originals did, but I did not. I had to learn my circumstances just as you did.'

'Then how', Dex said, 'how does the idea of maybe being meaningless sit well with you?'

Mosscap considered. 'Because I know that no matter what, I'm wonderful', it said. There was nothing arrogant about the statement, nothing flippant or brash. It was merely an acknowledgment, a simple truth shared." (ibid: 96–97)

In 2011, Ali Binazir played with this curious insight. The *The Huffington Post* contributor published an equal parts serious and jester article about the probability of any human being born. Needless to say, the numbers are impossible to comprehend, which could be translated as: humans were hardly ever meant to exist. We may ache for something more, but eternity is, after all, nothing but a second, and the very fact we exist is astonishing on itself. The conditions for conscious, self-aware, intelligent life to form are so unique and special that the odds were never, ever in our favour – and yet, here we are.

That is the real meaning of life for Brian Greene: not to search for the miracle that will grant us eternal life, but to live as the miracles we already are. To appreciate our existence, accept our limits and enjoy every second of being alive. "Life and thought likely populate a minute oasis on the cosmic timeline", and if we "take that in fully, envisioning a future bereft of stars and planets and things that think", our "regard for our era can appreciate toward reverence" (2020: 15).

Works Cited

Attenborough, David (2020): A Life on Our Planet: My Witness Statement and a Vision for the Future, London: Ebury.

Baggaley, Kate (2017): "'Cryosleep' May Open the Door to Deep Space. Here's How". In: NBC News, June 12 (https://www.nbcnews.com/m ach/tech/cryosleep-may-be-key-deep-space-missions-here-s-how-ncna770961).

Binazir, Ali (2011): "Are You a Miracle? On the Probability of Your Being Born". In: The Huffington Post, June 16 (https://www.huffpost.com/ entry/probability-being-born_b_877853).

Cameron, James (2009): Avatar [Film], 20th Century Fox.

Cameron, James (2022): Avatar: The Way of Water [Film], 20th Century Fox.

Chambers, Becky (2021): A Psalm for the Wild-Built, New York: Tordot-com.

Chambers, Becky (2022): A Prayer for the Crown-Shy, New York: Tordot-com.

Cholbi, Michael J. (2018): The Science of Immortality, John Templeton Foundation.

Clarke, Laurie (2022): "Why the sci-fi dream of cryonics never died". In: MIT Technology Review, October 14 (https://www.technologyreview .com/2022/10/14/1060951/cryonics-sci-fi-freezing-bodies/).

Cline, Ernest (2011): Ready Player One, New York: Crown.

Cline, Ernest (2020): Ready Player Two, New York: Ballantine.

Conant, Eve & Nowakowsi, Kelsey & Treat, Jason (2022): "How our cells age". In: The National Geographic Magazine, December 28 (https:// www.nationalgeographic.com/magazine/graphics/aging-hallmark s-damage-cells-disease-feature).

Crouch, Blake (2014): The Last Town, Seattle: Thomas & Mercer.

Dickinson, Emily (2016 [1955]): The Complete Poems, London: Faber & Faber.

Dihn, Jason P. (2022): "Immortal jellyfish genes identified that may explain their long lives". In: New Scientist, August 22 (https://www.

newscientist.com/article/2335495-immortal-jellyfish-genes-identif
ied-that-may-explain-their-long-lives/).

Eisenstein, Michael (2022): "Does the human lifespan have a limit?". In:
Nature, January 19 (https://www.nature.com/articles/d41586-022-0
0070-1).

Else, Liz (2012): "The wasteful quest for immortality". In: New Scientist,
June 13 (https://www.newscientist.com/article/mg21428690-400-th
e-wasteful-quest-for-immortality/).

Farrier, David (2016): "How the Concept of Deep Time Is Changing". In:
The Atlantic, October 31 (https://www.theatlantic.com/science/arch
ive/2016/10/aeon-deep-time/505922/).

Francavilla, Joseph V. (1984), "These Immortals: An Alternative View of
Immortality in Roger Zelazny's Science Fiction". In: Extrapolation
25/1, pp. 20–33.

Friese, Jantje & Odar, Baran bo (2022): 1899 [TV Series], Netflix.

George, Linda K. & Ferraro, Kenneth F. (Ed.) (2016): Handbook of Aging
and the Social Sciences, 8th Edition, London: Elsevier.

Gordon, Helen (2021): Notes from Deep Time: A Journey Through Our
Past and Future Worlds, London: Profile.

Greene, Brian (2020): Until the End of Time: Mind, Matter, and Our
Search for Meaning in an Evolving Universe, London: Allen Lane.

Grey, Aubrey de & Rae, Michael (2007): Ending Aging: The Rejuvenation
Breakthroughs That Could Reverse Human Aging in Our Lifetime,
New York: St. Martin's.

Grossman, Terry & Kurzweil, Ray (2004): Fantastic Voyage: Live Long
Enough to Live Forever, Emmaus: Rodale.

Horgan, John (2021): "Can Science Survive the Death of the Universe?".
In: Scientific American, June 16 (https://www.scientificamerican.co
m/article/can-science-survive-the-death-of-the-universe/#).

Humphries, Courtney (2018): "Digital immortality: How your life's data
means a version of you could live forever". In: MIT Technology Review, October 18 (https://www.technologyreview.com/2018/10/18/13
9457/digital-version-after-death/).

Immortality Institute (2004): The Scientific Conquest of Death: Essays
on Infinite Lifespans.

Kaeberlein, Matt & Martin, George M. (Ed.) (2016): Handbook of the Biology of Aging, 8th Edition, London: Elsevier.

Kalogridis, Laeta (2018–2020): Altered Carbon [TV Series], Netflix.

Kosoff, Maya (2016): "Peter Thiel wants to inject himself with young people's blood". In: Vanity Fair, August 1 (https://www.vanityfair.com/news/2016/08/peter-thiel-wants-to-inject-himself-with-young-peoples-blood).

Kurzweil, Ray (2005): The Singularity Is Near: When Humans Transcend Biology, London: Viking.

Lewis, Simon L. & Maslin, Mark A. (2018): The Human Planet: How We Created the Anthropocene, London: Pelican.

Liu, Ken (2014a): "The Gods Will Not Be Chained". In Adams, John Joseph & Howey, Hugh (Ed.), The End is Nigh, Self-published, pp. 57–73.

Liu, Ken (2014b): "The Gods Will Not Be Slain". In Adams, John Joseph & Howey, Hugh (Ed.), The End is Now, Self-published, pp. 137–155.

Liu, Ken (2015): "The Gods Have Not Died in Vain". In Adams, John Joseph & Howey, Hugh (Ed.), The End Has Come, Self-published, pp. 252–271.

Lovelock, James (2020): Novacene: The Coming Age of Hyperintelligence, London: Penguin.

MacAskill, William (2022): What We Owe The Future, New York: Basic.

McKie, Robin (2018): "No death and an enhanced life: Is the future transhuman?". In: The Guardian, May 6 (https://www.theguardian.com/technology/2018/may/06/no-death-and-an-enhanced-life-is-the-future-transhuman).

Merriam-Webster.com Dictionary, s.v., "eternal" (https://www.merriam-webster.com/dictionary/eternal).

Merriam-Webster.com Dictionary, s.v., "immortal" (https://www.merriam-webster.com/dictionary/immortal).

Merriam-Webster.com Dictionary, s.v., "timeless" (https://www.merriam-webster.com/dictionary/timeless).

More, Max & Vita-More, Natasha (Ed.) (2013): The Transhumanist Reader, Oxford: Wiley-Blackwell.

Morgan, Richard K. (2002): Altered Carbon, London: Victor Gollancz.

Morgan, Richard K. (2003): Broken Angels, London: Victor Gollancz.

Morgan, Richard K. (2005): Woken Furies, London: Victor Gollancz.

Pester, Patrick (2021): "Will humans ever be immortal?". In: Live Science, October 4 (https://www.livescience.com/could-humans-be-immortal).

Rothenberg, Jason (2014–2020): The 100 [TV Series], The CW Network.

Rushkoff, Douglas (2022): Survival of the Richest: Escape Fantasies of the Tech Billionaires, New York: W. W. Norton.

Sagan, Carl Edward (1994): Pale Blue Dot: A Vision of the Human Future in Space, New York: Random House.

Schaie, K. Warner & Willis, Sherry L. (Ed.) (2016): Handbook of the Psychology of Aging, 8th Edition, London: Elsevier.

Silverstein, Craig (2022): Pantheon [TV Series], AMC+.

Slusser, George & Westfahl Gary (Ed.) (1996): Immortal Engines: Life Extension and Immortality in Science Fiction and Fantasy, Athens: University of Georgia.

Smith, Fran (2022): "Can aging be cured? Scientists are giving it a try". In: The National Geographic Magazine, December 28 (https://www.nationalgeographic.com/magazine/article/aging-cure-longevity-science-technology-feature).

Smith, Fran (2023a): "'Zombie cells' could hold the secret to Alzheimer's cure". In: The National Geographic Magazine, January 10 (https://www.nationalgeographic.com/magazine/science/article/zombie-cells-could-hold-the-secret-to-alzheimers-cure).

Smith, Fran (2023b): "Can fasting help you live longer? Here's what the science says". In: The National Geographic Magazine, January 17 (https://www.nationalgeographic.com/magazine/article/can-fasting-help-you-live-longer-what-the-science-says).

Stamp, Elizabeth (2019): "Billionaire bunkers: How the 1% are preparing for the apocalypse". In: CNN, August 7 (https://edition.cnn.com/style/article/doomsday-luxury-bunkers/index.html).

Thacker, Eugene (2011): In the Dust of This Planet: Horror of Philosophy, vol 1, Winchester: Zero.

Thacker, Eugene (2015): Cosmic Pessimism, Minneapolis: Univocal.

Wallace-Wells, David (2019): The Uninhabitable Earth: Life After Warming, New York: Tim Duggan.

Weiner, Jonathan (2022): "The bird is fine, the bird is fine, the bird is fine, it's dead". In: MIT Technology Review, October 20 (https://www.technologyreview.com/2022/10/20/1060934/pursuing-immortality-consolations-mortality/).

Weisman, Alan (2007): The World Without Us, New York: St. Martin's.

Wolchover, Natalie (2019): "Physicists Debate Hawking's Idea That the Universe Had No Beginning". In: Quanta Magazine, June 6 (https://www.quantamagazine.org/physicists-debate-hawkings-idea-that-the-universe-had-no-beginning-20190606/).

Queering Time, Questioning Ageism Through Speculative Siction

Maricel Oró-Piqueras[1] *and Sarah Falcus*[2]

Abstract: *Speculative narratives offer particularly rich and complex explorations of time and aging, exhibiting a tendency to play with 'queer temporalities' and imagine the lifecourse and human chronology in alternative ways. In this article, we employ an ageing studies perspective in our analysis of time, the lifecourse and aging in four visual speculative narratives. We focus on recent film/TV about increased longevity/immortality. "San Junipero" (in TV Series Black Mirror, 2016), Mr Nobody (2009) and In Time (2011) imagine societies in which forms of technologically enabled extended longevity have been achieved. The Age of Adaline (2015), on the other hand, follows the tradition of speculative fiction about exclusive immortality, achieved only by one or a small number of persons. All four texts play with linear and chronological aging and juxtapose youth and age in provocative ways, exploiting the possibilities of the visual mode. In Time and Adaline seem to yearn for normative social order and present extended longevity as the source of unhappiness and social crisis. San Junipero and Mr Nobody, on the other hand, focus on the possibilities of temporal disorder as a way of escaping normative expectations. They draw attention to the constricting nature of normative times and combine utopian and dystopian elements to explore the tension between normative and queer temporal orders.*

Keywords: *speculative film/TV; queering time; aging; longevity; immortality*

---

1   University of Lleida.
2   Huddersfield University.

Introduction

The potential of literary gerontology to question ageist conceptions and identify alternative visions of aging in contemporary society has been proved in recent years. Literary gerontology offers different perspectives on the complexity of growing old (Chivers 2003: x), at the same time as it looks at the contradictions around the experience of aging (Falcus, 2015: 53). The richness in perspectives and possibilities of literary gerontology then intersects with other traditional literary approaches, such as gender, class, race and ethnicity. The already well-accepted perspective of the lifecourse within aging studies recognises that aging is lifelong and that stages of life cannot be considered in isolation. Literary gerontology reminds us of the fact that life is lived in and across time and that narrative is the mode through which we explain, and relate to, our own experiences. As Margaret Morganroth Gullette states in *Agewise*, "Whatever happens in the body, and even if nothing happens in the body, aging is a narrative. Each of us tells her own story." (2010: 5) Narrative gerontologists Jan-Erik Ruth and Gary Kenyon highlight the importance of narrative in making sense of our life trajectories and in discerning how the stories of our individual lives fit into "cultures, subcultures, or family patterns" to either conform to such patterns or to expand "the possibilities and limits set by the historical time period in which we live" (Ruth and Kenyon 1996: 2). Narrative imbues life with meaning and this meaning can change and expand as one grows older.

Moreover, in the same way as we live in time, we narrate our or others' stories in time; as Ruth and Kenyon state: "as we grow, mature and age in time, we gradually form and reform ourselves and the stories we tell about ourselves" (1996: 7). Thus, there is a difference between "inner time" and "outer time" (Kenyon 1996), terms corresponding to Jan Baars' "chronological time" and "lived time" (2012: 143). Whereas Kenyon considers that "the time in which we live includes both physical (outer) and psychological (inner time)" (1996: 30), for Baars "we are always already living in time, and in some sense, we are always already living time"; in other words, chronological time does not usually coincide with lived time and, moreover, lived time may be modified by memory and perspective. As Kenyon states: "there are individual experiences and perspectives of time, and those time perspectives may change over the lifespan" (1996: 30). Narrative is key in relating these two dimensions of time within human beings: "Not only are narratives needed to relate chronometric time to the world, they are also crucial to interrelate the dimensions of lived time: the past, the present and the future." (2012: 143) However, even though narrative relates us to the world, Kenyon considers that the narrative we construct is essentially "storytime" and adds "Where clock time epitomizes objective time, storytime epitomizes subjective time, the time of our lives." (Randall and Kenyon 2004: 334)

Chronological time and the specific social expectations related to each life stage may, then, differ from lived time. Depending on the social and cultural organisation in which we live, "people judge themselves to be on-time or off-time in their life course" (Kenyon 1996: 30). This idea of the dominance of clock time and its juxtaposition with lived time was further developed by Judith Halberstam in *In a Queer Time and Place*, where she defines "queer time" as living and organizing one's life outside "the conventions of family, inheritance and child rearing" (2005: 5) and highlights the potentiality of "queerness" to "open up new life narratives and alternative relations to time and space" (2005: 5). Halberstam understands "queer time" as moving away from the ordering of the lifecourse by strict "bourgeois rules" (2005: 5) that are seen as "natural". For Halberstam: "[q]ueer uses of time and place develop, at least in part, in opposition to the institutions of family, heterosexuality, and reproduction" (2005: 1), so that alternative ways of organizing and establishing relationships are brought centre-stage. Halberstam defines queer as "non-normative logics and organizations of community, sexual identity, embodiment, and activity in space and time" (2005: 6). Within literary and cinematic analysis, Cynthia Port (2012) and Eva Krainitzki (2014) have applied Halberstam's concept of queer temporalities to Amis's novel *Time's Arrow* and Fincher's film *The Curious Case of Benjamin Button*, and the character of M in the Bond films respectively. Whereas Port suggests that disruptive representations of youthing and aging contribute to disorienting the viewers' internalized sense of cultural temporality, Krainitzki argues that "M's disruption of chrono-temporality [...] allow viewers to imagine an ageing process outside paradigmatic markers" (2014: 34). These analyses make clear the ways in which literary narratives may engage with the "queering" of time to allow us to reimagine age and aging across the lifecourse.

Speculative narratives are a particularly important genre in relation to time and aging. Considering speculative narratives of rejuvenation, for example, Teresa Mangum argues that they "lead[...] us far from varicose veins and shrinking bone mass; often these fantasies turn outward and become embroiled in larger concerns about time" (2002: 80). Speculative fiction and film exhibit a tendency to play with 'queer temporalities', addressing, for example, immortality, rejuvenation, longevity, and demographic change, and imagining the lifecourse and human chronology in alternative ways, on both macro and micro scales. Addressing hopes and fears around aging and death, speculative narratives explore specific cultural conceptions attached to youth and old age as well as the value attributed to different life stages. In this paper, then, we analyse four visual speculative narratives to explore the ways in which they offer us alternative, not always straightforward, visions of time, the lifecourse and aging. We focus on film/TV that explores longevity, whether that be achieved through accident or – as is more often the case – technological innovation. "San Junipero" (in TV Series *Black Mirror*, directed by Owen Harris, 2016), *Mr Nobody* (directed by Jaco Van Dormael, 2009) and *In Time* (directed by Andrew Niccol, 2011) imagine societies in which forms of technologically enabled longevity have been achieved, whether through biomedical or virtual means. *The Age of Adaline* (directed by Lee Toland Krieger, 2015), on the other hand, follows the tradition of speculative fiction about exclusive immortality, achieved only by one or a small number of persons. All four texts play with linear and chronological aging and juxtapose youth and age in provocative ways, exploiting the possibilities of the visual mode. *In Time* and *Adaline* seem to yearn for normative social order, and follow the idea that longevity will always lead to unhappiness and social crisis. *San Junipero* and *Mr Nobody*, on the other hand, focus on the possibilities of temporal disorder as a way of escaping normative expectations. They draw attention to the constricting nature of normative times and combine utopian and dystopian elements to explore the tension between normative and queer temporal orders.

Superposition of Young and Old in Speculative Visual Texts

Speculative visual texts offer especially rich presentations of disruptions of time and the lifecourse through the recurrent superimposition of younger and older versions of characters. The plots that prompt this superimposition often centre around extended longevity/immortality and physical agelessness, but may also include what Peter Goggin and Ulla Kriebernegg (2023) call 'youthing' (where older characters suddenly experience temporal reversal that makes them physically young again) and even multiple and alternative memories that destabilise the linear lifecourse. These longstanding speculative tropes are now part of a wider interest in temporal and narrative experimentation in mainstream television and film, as Melissa Ames (2012) argues. For Ames, "the co-existence of these competing experiences of time allows new conceptions of history and posthistory to emerge" (2012, 6) often through non-normative narrative structures. Ames's research on temporal narrative in film and TV establishes a dialogue with Halberstam's theories on queer time and place as well as with Mangum's, Port's and Krainitzi's readings of temporal disruption in relation to aging and the lifecourse. The visual management – or rather dismantling – of normative time in speculative visual texts is a powerful way to explore and challenge our sense of time, the lifecourse and memory.

The Age of Adaline and In Time focus on the dystopian possibilities of temporal disorder and provide a way in to our analysis of speculative visual texts and queering age. Following a long trend in science and speculative fiction, they point to the negative social and personal repercussions of extended lifespans (see Lebow 2012; Mangum 2002). The Age of Adaline is a sci-fi romance by director Lee Toland Krieger. It focuses on one character, Adaline Bowman, who despite being 107 years old looks 29 due to an accident that provoked her heart to stop for a few seconds and made her "immune to the ravages of time". What the film makes clear is that living out of normative, chronological time like this ultimately leads to isolation, alienation and unhappiness. Adaline increasingly lives disconnected from others in a peripatetic existence forced on her by the need to disguise her posthuman condition. Every few years she moves to a new city and changes her identity completely in order to make sure that no one recognises her and becomes aware of the fact that she has not aged at all. This isolation is also generational: she cannot share her life experiences with a birth cohort or take her place in a genealogical order (see Falcus and Oró-Piqueras 2023). More specifically, in a film focussed on heterosexual romance, she cannot follow her desires and take her place in a heterosexual order, presumably also giving birth to the next generation. The utopian possibilities of life extension are, as Mark Brand argues about narratives of longevity more broadly, increasingly dystopian (2016: 3).

In Time, on the other hand, extends longevity to the whole society. In this future dystopian world everyone is designed to live 'freely' for twenty-five years, but at that point, they have to earn their time in order to continue living. As the main protagonist says: "Time is now the currency. We earn it and spend it. The rich can live forever. And the others? I just want to wake up with more time in my hand and hours a day." Thus, the society in *In Time* is divided into time zones based on wealth, making explicit Frederic Jameson's argument that the longevity narrative is about class and wealth disparity (2005). Again, a dystopian world is fashioned on the premise that life extension will lead to inequality, alienation and boredom.

Despite what might be seen as the conservative narrative propulsion of both of these films, they nevertheless offer themselves to fruitful analysis from an age-studies perspective, working to introduce our discussion of queering time in speculative, visual texts. Whilst both films ultimately work to restore a (heteronormative) sense of social order and history, their effects on the viewer do exceed this. In both films, a sense of visual anachronism is exploited through characters who look, often significantly, younger than their chronological age, complicating the dichotomy old/young. Undeniably, *The Age of Adaline* relies for its visual effects upon the youthful and attractive appearance of its star, Blake

Lively, something enhanced by the frequent and striking changes of costume and hairstyle across the decades of the storyline. Nevertheless, this youthful appearance is at odds with the increasing chronological age of the character, something we are forced to confront at specific moments of the film. For example, Adaline meets her daughter and whereas Adaline looks like a young woman in her twenties, her daughter is an old woman with white hair. The daughter tells Adaline that she is thinking of moving to a retirement community where she can be taken care of as she gets older. On one level, this conversation emphasises the film's central message about normative temporal structures and generational order: Adaline is out of time here and not succumbing to generational succession and to age itself (she should presumably have been in a nursing home before her daughter). At the same time, as a viewer, we are forced into an uncomfortable double vision that makes us reflect on normative temporal structures: Adaline both is and is not old and young. We are made aware of the signifiers we use to determine age (largely physical in a visual text) and may question what age, then, actually means. In a further example of this double vision, in one of the first scenes of the film, the camera goes around Adaline's apartment and shows a sepia photo of her looking exactly as she does in the present of the film. In the next scene, Adaline is in her job checking films from the beginning of the century; in one of them she sees images of the construction of the Golden Gate that takes her back to memories of walking with her mother and observing the construction of the Gate. Once again, Adaline looks exactly the same in the 1920s as in the present moment of the film, the 2010s.

In Time relies on a fairly conservative vision of temporal social orders, one based upon generational, class conflict: an older gerontocratic elite is quite literally stealing the time (and the lifeblood, in a pseudo-vampiric way) of the young. The text is again driven by a heterosexual romance plot, this time underpinned by a battle between young and old, rich and poor. Like *The Age of Adaline*, it relies upon the visual pleasure given by youthful, active, attractive bodies – in this case, contrasted with the sculpted, artificial youthfulness of those who have achieved extended mortality. Nevertheless, as in *The Age of Adaline*, the status of some of the

characters as youthful and yet long lived presents the viewer with a dialogic and palimpsestic vision of age itself. In one scene in the film, protagonist Will Salas enters zone one, where rich people live – that is, the
people who have lived for a long time and still have a great amount of
time on their 'watches' – and is introduced to the family of a woman he
meets there. The three women of the family appear to be in their twenties and yet it is clear that they are daughter, mother and grandmother,
unsettling generational and chronological aging and order. The father of
the family draws attention to this when he asks Will, "Is she my sister,
my mother or my daughter? Colluding times. They say it was easy in the
past." *In Time* is unsettling precisely because it is impossible to use embodied, visual markers as a determinant of age, experience and generational location. Age becomes a performative construct that echoes what
Judith Butler argues about drag and gender. In drawing attention to the
markers of age, our assumptions about aging are interrogated.

"San Junipero" and *Mr Nobody* go further than *The Age of Adaline* and
In Time in their exploration of age, embodiment and temporal orders,
though they also rely upon the visual juxtaposition of age and youth for
specific effects. "San Junipero" is the fourth episode in season three of
anthology TV Series *Black Mirror*, created by Charlie Brooker.[3] As Duarte
and Battin (2021) argue in their recently published volume on the series,
it questions the uses, limitations and ethics of new technologies in a time
in which humanity seems to accept them almost blindly. The episode interrogates chronological conceptions of time, life and death by offering
an alternative to dying; namely, life in the virtual seaside resort of San
Junipero after one's memories are uploaded to the system on the death
of the body. However, before death, clients can visit San Junipero for a
maximum of five hours a week as a form of elder care called 'immersive
therapy'. This is when the two protagonists of the episode meet: Yorkie,
a 61-year-old woman who has been paralysed for forty years, and Kelly,
a woman of the same age who is suffering from a terminal cancer. The

---

3   *Black Mirror* was initially aired on UK's Channel 4, moving to Netflix in later se-
     ries. It ran for five series (2011–19) and attracted significant viewer and critical
     response.

episode offers a vision of queered and palimpsestic time at the same time as it indicates the drawbacks of living a digital eternal life.

Initially, the episode immerses the viewer in a very nostalgic 1980s world – clothing, computer games, music, cars. As it progresses, we become aware that all is not as it seems – something we are prepared for as viewers of *Black Mirror*, where nothing is ever straightforward and various nova disrupt any kind of contemporary realist setting. Once the episode begins to move between real and simulated worlds – making clear the premise on which it is based – we experience human time and aging as palimpsestic, in just the way that Brand explains our experience of time and the lifecourse: "one might not be young or old at any given moment, but barring premature death one could expect to be both of those things, and every other stage in between, in his or her lifetime" (2016: 1). As Isra Daraiseh and Keith Booker point out, the emphasis upon popular culture of the eighties (film, TV, music, video games) in San Junipero functions to emphasise the "sort of heavily mediated environment in which we all live, immersed in a constant stream of manufactured images that makes the distinction between 'real' and 'virtual,' on which the episode apparently hinges, extremely blurry and unstable" (2019: 156). That blurring of real and virtual in the episode extends to its treatment of old and young, which are no longer stable binaries based on memory and retrospect. We see Kelly and Yorkie in their twenties and in their sixties and are encouraged to read these representations as a palimpsest. Of course, this is not unusual in TV and film: characters are frequently aged or youthed (through chronology or through flashback and memory, see Goggin and Kriebernegg 2023), but this episode takes that further by making Kelly and Yorkie both ages at the same time. This works on a number of levels. The plot obviously connects the characters in the time of the film – they move between worlds (and ostensibly between times), but once we know that they are older, we are aware as viewers that even when we see the young characters, we are reading the lives of older people. This creates a sense of dissonance as we move between older and younger bodies. That productive dissonance is fuelled in other ways, too. In particular, we become increasingly aware that the inhabitants of San Junipero remember and are very aware of who they were/are and the experiences they had in their 'real' lives. Kelly, for example, converses with a man at a bar who is telling her about his failing knees, something that we inevitably relate to the fact that he is either older or dead, though he is living in a young body in San Junipero. That kind of dissonance – between the young body and the life experiences that appear to exceed this – is developed as Kelly and Yorkie talk (and argue) about their real lives, particularly Kelly's marriage and the loss of her daughter. In an argument about the lack of understanding Yorkie has of that life, we come closest to bridging the gap between younger body and long life as we begin to see younger Kelly both as older and young. Through dissonance and palimpsestic aging, then, "San Junipero" forces us to recognise the complexity of aging itself and the ways in which it exceeds – and cannot be limited to – the chronological.

This juxtaposition of young and old is in many ways similar in *Mr Nobody*. The protagonist is Nemo, a 118-year-old man who is presented as "the last man on Earth to die of old age" in a time where quasi-immortality has been achieved through the endless replication of cells. The older Nemo is depicted in a sterile, white room (disassociated from the wider world) where a scientist/doctor and a journalist visit him to try to learn more about his story and help him to recover his seemingly lost memories. The treatment of past and present is more complicated than in "San Junipero", however, as *Mr Nobody* offers a number of alternative pasts/lives for Nemo. Nemo remembers and narrates his life to the doctor and journalist, but there is not just one version of the past; instead, he seems to have lived many different lives. Specifically, he offers two versions of what happened after his parents divorced: in one he stayed with his father and in the other, with his mother. Moreover, he seems to have had three adult lives in which he married three different women, with each of whom he had a different fate. The experience of viewing this film is one of disorientation and confusion, as the viewer tries to make sense of seemingly contradictory narratives and constantly revises assumptions in the face of additional evidence. Viewing the film, then, echoes the process of remembering and making sense of unstable and multiple pasts. These complicated alternative pasts undermine the idea of memory as reliable and based solely on recall. Instead, memory becomes a series of possibilities and multiple rather than singular. The lifecourse is then not a linear trajectory, but a series of intersections and overlapping, sometimes contradictory, narratives.

As in "San Junipero", *Mr Nobody* juxtaposes scenes of characters in older and younger age. Here, we see older Nemo and Nemo as a child, as a teenager and as an adult man. This again creates a palimpsestic vision of aging that interrogates a chronological, linear model. The older, infirm Nemo is also, at the same time, a younger man and even a child. On one level, this challenges a reductive, ageist view, something Nemo articulates when he confronts the journalist and insists that he is not simply a grumpy old man who can't remember, but is also a boy of nine and a teenager of fifteen. Multiple possible lifecourse trajectories and the relation between young and old selves destabilise a linear model that reinforces aging as decline.

At the same time, the film relies for its effects and affects on the juxtaposition of age and youth, something we also see in "San Junipero". Eszter Ureczky argues that despite its seeming challenges to stereotypical ideas about aging and the life course, "San Junipero" still devotes significantly more screen time to younger bodies (and actors), offering relatively limited representations of older bodies on screen (2023). The same could be said of *Mr Nobody*, in which the scenes from Nemo's earlier life take up much more screen time than his 'present' older self. Like other science and speculative fiction, the film also relies upon images of age which verge on the grotesque in order to achieve its effects. Here, the older Nemo is seen in a sterile, static environment; he is significantly aged, with all of the usual tropes of older age very prominent: wrinkles, sparse hair etc. When he looks at his older self in a mirror, the sense of shock and repulsion is evident (and felt by both character and viewer). The film also exploits other common tropes in representations of older characters, with Nemo a grumpy, even angry, old man and increasingly forgetful.

By the end of the film, older Nemo appears on a screen in front of young Nemo and tells him: "What you are living now is the past. I'm 70 years younger. [...] To me, life is inverted", showing a disruption of lived time which also underlines the complexity of the aging experience. What is not clear in the film is its position on aging and (im)mortality: if the fact that people will not die deprives them of such complex life experience and whether that is a loss for them. In any case, Nemo is presented as a rarity: someone who has lived a long life, making many choices as he ages across the lifecourse.

Queering Time, Questioning Ageism?

By erasing the constraints of chronological and lifecourse time as described in Baar's and Halberstam's work, these four texts explore and foreground questions related to contemporary conceptions of age and, in the case of "San Junipero", gender and sexuality. Yet, they ultimately differ in their openness to temporal disruption and its relationship to normative lifecourse models.

In *The Age of Adaline*, the immortality of Adaline does not question the heterosexual system but it alters the order of generations, if only for a short time, while Adaline's immortality lasts. Adaline's avoidance of commitment and stasis is the obstacle to satisfactory heterosexual (and narrative) fulfilment in this popular romance film. The plot sees her try to overcome this obstacle in her relationship with Ellis. However, on meeting his parents, she realises that she had had a relationship with Ellis's father, William, when he was a young man, decades ago. Adaline introduces herself to William as Adaline's daughter; however, William feels impressed by the resemblance between the supposed Adaline's mother and herself and confesses to his wife: "I'm remembering things that I don't even know I remembered." In this sense, the appearance of Adaline in William's life after all this time alters the sense of the linearity of his own life, at the same time as it alters the generational logic of William and Ellis's family, since both William and Ellis have fallen in love with the same, physically unchanged woman. This creates conflict within the family since Ellis feels disoriented and William's wife feels she was only his second choice. In the film, this disruption of time and generation is symbolised through William's research on the orbit of a specific comet, which comes back to Earth fifty years later than his research had predicted, thus proving that time is not linear. By the end of the film, Adaline has – conveniently – suffered another car accident, one that reverses her immortal condition. The film then finishes with Adaline finding her first white hair in front of the mirror, a rather stereotypical sign of her physical aging. Thus, the disruption provoked by Adaline's longevity is solved by the end of film, restoring the heterosexual order. The film, however, despite ending with the restoration of the heterosexual family and bourgeoisie time – as defined by Halberstam –, points to the possibility of immortality and time disruption being scientifically plausible, highlighting, thus, the constructed nature of human time and generational division based on heterosexual normativity.

In Time is similarly driven by a heterosexual romance plot: that of Will and Sylvia. Unlike *The Age of Adaline*, *In Time* presents a society fundamentally altered by extreme longevity. This is not, then, the story of a protagonist trying to reconcile her own non-normative condition, but the much more common dystopian narrative of a (young) protagonist fighting the system. A thriller narrative, the film is driven by action and pursuit, as the young couple battles against the gerontocracy and the forces that uphold this state of affairs. Significantly, this takes a genealogical form as Sylvia's father represents all that they fight against. Youth is, then, prioritised and the plot of the film is premised upon the necessity of generational succession and the redundancy of older people. The disruptive potential of the visual juxtaposition of age and youth in this film, and the ways in which it draws attention to our conceptions of aging and the life-course, are firmly located within a narrative that works to restore social and generational order, and with it the dominance of chronometric and normative time.

"San Junipero" offers a much more subversive vision of temporal disorder in its queer love story, whilst at the same time drawing attention to the way this is framed by a dystopian system of (temporal) control. On one level, San Junipero offers the characters a heterotopic space (see Ureczky 2023) in a parallel time to that of their lives: they can move between decades at will; they are young and not in their limiting older bodies. Importantly, they can live a story that is different from the one that they have lived in the real world. Primarily, they can explore sexual preferences that they were unable to act on in the real world: Kelly because she stayed in a long marriage; Yorkie because she becomes disabled, seemingly quadriplegic, after the accident, something which is used as prosthesis in the episode. Their love story – the primary narrative drive in the text – offers what can be read as a queer time, in the Halberstam sense, since San Junipero opens up new life narratives and alternative relations to time and space for Kelly and Yorkie. In San Junipero they can choose to live the way they want and do not have to fulfil specific objectives related to life stages. Explicitly juxtaposed to the narratives of their real lives, San Junipero is a space where they apparently escape social and cultural constraints.

Nevertheless, the programme constantly reminds us of the limited nature of that escape: even before we are fully aware of the exact nature of San Junipero, clock time is a dominant feature of life there. Yorkie and Kelly are limited to 5-hour visits, one per week Characters frequently refer to the time they have left in the online world. For many, their time there ends at the fairytale-esque midnight (as is the case for Kelly and Yorkie). The titles that frame the visits to San Junipero emphasise real-world temporality and chronology: one week later. Yorkie and Kelly's relationship, therefore, free as it may seem in San Junipero, is always framed by a vague, undetermined external power that controls time there. This juxtaposition of times reminds us that queer time is precariously opposed to heteronormative, linear time, and, in this episode at least, it seems that, in the tradition of dystopian scenarios, freedom from real-world time is controlled.

The end of "San Junipero" emphasises this ambivalent vision of freedom and constraint. Kelly and Yorkie choose to euphemistically 'pass over' and stay permanently in San Junipero. Ostensibly, then, they escape the power of the real world, their failing bodies and the limits on their time in the simulated world. Driving along the coast in a sports car to the sound of 'Heaven Is a Place on Earth', they appear to have achieved a blissful, queer immortality. Indeed, many popular responses to this episode see it as the most optimistic of all of Black Mirror's dystopian-fuelled visions. And in their analysis of pop culture in the episode, Daraiseh and Booker argue that "Ultimately, the happy-ever-after ending of the episode appears to be largely free of irony, so that the episode endorses the notion of uploading human consciousnesses into computer-simulated worlds, even as a replacement for biological life, which can then be removed from the equation by euthanasia." (2019: 156) Nevertheless, as Daraiseh and Booker acknowledge, the enabling queer time in "San Junipero" is shadowed by an oppressive system time – that of TCKR Systems, the presumably capitalist venture that provides the virtual reality. The very fact that the freedom Kelly and Yorkie enjoy can only be imagined in a nostalgic vision of the 1980s points to the limits of a corporate system that is itself an evolutionary outcome of 1980s capitalism. That sense of 'ustopian' (Atwood 2011: 66) limitations is reiterated at the end of the text. The scene in which Kelly and Yorkie drive off into the sunset in "San Junipero" is followed by the cut to a high-tech storage room in which a robot manages a massive, shining chrome and black bank of plugs that represents the downloaded memories of those who live in San Junipero, a visual contrast that emphasises the complexity of utopian/dystopia in this episode. 'Heaven Is a Place on Earth' continues to play in the background, an ironic and sinister set of lyrics when juxtaposed with the image. As James Cook (2020) points out, this technological forever is deeply inserted in a capitalist system.

More fundamentally disturbing are the obvious questions raised in the episode about euthanasia, care and wealth. Care here is very advanced and takes place in hi-tech, expensively designed environments. The questions of who pays for that care, how they pay and who, then, is unable to pay are left unresolved and unaddressed in the series. Euthanasia as a solution to serious disability or terminal illness is also a question that is inevitably raised in the episode, though largely passed over in the episode's emphasis upon and representation of the ease with which death is ensured.

Like "San Junipero", *Mr Nobody* draws attention to aging, time and the lifecourse, in this case playing with images in which time and space are somehow eliminated. The film includes repeated images of space and space travel. We see Nemo as a teenager typing a story about space travel and humans in suspended animation on the way to Mars. This image of travel to Mars is seen more than once in the film: early in the narrative, Nemo seems to remember being one of those human travellers and later he seems to remember waking up from hibernation and arriving on Mars. Other, visual images self-reflexively comment on temporal instability, such as Nemo walking across the sand and into his own footsteps, that then disappear. Similarly, he invests in time-lapse photography in which he reverses images of decay and putrefaction. Further drawing attention to the destabilisation of time are Nemo's memories of life as a popular scientist, appearing on TV to explain string theory, dimensions and time. These images and memories function as a kind of metanarrative comment on the constant temporal reversal and even confusion that characterises the narrative of Nemo's life.

Unlike "San Junipero", *Mr Nobody* does not offer any kind of 'queer utopia' (see Ureczky). In fact, the emphasis seems to be on heterosexual relationships and normative familial structures. Nemo's memories centre on his parents' divorce, his mother's new relationship and his own three marriages. Suburban settings and domestic environments dominate his memories. Nevertheless, the film draws attention to the constructed nature of these environments and offers what might be seen as a knowing and ironic vision of twentieth-century American life. The combination of the real and the fantastic in the speculative mode is exploited here. For example, the childhood suburbia Nemo remembers also features as a toy in the child's bedroom. Early in the film, Nemo's memories are presented as a hyperreal version of the past reminiscent of *The Truman Show*. That sanitised version of 1970s, suburban America suggests a self-conscious presentation of the past and nostalgia that presents the dominance of the heterosexual as itself part of an imagined, unstable narrative of American life in which, at the same time, old age seems to have disappeared. Exacerbating this sense of the instability of this heterosexual ideal are the relationships themselves: Nemo's memories centre around his parents' divorce and his own story is dominated by three versions of heterosexual romance, none of which seems to be successfully realised. In these ways, then, *Mr Nobody* queers the dominance of the heterosexual lifecourse model, drawing attention to its instability and, potentially, redundancy.

Conclusion

Longevity is explored in these four narratives; however, none of them seems to unproblematically advocate for longevity and immortality as either desirable or remotely close to happiness, making them characteristic of many narratives of rejuvenation and longevity (see Mangum 2002: 70 and Lebow, 2012). In *In Time*, the dystopian consequences of extended longevity are clear in the inequality that permeates the world. The individual effects of extended life spans are made clear in characters such as Henry, who gives all of his remaining time to Will, having lived more than one hundred years and found himself simply tired and bored. That desire for mortality and finitude is also seen in *Mr Nobody* and *The Age of Adaline*. *Mr Nobody* finishes with Nemo dying and declaring that this is the happiest day of his life. In *The Age of Adaline*, the protagonist is actually happy to discover that she has her first white hair and is thus physically aging, since her life has been in a state of static isolation. In both narratives, then, aging and finitude ensure meaning in the lives of the protagonists.

"San Junipero" may be viewed as an exception amongst these narratives, since Kelly and Yorkie will stay young and happy forever in the dream-like world of San Junipero. However, the episode does subtly indicate the potential limitations of this world (not only through its dystopian system of capitalist control). As Cook, drawing on Wulandhani and Wijaya, points out, the lack of mortality in San Junipero constitutes a world without risk and goals, and therefore an existence without meaning (Cook 2020: 115), something further emphasised in San Junipero through repetition since life there is presented like a holiday in which every day is very similar to the next one. In fact, the queering of time and lack of lifecourse markers in this *Black Mirror*'s episode may lead to unhappiness rather than freedom; this is one of the arguments Yorkie initially uses in her refusal to stay in San Junipero permanently, since she believes that those who do are bored and lack affective and emotional satisfaction.

Whilst all of the narratives embrace finitude, they take differing approaches to their explorations of aging and the lifecourse. All of the texts juxtapose older and younger ages in productive ways, often through the visual and palimpsestic presentation of older and youthful bodies. They can all be said to be texts that to some extent queer our understanding of age itself. Nevertheless, it is clear that *Mr Nobody* and "San Junipero" go further than *In Time* and *The Age of Adaline* in their explorations of temporal order and aging. Whilst the latter texts situate their representations of aging within fairly conservative narratives of heterosexual fulfilment and genealogical security, "San Junipero" and *Mr Nobody* more fundamentally disrupt our conceptions of the (heterosexual) lifecourse. Whilst the dystopian elements of both narratives offer constant reminders of the limited nature of any utopian alternatives to chronometric time, they nevertheless draw attention to the possibility of queering that time and offering alternative ways of conceptualising our progression along the lifecourse, making clear the potential of speculative fiction to contribute to the ways in which we understand aging itself.

Works Cited

"San Junipero" (2016). In: Black Mirror (TV Series). Director Owen Harris.

Ames, Melissa (2012): Time in Television Narrative: Exploring Temporality in Twenty-First-Century Programming. University Press of Mississippi.

Amis, Martin (1991): Time's Arrow, London: Vintage Books.

Atwood, Margaret (2011): *In Other Worlds: SF and the Human Imagination*, London: Virago.

Baars, Jan (2012): "Critical Turns of Aging, Narrative and Time." In: International Journal of Aging and Later Life 7/2, pp. 143–65.

Brand, Mark R. (2016): "Growing Old in Utopia: from Age to Otherness in American Literary Utopias." In: Age, Culture and Humanities, 3. Available online: https://ageculturehumanities.org/WP/growing-old-in-utopia-from-age-to-otherness-in-american-literary-utopias/ (accessed 20 Nov 2021).

Chivers, Sally (2003): From Old Woman to Older Women: Contemporary Culture and Women's Narratives, Columbus, OH: Ohio UP.

Cook, James (2020): "San Junipero and the Digital Afterlife. Could Heaven be a Place on Earth?" In: David Kyle John (ed.), Black Mirror and Philosophy: Dark Reflections, John Wiley, pp. 109–117.

Daraiseh, Isra/Booker, Keith (2019): "Unreal City: Nostalgia, Authenticity, and Posthumanity in "San Junipero"." In: Terence McSweeney/Joy Stuart (eds.), Through the Black Mirror: Deconstructing the Side Effects of the Digital Era, London: Palgrave Macmillan, pp. 151–163.

Duarte, German A./Battin, Justin Michael, eds. (2021): Reading "Black Mirror": Insights into Technology and the Post-Media Condition, transcript Publishing.

Falcus, Sarah (2015): "Alternative futures: Ageing and Identity in Contemporary Women's Writing." In: Flocel Sabaté (ed.), Conditioned Identities: Wished-for and Unwished-for Identities. Berlin: Peter Lang, pp. 303–32.

Falcus, Sarah/Oró-Piqueras, Maricel, eds. (2023): Age and Ageing in Contemporary Speculative and Science Fiction, London and New York: Bloomsbury.

Goggin, Peter/Kriebernegg, Ulla (2023): "Ageing and Youthing: Portrayals of Progression and Regression in Recent Science Fiction Film and TV." In: Sarah Falcus and Maricel Oro-Piqueras (eds.), Age and Ageing in Contemporary Speculative and Science Fiction, London and New York: Bloomsbury, pp. 29–48.

Gullette, Margaret (2011):. Agewise: Fighting the New Ageism in America, Chicago and London: University of Chicago Press.

Halberstam, Judith (2005): In a Queer Time and Place: Transgender Bodies, Subcultural Lives, New York: New York UP.

In Time. (2011). Director Andrew Niccol.

Kenyon, Gary (1996): "The Meaning/Value of Personal Storytelling." In: James E. Birren et al. (eds.), Aging and Biography. Explorations in Adult Development, New York: Springer Publishing Company, pp. 21–38.

Krainitzki. Eva (2014): "Judi Dench's Age-inappropriateness and the Role of M: Challenging Normative Temporality." In: Journal of Aging Studies 29, pp. 31–40.

Lebow, Richard N. (2012): The Politics and Ethics of Immortality, Cambridge: Cambridge University Press.

Mangum, Theresa (2002): "Longing for Life Extension: science fiction and late life." In: Journal of Aging and Identity 7/2, pp. 69–80.

Mr. Nobody (2009). Director Jaco Van Dormael.

Port, Cynthia (2012): "No Future? Aging, Temporality, History and Reverse Chronologies." In: Occasion: Interdisciplinary Studies in the Humanities 4/31, pp. 1–19.

Randall, William/Kenyon, Gary (2004): "Time, Story and Wisdom: Emerging Themes in Narrative Gerontology." In: Canadian Journal of Aging 23/4, pp. 333–46.

Ruth, Jan Erik/Kenyon, Gary (1996): "Biography in Adult Development and Aging." In: James E. Birren et al. (eds.), Aging and Biography. Explorations in Adult Development, New York: Springer Publishing Company, pp. 2–20.

The Age of Adaline (2015). Director Lee Toland Krieger.

The Curious Case of Benjamin Button (2008). Director David Fincher.

The Truman Show (1998). Director Peter Weir.

Ureczky, Eszter (2023): "A cure for ageing: Digital cloning as utopian end-of-life care in the "'San Junipero' episode of Black Mirror." In: Sarah Falcus/Maricel Oró-Piqueras (eds.), Age and Ageing in Contemporary Speculative and Science Fiction, London and New York: Bloomsbury, pp. 173–94.

Authors

Ryan Bell is a writer, musician, educator, and PhD candidate in English at the University at Buffalo. His current research focuses on 20th-century poetics, experimental music, interdisciplinary avant-gardes, and vocality. His dissertation, tentatively titled "Expanded Voice: Mapping Non-Normative Vocal Performance," examines the ideological, historical, echnological, and modal negotiations that inform the shifting distinctions between sound poetry, rt music's extended vocal techniques, and other forms of innovative and non-normative vocal erformance in 20th-century art. He received his BA and MA, both in English, from University of North Florida.

Mariana Castelli-Rosa is a PhD student (Cultural Studies) at Trent University, Canada. She has two MAs (English Studies from the University of Heidelberg, Germany and Public Texts from Trent University, Canada) and a BA in English and Portuguese and a Teaching Degree from the University of São Paulo, Brazil. Her areas of interest are Canadian and Indigenous literatures, cultural understandings and images of aging; translation and tensions in intercultural encounters; interactions between countries and individuals from the Global South and so-called developed countries and how these may shape identity; trauma, popular culture, identity, gender. She currently works as a Teaching Assistant and Marker at the Department of Gender and Social Justice at Trent University. She also works as a Research Assistant editing and annotating through coding the journal that Canadian poet PK Page wrote during her time in Brazil and Robertson Davies' Massey College diaries. She is an aspiring academic and translator and her doctoral research is on the experience of aging in Indigenous communities in Canada through the analysis of works of life writing and novels.

Carmen Concilio is Full professor of English and Postcolonial literature at the University of Turin: Department of Foreign Languages, Literatures and Modern Cultures. She is the recipient of Canada-Italy Innovation Award 2021. She is past president of AISCLI (www.aiscli.it) and she has recently published *Imagining Ageing. Representation of Age and Ageing in Anglophone Literature* (transcript 2018) and *New Critical Patterns in Postcolonial Discourse. Historical Traumas and Environmental Issues* (2012). She has co-edited *Trees in Literatures and the Arts. Humanarboreal Perspectives in the Anthropocene* (2021). Her research fields are Anglophone Postcolonial Literature, Ageing Studies and Gender, Migration and Diaspora, Human and Environmental Rights, Digital and Environmental Humanities.

Michael Davidson is Distinguished Professor Emeritus at the University of California, San Diego. His work has focused on modern and contemporary American poetry, gender and sexuality studies, disability studies and deaf studies. His books on poetics include *The San Francisco Renaissance: Poetics and Community at Mid-Century* (Cambridge U Press, 1989), *Ghostlier Demarcations: Modern Poetry and the Material Word* (U of California Press, 1997), *Guys Like Us: Citing Masculinity in Cold War Poetics* (U of Chicago, 2003), and *Outskirts of Form: Practicing Cultural Poetics* (Wesleyan U Press, 2011). His work in disability studies includes *Concerto for the Left Hand: Disability and the Defamiliar Body* (U of Michigan, 2008), *Invalid Modernism: Disability and the Missing Body of the Aesthetic* (Oxford U Press, 2019) and *Distressing Language: Disability and the Poetics of Error* (New York U Press, 2022). He is also the author of six books of poetry, the most recent of which is *Bleed Through: New and Selected Poems* (Coffee House Press, 2013). He is the co-author, with Lyn Hejinian, Barrett Watten, and Ron Silliman, of *Leningrad* (Mercury House Press, 1991). He is the editor of *The New Collected Poems of George Oppen* (New Directions, 2002).

Sarah Falcus is a Reader in Contemporary Literature at the University of Huddersfield. She is interested in the intersection of ageing studies and literary studies, and is the co-author of *Contemporary Narratives of Dementia: Ethics, Ageing, Politics* (with Katsura Sako, 2019) and co-editor of *Contemporary Narratives of Ageing, Illness, Care* (with Katsura Sako, 2022). Her current work centres on two main areas: children's literature and ageing; and ageing/the lifecourse in science and speculative fiction. She is the Primary Collaborator on the project 'Ageing and Illness in British and Japanese Children's Picturebooks 1950–2000: Historical and Cross-Cultural Perspectives', funded by the Japan Society for the Promotion of Science. She is the co-director of the Dementia and Cultural Narrative Network.

Jade Elizabeth French works on ageing, care and intergenerationality. She is currently a Doctoral Prize Fellow at Loughborough University developing the project 'Imagining the Care Home in Post War British Literature'. Previously, she was a research fellow as part of the ESRC-funded project 'Reimagining the future in Older Age'. She has written on modernism and ageing in articles for *Feminist Modernist Studies*, *Women: A Cultural Review* and *Modernism/modernity Print Plus*.

João Paulo Guimarães holds a PhD in English from SUNY Buffalo and is a full-time researcher at the University of Porto. He specializes in contemporary American experimental poetry and science studies. His first book, *American Experimental Poetry and the New Organic Form* is forthcoming from Bloomsbury's Studies in Critical Poetics series. He is editing another essay collection for transcript publishing titled *Fear of Aging: Old Age in Horror Fiction and Film*. His current book project focuses on representations of aging in recent innovative American poetry.

Heunjung Lee is a Ph.D candidate in Performance Studies at the University of Alberta. She is also a dancer and dramaturg and teaches undergraduate drama courses. Crossing Performance Studies, Age Studies, Disability Studies, her research investigates cultural constructions of ageing and older adults living with dementia. Her research explores how performance practices and theories can offer counter-narratives of the dominant narrative of decline associated with ageing and produce empowering images of old age.

Jiwon Ohm is a PhD candidate in the Department of English at the University at Buffalo. Her research focuses on the formation of the modern fantasy genre, as well as the imagining and forming of national identities in/through 20th- to 21st-century neo-medievalist fantasy. She is particularly interested in the history behind the publications of J.R.R. Tolkien's *The Hobbit* and *The Lord of the Rings* and the ways in which these works have shaped the trajectory of the fantasy genre in popular culture and the market.

Maricel Oró-Piqueras is Associate Professor at the Department of English and Linguistics, Universitat de Lleida. Since 2022, she is coordinator of research group "Grup Dedal-Lit" which has recently been granted a three-year-long project on ageing, old age and intergenerational relations (funded by the Spanish Ministry of Science and Innovation). Her research interests include ageing and old age in contemporary fiction as well as representations of gender and ageing in film and TV series. She is co-editor of *Serializing Age: Ageing and Old Age in TV Series* (with A. Wohlmann, 2016), *Re-Discovering Age(ing): Narratives of Mentorship* (with N. Casado-Gual and E. Domínguez-Rué, 2019) and *Age and Ageing in Contemporary Speculative and Science Fiction* (with S. Falcus, 2023). ORCID: htt ps://orcid.org/0000-0001-6868-9113

Patricia Silva is Associate Research Fellow at the Centre for Social Studies (CES), University of Coimbra. Her research centers on Luso- and Anglophone transnational modernist networks and movements, and on Transcultural Modernism. She holds a PhD in Portuguese & Brazilian Studies from King's College London, was Visiting Research Fellow at University of London School of Advanced Study, Queen Mary University of London, and UniFESP (Brazil), and taught at KCL, UCL, and the University of Cambridge. She is the author of *Yeats and Pessoa: Parallel Poetic Styles* (2020; rpt. 2010) and co-editor of *Pessoa Plural* 11,

"Portuguese Modernisms 1915–1917: Contexts, Facets & Legacies of the *Orpheu* Generation" (2017). She has published on Modernism, Modernist Magazines, Lusophone Literary & Cultural Studies, and Comparative Literature in numerous refereed journals, notably *Portuguese Studies*, *Portuguese Literary & Cultural Studies*, and *Comparative Critical Studies*, and has forthcoming chapters on Brazilian Modernists and the Avant-Garde in *Peripheral Modernisms* (Palgrave, 2023), and on Brazilian modernist magazines in the volume of *The Oxford Critical and Cultural History of Global Modernist Magazines* about *South America, Central America, and the Caribbean* (OUP, 2024).

Sofia Matos Silva is a journalist, photojournalist, photographer, writer, and a perpetually-researcher-of-something, but she is mostly just a work in progress. Currently a freelancer, she holds a major in Communication Sciences: Journalism, Public Relations and Multimedia, and is working her way through her master's thesis in Literary, Cultural and Interartistic Studies. She is a twenty-something from Portugal.

Cultural Studies

Gabriele Klein
Pina Bausch's Dance Theater
Company, Artistic Practices and Reception

2020, 440 p., pb., col. ill.
29,99 € (DE), 978-3-8376-5055-6
E-Book:
PDF: 29,99 € (DE), ISBN 978-3-8394-5055-0

Markus Gabriel, Christoph Horn, Anna Katsman, Wilhelm Krull,
Anna Luisa Lippold, Corine Pelluchon, Ingo Venzke
Towards a New Enlightenment –
The Case for Future-Oriented Humanities

October 2022, 80 p., pb.
18,00 € (DE), 978-3-8376-6570-3
E-Book: available as free open access publication
PDF: ISBN 978-3-8394-6570-7
ISBN 978-3-7328-6570-3

Sven Quadflieg, Klaus Neuburg, Simon Nestler (eds.)
(Dis)Obedience in Digital Societies
Perspectives on the Power of Algorithms and Data

March 2022, 380 p., pb., ill.
29,00 € (DE), 978-3-8376-5763-0
E-Book: available as free open access publication
PDF: ISBN 978-3-8394-5763-4
ISBN 978-3-7328-5763-0

All print, e-book and open access versions of the titles in our list
are available in our online shop www.transcript-publishing.com

Cultural Studies

Ingrid Hoelzl, Rémi Marie
Common Image
Towards a Larger Than Human Communism

2021, 156 p., pb., ill.
29,50 € (DE), 978-3-8376-5939-9
E-Book:
PDF: 26,99 € (DE), ISBN 978-3-8394-5939-3

Anna Maria Loffredo, Rainer Wenrich,
Charlotte Axelsson, Wanja Kröger (eds.)
Changing Time – Shaping World
Changemakers in Arts & Education

September 2022, 310 p., pb., col. ill.
45,00 € (DE), 978-3-8376-6135-4
E-Book: available as free open access publication
PDF: ISBN 978-3-8394-6135-8

Olga Moskatova, Anna Polze, Ramón Reichert (eds.)
Digital Culture & Society (DCS)
Vol. 7, Issue 2/2021 –
Networked Images in Surveillance Capitalism

August 2022, 336 p., pb., col. ill.
29,99 € (DE), 978-3-8376-5388-5
E-Book:
PDF: 27,99 € (DE), ISBN 978-3-8394-5388-9

**All print, e-book and open access versions of the titles in our list
are available in our online shop www.transcript-publishing.com**

GPSR Authorized Representative: Easy Access System Europe, Mustamäe tee
50, 10621 Tallinn, Estonia, gpsr.requests@easproject.com

www.ingramcontent.com/pod-product-compliance
Lightning Source LLC
Chambersburg PA
CBHW061736120626
46550CB00005B/1811